THE BEGINNINGS OF METHODISM IN ENGLAND AND IN AMERICA

John and Charles Wesley, George Whitefield. The Founders of Methodism

THE
BEGINNINGS OF METHODISM
IN
ENGLAND AND IN AMERICA

FRANCIS H. TEES
Pastor, Old St. George's, 1931—

Author, *The Story of Old St. George's;*
Co-author, *Pioneering in Penn's Woods.*

Francis H. Tees

WIPF & STOCK · Eugene, Oregon

Wipf and Stock Publishers
199 W 8th Ave, Suite 3
Eugene, OR 97401

The Beginnings of Methodism in England and America
By Tees, Francis H.
Softcover ISBN-13: 978-1-7252-8484-5
Hardcover ISBN-13: 978-1-7252-8485-2
eBook ISBN-13: 978-1-7252-8487-6
Publication date 7/15/2020
Previously published by Parthenon Press, 1940

This edition is a scanned facsimile of the original edition published in 1940.

FOREWORD

The *Methodist Home Journal* of Saturday, July 19, 1873, printed the following from the proceedings of the 100th Anniversary of the First Conference of American Methodism held in St. George's July 14, 15, 1773.

"Monday evening, July 14, Dr. Robert H. Pattison of this city (Philadelphia) read an admirable essay on the First Churches. He enlightened and instructed even old men of antiquarian research, and has the honor of securing to Methodism the most valuable manuscript Journal of the Reverend Joseph Pilmoor, D.D., containing a history of Methodism in America from 1769 to 1774.

"The future historians of Methodism will not venture to write of early Methodism without consulting this invaluable document."

The manuscript referred to, containing 309 pages 8x13, is now in the possession of the Philadelphia Conference Historical Society.

In spite of the prediction of the *Home Journal*, many have "ventured to write of early Methodism" without access to and therefore "without consulting this invaluable document," or Journal, of Pilmoor.

The author of the following pages, however, has not so ventured. While brief quotations from Pilmoor's Journal have been printed in several volumes no such frequent or copious quotations appear as they do here.

Nor has the author ventured to confine himself largely to other than original sources. Most of the matter contained herein has been gotten directly from the Journals of Whitefield and of the Wesley's, the letters, "Ecclesiastical History," and other miscellaneous writings of John Wesley, the Journals of Pilmoor and Asbury; from the British Conference Minutes, the early American Conference Minutes, and the General Conference Journals, 1792-1824; the Autobiography of Benjamin Franklin, the Philadelphia and the Pennsylvania Gazettes, Lee's

"History of the Methodists in the United States," Watson's Annals of Philadelphia and Pennsylvania; the Archives of the Philadelphia Conference Historical Society, the Archives of Old St. George's and, indirectly, from the Archives of "John St." through the "Story of Old John St." by Dr. Upham and J. B. Wakeley's "Lost Chapters" and from articles by Dr. Frederick Platt, Warden of the "New Room" (Bristol).

The reader will not find herein an exhaustive history of Methodism nor Methodist history down to date. As the title suggests we simply present the beginnings of Methodism culled mostly from various original sources and, as far as possible, dovetailed together and set down in chronological order.   FRANCIS H. TEES.

Philadelphia, 1940.

CONTENTS

CHAPTER		PAGE
	Foreword	5
	Introduction	9
I.	The Founders	15
	Visits to America, Period 1735-1738.	
II.	Laying the Foundations	30
III.	Rise of the Society, Class, Itinerant, Conference, etc.	42
IV.	Whitefield and Early American Methodism	61
V.	American Societies—How Recruited	77
	First Societies and Meeting Houses.	
VI.	Arrival and Initial Activities of Williams, Pilmoor, and Boardman	100
VII.	An Important Statement of Faith	114
	Inauguration of the Prayer Meeting, "Watch-Night," "Love Feast," etc.	
VIII.	Arrival of King, Asbury, and Wright	120
IX.	Appointment and Arrival of Rankin and Shadford Extended Labors of Pilmoor and Boardman	128
X.	First Conference of American Methodism	137
XI.	Organization of The Methodist Episcopal Church General Conferences to 1824.	149
XII.	Bishop Asbury's Labors	171
	Coke's Attempt to Unite the Methodist Episcopal Church and the Episcopal Church.	
XIII.	The Book Concern and the Chartered Fund	179
XIV.	The Sunday School, Cokesbury College, First Missionaries	196
XV.	The Colored People in Early American Methodism	205
XVI.	Some Early Methodist Customs	210
	Bibliography	221

INTRODUCTION

In the latter part of the eighteenth century, America experienced vital and stirring movements. In the political world, there was a new expression of democracy, and an experiment was being worked out by means of a document, which since has been called the greatest expression of human liberty. Along with the development of this notion of liberty was the idea of a federation of colonies to make a union of states. The greatest minds and souls of the new world were determined to provide a new nation founded on the principles of liberty and democracy. In the religious world of America, another great struggle was in progress. A native church was needed to care for the people who wanted a church that should have its leadership in the new world, which already had shown signs of rebellion from the control of the old world.

For fifty years the city of Philadelphia was the scene of action of much that was in both of these realms. George Washington and Thomas Jefferson, with all the other founders of the republic, were figures in the life of Philadelphia. Shrines of American liberty and national life are here. Here also were the leaders of the new American church, whose history, as well as whose form of government, closely parallels the form of government and history of our republic. The founding fathers of American Methodism were frequent visitors to St. George's Church, and several of them served as pastors for the short terms which were then the requirement. Old St. George's, where they served, where the early conferences were held, and where the Methodist Book Concern was initiated under the leadership of John Dickins, is hard by Independence Hall and Carpenters' Hall, both shrines of American liberty. This church has been called the "Church of the Arrival," and the "Welcoming, Receiving Station." Indeed, it was at Philadelphia that Francis Asbury first landed in America on October 27, 1771. He preached his first sermon, in this newly developing country, in St. George's Church,

October 28, 1771, and here began his journeys as the "Prophet of the Long Road."

It is fitting, therefore, that "The Beginnings of Methodism in England and America" should be recorded by the pastor, at the present time, of "Old St. George's" in Philadelphia. No complete story of American Methodism, nor indeed of world Methodism, could be told without the records of St. George's Church. Out of these priceless records and the archives of the Philadelphia Conference Historical Society, Dr. Tees has been in a position to gather these materials as no one else has done. This book, the result of years of research on the part of the author, will be welcomed by every student of early Methodism. It will be found necessary for the full understanding of the "Beginnings."—CHANNING A. RICHARDSON, Department of City Work, Board of Home Missions and Church Extension. Philadelphia, Pa.

Methodism will make its best progress forward by frequently looking back. It was a providence in timeliness that the celebration of the Aldersgate experience of John Wesley came the year before the consummation of the union of American Methodism. The warming of the heart made ready for the joining of hands. It is evident to all thoughtful students of the times, who know the weaknesses which have crept into churches and who appreciate their potential powers, that Methodism must recover some of her initial experiences and return to first principles in church work if she is to serve the present day in proportion to her resources as she served the days that are past. History is the basis of our hope.

The witnesses of the personal experience of the grace of God in the single soul and the record of the guidance of God in local churches are the most valuable material we possess in Methodist literature. From the beginning those who told the stories of our Church have dealt with the concrete. The most vital histories of Methodism have been concerned with specific localities and institutions. The whole Church has been urged to do greater things by knowing what churches have done.

For reasons like these the chronicle of Old St. George's

IN ENGLAND AND IN AMERICA

Church, Philadelphia, is more than the record of a single church. The spiritual quality which vitalized this one household of God's people has spread throughout the whole of Methodism and the might of the aggregate has been seen in this one section of a movement. The life of Old St. George's required many new activities and this became a church of beginnings. How many initiations and how important they were will be recounted in this interesting volume. We can only say that if some of the things which came to birth in this noble church had never happened Methodist history would have been profoundly different and, we think, less notable. It is a wholesome exercise of the mind to go back and study origins in order to check our activities and see if we have been faithful to the past.

While possessing records of an unbroken church life from the beginning and holding within its treasure rooms priceless relics, Old St. George's has very much more than precious mementos. The church has served and is still serving its days and generations. The program has been adapted to changing conditions in the community. From a large city church, ministering to a fine residential section, it has become a mission church in lower downtown, but when one worships in this sanctuary and sees the work performed in the Sabbath school, he knows that service is still the major objective of the organization. The gospel for our day is preached from a Bible once used by Francis Asbury and the pulpit in which the preacher stands was sanctified by the tired feet of "the prophet of the long road" but the ministry is to those who need the comfort of Christ today.

The pastor of Old St. George's, the author of this book, is an active minister serving with effectiveness his parish. He sees the inspirational value of the old and utilizes the treasures of the past to enhance his message. He would serve his day with strength and resources gained from other days. Having in hand the records of his church and having access to the distinctive treasures of the Philadelphia Conference Historical Society he has been able to gather very much material of deep interest which has not hitherto been published. This unique matter he has correlated with the work done by early historians of the Methodist Church in America and he has made his digest of records more than a bare recital of facts. Added to unusual opportunities of contrast with original sources there has been patient and intelligent research through many years. The combination of circumstances in his privileges and his own personal talents have produced a book which is an invaluable addition to the historical literature of The Methodist Church. It has been a pleasure to read the book which will have a permanent place in the libraries of all who wish to be informed about the way our Church has gone and who desire to gain from the road we have traveled a better chart for the way ahead.—RICHARD L. SHIPLEY, Editor, *Methodist Recorder*, Baltimore, Md.

On one occasion Bishop Francis Asbury wrote in his Journal these words: "I have well considered my Journal; it is inelegant, yet it conveys much information of the state of the religion and country. I make no doubt the Methodists are, and will be, a numerous and wealthy people, and their preachers who follow us will not know our struggles but by comparing the present improved state of the country with what it was in our day as exhibited in my Journal and other records of that day." Bishop Asbury's prophecy that the American Methodists would become a numerous and wealthy people has been fulfilled. In The Methodist Church alone there are 8,000,000 members and the annual budget is at least $75,000,000. Instead of the crude churches of Asbury's era the value of church property approximates $600,000,000. Instead of one college there are now one hundred and thirty-nine educational institutions with an enrollment of 93,000 students. The Methodist Church has material resources never dreamed of by the pioneer American Methodists.

Bishop Asbury's fear that the future Methodists would forget about the struggles, hardships, and privations of the pioneer Methodists seems also to have been justified for there are thousands of American Methodists who are ignorant of the early history of their church. A great contribution, therefore, can be made by Methodist scholars in presenting the picture of the heroic era of pioneer Methodism.

IN ENGLAND AND IN AMERICA

The author of this book, Dr. Francis H. Tees, has rendered a vital service in preparing a volume which tells of those early days of American Methodism referred to by Bishop Asbury. Dr. Tees for nine years has been the pastor of Old St. George's Methodist Church in Philadelphia, the oldest church in American Methodism. Despite a busy pastorate Dr. Tees has found time to examine records not always available to historical students and has presented this material in an accurate and historical attitude.

Dr. Tees has done more than record historical data for the readers of this volume will be inspired to emulate the courage, devotion, and warmth of heart that characterized the leaders of pioneer American Methodism. Dr. Tees has made a valuable contribution to Methodist literature.—PAUL NEFF GARBER, Duke University, October 26, 1939.

CHAPTER I

Brief Sketches of the Founders. Visits to America, 1735-1738
The religious movement which resulted in the foundation of Methodism began at Oxford University, Oxford, England, sometime in or prior to 1729 with a group of undergraduates who formed themselves into a society to assist and encourage one another in their studies, to read the Scriptures in the original languages and to aid one another in spiritual improvement. The group was probably first called "The Methodists."

Concerning the epithet "Methodist" John Wesley wrote in 1739: "Let it be well observed, that this is not a name which they take to themselves but one fixed upon them by way of reproach, without their approbation or consent. It was first given to three or four young men (of whom Charles Wesley was the leader) at Oxford, by a student of Christ Church, either in allusion to the ancient sect of physicians, so called from their teaching that almost all diseases might be cured by a specific *method* of diet and exercise, or from observing a more regular *method* of study and behavior than was usual with those of their age and station."

"The world, not themselves," said Whitefield, "gave them the title of Methodists, I suppose from their custom of regulating their time and planning their business of the day every morning."

On the return of John Wesley to Oxford in November, 1729, a new and deeper turn was given to the aim of the group over which he assumed leadership. "In 1729," says he, "my brother and I by reading the Bible saw inward and outward holiness therein; followed after it and incited others so to do"; and "Never did persons," wrote Whitefield, "I believe strive more earnestly to enter in at the straight gate. They kept their bodies under even to an extreme. They were dead to the world and willing to be accounted as the dung and offscouring of all things so that they might win Christ. Their hearts glowed with the love of God."

To the group was eventually applied also names that indicated not their claim but the object of their aim and methods—"The Holy Club," "The Holy Bigots," and "The Godly Club." John Wesley was called the "Curator of the Holy Club."

The original Oxford group was composed of Charles Wesley, Richard Morgan, a Mr. Kirkman, and John Wesley. In 1730 two or three of John Wesley's pupils joined. In 1732 Benjamin Ingham, a Mr. Broughton, a Mr. Clayton, James Harvey, and several others were added. In 1732 there was the very notable addition, also, of George Whitefield. Whitefield states that "Many came amongst them for a while who in the time of temptation fell away."

The names most familiar are those of the chief leaders and actual founders of Methodism—John Wesley, Charles Wesley, and George Whitefield.

John Wesley

John Wesley, the fifteenth of nineteen children, was born at Epworth, Lincolnshire, England, on June 17, 1703, to Susanna and Samuel Wesley, rector of Epworth. Wesley's mother has been credited with most of his early training and elementary education. At the age of eleven he was admitted to the Charterhouse School, London. At sixteen John Wesley was elected to Christ Church College, Oxford, and at twenty-three, to the fellowship of Lincoln College. In September, 1725, he was ordained deacon in the Church of England and in 1728, priest. From 1725 to 1729 his time was spent partly at Epworth, as his father's curate, and partly at Oxford.

The College authorities having insisted on his residence at Oxford, Wesley accordingly returned in November, 1729, and resumed the duties of his fellowship.

In 1735 he was persuaded to accompany Gen. Oglethorpe, first Governor and founder of that province, to Georgia. Charles Wesley, also, was induced to take the journey; John going as a missionary to the Indians, Charles as "Secretary for Indian Affairs." John Wesley's underlying motive, however, is revealed in the following note in his Journal under date of Tuesday, October 14, 1735: "Our end in leaving our native country was not to avoid want, ... nor to gain the dung or dross of riches or honor; but singly this—to save our souls; to live wholly to the glory of God."

In May, 1738, he wrote: "In my continual endeavor to keep the whole law, inward and outward, to the uttermost of my power, I was persuaded that I should be accepted of Him, and that I was even then in a state of salvation. In this vile abject state of bondage to sin I was indeed fighting continually, but not conquering. In this refined way of trusting to my own righteousness, I dragged on heavily, finding no comfort or help therein till the time of my leaving England."

On December 10, 1735, John Wesley, Charles Wesley, Benjamin Ingham, Charles Delamotte, James Hutton, Dr. Burton of Corpus Christi College, Oxford, and Charles Morgan, brother of Richard, set sail on the "Simmonds" from Cowes for Savannah, Georgia. Beside the crew and eighty English passengers was a company of immigrants, the fifth that had gone to Georgia, among them twenty-six Moravians under the leadership of their Bishop, David Nitschman.

"On shipboard, however," Wesley continues, "I was again active in outward works, when it pleased God of his free mercy, to give me twenty-six of the Moravian brethren for companions, who endeavored to show me a more excellent way."

The voyage proved an exceedingly stormy one but it afforded the Moravians an opportunity of displaying such humility, meekness, faith, and fearlessness as Wesley never forgot.

"Sunday, January 25, 1736.—At noon our third storm began. .... At seven I went to the Germans, I had long before observed the great seriousness of their behaviour. Of their humility they had given a continual proof, by performing those servile offices for the other passengers which none of the English would undertake; for which they would receive no pay, saying 'It was good for their proud hearts' and 'their loving Saviour had done more for them.' And every day had given them occasion of showing a meekness, which no injury could move. .... There was now an opportunity of trying whether they were delivered from a spirit of fear as well as from that of pride, anger, and revenge. In the midst of the psalm wherewith their service began, the sea broke over, split the mainsail in pieces, covered the ship, and poured in between the decks. .... A terrible screaming began among the English. The Germans calmly sang on. I asked one of them afterward 'was you not afraid?' He answered, 'I thank God, no.' I asked, 'But were not your women and children afraid?' He replied mildly, 'No, our women and children are not afraid to die.'"

Later commenting on this example of the Moravians Wesley said, "But I understood not at first. I was too learned and too wise. So that it seemed foolishness unto me. And I continued preaching and following after and trusting in that righteousness whereby no flesh can be justified."

"Friday, February 6, 1736.—About eight in the morning we first set foot on American ground .... a small uninhabited island over against Tybrie. Mr. Oglethorpe led us to a rising ground where we kneeled down to give thanks. He then took a boat to Savannah. Saturday Mr. Oglethorpe returned from Savannah with Mr. Spankenberg, one of the pastors of the Germans. I soon found out what spirit he was of and asked his advice with regard to my own conduct. He said, 'My brother I must first ask you one or two questions. Have you the witness within yourself? Does the spirit of God bear witness with your spirit that you are the child of God?'" Wesley hesitated over the answer. Again, he was asked, "Do you know Jesus Christ?" He answered, "I know he is the Saviour of the world." "True," said Spankenberg, "but do you know that he hath saved you?" Wesley answered, "I hope He has died to save me." "Do you know yourself?" persisted Spankenberg. To this Wesley replied. "I do. But," commented he, "I fear they were vain words."

Without any solicitation from him and "without either his desire or knowledge" John Wesley had been appointed by the Trustees of Georgia as minister of Savannah. While he did not refuse to serve, he declared (Journal, November 23, 1736) in answer to Oglethorpe's remark, "You cannot leave Savannah without a minister," "I know not that I am under any obligation, to the contrary, I never promised to stay here a month. I openly declared both before and ever since my coming hither, that I neither would nor could take charge of the English any longer than till I could go among the Indians."

The Moravians, sixteen in number, Wesley found in Georgia, had been conducted there the year before by Spankenberg and had been assigned two lots of ground upon which they had built a "Brotherhood House."

"Tuesday, February 24," Wesley writes at Savannah, "Mr. Quincey [whom he succeeded as rector of Christ Church] being in the house wherein we afterward were, Mr. Delamotte and I took up our lodging with the Germans. We had now an opportunity day by day of observing their whole behaivour..... They were always employed,.... cheerful.... and in good humor .... they had put away all anger, strife, bitterness, wrath, clamour, evil speaking; they walked worthy of the vocation wherewith they were called and adorned the Gospel of our Lord in all things.

"Sunday, March 7.—I entered," says Wesley, "upon my ministry at Savannah, by preaching on the Epistle for the day, being the thirteenth of the first of Corinthians..... Monday, 15.—Mr. Quincey going for Carolina, I removed into the minister's house. It is large enough for a larger family than ours, and has many conveniences besides a good garden. I could not but reflect on the well-known epigram, 'How short a time will it be before its present possessor is removed, perhaps to be no more seen.'... Monday, May 10.—I began visiting my parishioners in order from house to house; for which I set apart (the time when they cannot work, because of the heat), viz. from twelve till three in the afternoon."

While in Savannah Wesley tells us he followed a general method of "catechising the children and instructing the youth." Delamotte, it seems, "taught between thirty and forty children to read, write, and cast accounts." Both Delamotte and Wesley instructed and catechised the children on Sundays and Saturdays.

Some of the boys in Delamotte's school ridiculed others who came without shoes or stockings. On one occasion, therefore, Wesley, barefoot, took Delamotte's place. The ridicule ceased.

Besides ministering at Savannah, whose entire population was only about five hundred, Wesley ministered elsewhere, particularly at Frederica. It is estimated that he had at least seven hundred souls directly under his care.

On the whole Wesley's ministry in America does not appear to have been very encouraging or successful. Certainly his mission to the Indians, in spite of a number of contacts with them, was an admitted failure.

After nearly ten months in America Wesley declared (November 23, 1736), "Mr. Oglethorpe sailed for Europe leaving Mr. Ingham, Mr. Delamotte, and me at Savannah; but with less prospect of preaching to the Indians than when we had the first day set foot in America." October 7, 1737, he writes: "I consulted my friends, whether God did not call me to return to England? The reason for which I left it had now no force; there being no possibility as yet of instructing the Indians; neither had I, as yet, found or heard of any Indians on the continent of America, who had the least desire of being instructed..... Besides, there was a probability of doing more service to that unhappy people in England than I could do in Georgia."

Wesley's experience with certain women did not result happily for him. In 1748 he proposed marriage to Grace Murray, a young widow, who in every way seemed fitted for him but interference on the part of his brother Charles, because of her station in life, led to the engagement being broken. In 1751 after consulting with friends and being "clearly convinced" that he ought to marry, Wesley did so, marrying, to his sorrow, the widow of a London merchant, Vazeille by name. However, long before either of the above crossed his path, while at Savannah in 1737, Wesley contemplated but was advised against marriage with a Sophia Hopky.

On July 3, after Communion, Wesley reproved Sophia (now Mrs. Williamson) for some things he thought "reprovable in her behavior" and a month later, for Disciplinary reasons, repelled her from the Communion. As a result Wesley was sued for $1,000 for defamation of character. Mrs. Williamson made an affidavit which, Wesley says, "insinuated more than it asserted" and her uncle preferred charges against him of "spiritual tyranny" and the "usurpation of a new and illegal authority over their consciences."

This unfortunate affair, apparently, hastened the end of a visit that had already proven disappointing. Although the minority of the Grand Jury, to whom the presentments against Wesley were made, were favorable to him, nevertheless, feeling that he could never obtain justice, on November 3 he consulted friends a second time about leaving America. "This time," says he, "they agreed with me that the time we looked for was come."

On the 27th of November, 1737, Wesley left Savannah. On December 2, "I shook off the dust of my feet and left Georgia after having preached the Gospel," says he, "not as I ought, but as I was able, one year and nearly nine months." On December 13 he arrived at Charleston, South Carolina. On December 22 he writes, "I took my leave of America (though, if it please God, not forever)."

Writing on February 1 John Wesley says: "I left my native country in order to teach the Georgia Indians the nature of Christianity; but what have I learned myself in the meantime? Why (what I least of all suspected), that I who went to America to convert others was never myself converted to God. (I am not sure of this) I am not mad, though I thus speak; but I speak the words of truth and soberness, if haply some of those who still dream may awake, and see that as I am so are they."

Charles Wesley

Charles Wesley, known as the hymnist of Methodism, and "celebrated also, as a preacher and coadjutor of his brother John in the great evangelistic and ecclesiastical movement of their lives and times" was born at Epworth, December 18, 1707, the eighteenth child and youngest son of Samuel and Susanna Wesley.

At eight years of age Charles was enrolled at Westminster School and at nineteen he was elected to Christ Church College.

In the fall of 1735 Charles Wesley was ordained deacon and, shortly after, priest. In the same year he was persuaded to accompany John on the mission to Georgia. After a brief stay in America, ostensibly on business for Oglethorpe but sick and disappointed, he set sail from Charleston for England on August 11. His ship being forced to put in to Boston for repairs, he spent several weeks in that city and on October 5 resumed his voyage, arriving in England two months later.

In 1738 Charles met Peter Bohler, the Moravian. Charles instructed Bohler in English and he, together with John Bray, taught Charles, as he did John, the way of salvation by faith. The story of Charles' conversion is best told by himself in his Journal.

"Monday, February 20 [1738].—I began teaching Peter Bohler English.

"Friday, February 24.—At six in the evening, an hour after I had taken my electuary, the toothache returned more violently than ever. I smoked tobacco; which set me a-vomiting, and took away my senses and pain together. At eleven I waked in extreme pain, which I thought would quickly separate soul and body. Soon after Peter Bohler came to my bedside. I asked him to pray for me. He seemed unwilling at first, but, beginning very faintly, he raised his voice by degrees, and prayed for my recovery with strange confidence. Then he took me by the hand, and calmly said, 'You will not die now.' I thought within myself, 'I cannot hold out in this pain till morning. If it abates before, I believe I may recover.' He asked me, 'Do you hope to be saved?' 'Yes.' 'For what reason do you hope it?' 'Because I have used my best endeavours to serve God.' He shook his head, and said no more. I thought him very uncharitable, saying in my heart, 'What, are not my endeavours a sufficient ground of hope? Would he rob me of my endeavours? I have nothing else to trust to.'"

Thursday, May 11.—"I was just going to remove to old Mr. Hutton's when God sent Mr. Bray to me, a poor ignorant mechanic who knows nothing but Christ; yet by knowing Him knows and deserves all things. . . . . Mr. Bray is now to supply Bohler's place. We prayed together for faith."

On Pentecost Sunday, May 21, 1738, Charles still sick, John and some friends came to see him at 9 o'clock in the morning at Bray's home. While they were singing a hymn, Bray's sister drew near to Charles and said, "In the name of Jesus of Nazareth, arise, believe, and thou shalt be healed of all thy infirmities." Referring to this, Wesley continues in his Journal:

"I wondered how it should enter into her head to speak in that manner. The words struck me to the heart. I sighed, and said within myself, 'Oh, that Christ would but speak thus to me!' I lay musing and trembling: then thought, 'But what if it should be Him? I will send at least to see.' I rang, and, Mrs. Turner coming, I desired her to send up Mrs. Musgrave. She went down, and, returning, said, 'Mrs. Musgrave has not been here.' My heart sunk within me at the word, and I hoped it might be Christ indeed. However, I sent her down again to inquire, and felt in the meantime a strange palpitation of heart. I said, yet feared to say, 'I believe, I believe!' She came up again and said, 'It was I, a weak, sinful creature, spoke; but the words were Christ's: He commanded me to say them, and so constrained me that I could not forbear.'

"I sent for Mr. Bray, and asked him whether I believed. He answered, I ought not to doubt of it: it was Christ spoke to me. He knew it; and willed us to pray together: 'But first,' said he, 'I will read what I have casually opened upon: "Blessed is the man whose sin is covered: blessed is the man to whom the Lord imputeth no sin, and in whose spirit is no guile." ' Still I felt a violent opposition and reluctance to believe; yet still the Spirit of God strove with my own and the evil spirit, till by degrees He chased away the darkness of my unbelief. I found myself convinced, I knew not how nor when; and immediately fell to intercession. . . . .

"I rose and looked into the Scripture. The words that first presented were, 'And now, Lord, what is my hope? truly my hope is even in Thee.' I then cast down my eye, and met, 'He hath put a new song in my mouth, even a thanksgiving unto our God. Many shall see it, and fear, and shall put their trust in the Lord.' Afterwards I opened upon Isa. 11: 1: 'Comfort ye, comfort ye My people, saith your God: speak ye comfortably to Jerusalem, and cry unto her, that her warfare is accomplished, that her inquiry is pardoned; for she hath received of the Lord's hand double for all her sin.'

"I now found myself at peace with God, and rejoiced in hope of loving Christ."

Three days after Charles' conversion, on May 24, his brother John was converted at the Society meeting in Aldersgate Street.

Shortly after his conversion, Charles Wesley was appointed curate of St. Mary's, Islington, London. Although faithful to the Church of England to the last, this was his only appointment.

In 1739 he was summoned to appear before the Archbishop of Canterbury to answer to the charge of preaching in churches to which he had no canonical appointments. He was dismissed from the church and the clergy were forbidden to permit the Wesleys to preach in their churches. The Sunday following the dismissal Charles preached to ten thousand people in Moorfield from the text, "Come unto me all ye that travail."

In 1749 Charles Wesley was married to Sarah Gwynne, described as a "Welsh lady of piety, refinement, and fortune." Unlike his brother's, the married life of Charles was a happy one. Four sons and four daughters blessed the union.

For a number of years Charles itinerated throughout England and Wales. After his marriage he ceased to itinerate and settled in Bristol where, for twenty years, he ministered to the Society that worshiped in the "New Room," preaching regularly in its pulpit. In 1780 he attended his last Conference at Bristol. He died in London on March 29, 1788.

Charles Wesley's fame rests largely on his hymns and poetical works. From 1739 to 1785 he produced no less than 4,644 hymns, 2,030 of these "Short Hymns on Select Passages of Holy Scripture," in two volumes were published in 1762. Most of Charles' hymns were composed or written in the house at No. 4 Charles Street which he had rented at £11 a year and to which he had brought his bride. Others of his hymns he wrote as he rode or walked about the countryside.

George Whitefield

George Whitefield, the sixth son of Thomas and Elizabeth Whitefield, was born at Gloucester, England, December 16,

1714. At the age of two his father, who ran the Bell Inn, died and his mother continued to run the Inn. When George was ten his mother married again. Her marriage not being particularly happy and her circumstances having declined, Whitefield was compelled to assist in the public house—washing mops, cleaning rooms, and in a word, using his expression, he "became a professed and common drawer for nigh onto a year and a half."

"I was froward," wrote Whitefield, "from my mother's womb." He tells us that he was addicted to lying, filthy talking, foolish jesting, cursing and stealing, although he often stole to give to the poor. Early, however, he had convictions of sin and when the Inn was closed for the night he sat at the window reading the Bible by the light of the candle. Again, he tells us, he was "fond of playing and imitating clergymen." He tells us, also, that he composed two or three sermons and dedicated one to his elder brother. "A dear youth, now with God," says he "would often entreat me, when serving at the bar, to go to Oxford. My general answer was, 'I wish I could!' "

On his return from a visit to his brother at Bristol, Whitefield lived with his mother, who had given up the Inn. Providentially they were visited by an Oxford student, a servitor in Pembroke College. In the course of a conversation the student remarked that after all expenses at college for the quarter had been paid he had one penny left. Mrs. Whitefield at once exclaimed, "This will do for my son!" Then turning to George she said, "Will you go to Oxford, George?" He immediately answered, "With all my heart."

Returning to the grammar school of St. Mary de Crypt, Whitefield, it is said, not only resumed his studies with greater diligence, but endeavored to promote religion and virtue among his associates. In 1732, at the age of eighteen, he went to Oxford and was admitted, as a servitor, into Pembroke College.

At Oxford Whitefield met the Wesley's and was introduced by Charles into the "Holy Club," becoming its leader on the departure of the Wesleys for America in December, 1735.

Shortly after his entrance at Oxford, Whitefield was converted. "Under the influence of religious impressions," says Hutton, a personal friend, "his enthusiastic disposition was rapidly kindled." After days of bitter penitence marked by "lying whole days and nights on the ground in silent or vocal prayer; leaving off the fruits of the earth; choosing the worst food; thinking it unbecoming a penitent to have his hair powdered, wearing woolen gloves, a patched gown and dirty shoes, to acquire a habit of humility," Whitefield finally obtained peace and the consciousness of pardon.

"Indications of a spiritual turn of mind being reported," continues Hutton, "to Dr. Benson, Bishop of Gloucester, he offered Whitefield ordination." "The bishop sent for him," said Wesley, "and told him, 'Though I had purposed to ordain none under three and twenty, yet I will ordain you whenever you come.'" After much prayer and study of the thirty-nine Articles, Whitefield accepted the offer and in 1736 was ordained deacon. On the Sunday following his ordination he preached his first sermon in his native town of Gloucester.

After his ordination as deacon Whitefield returned to Oxford for his bachelor's degree. Shortly after receiving his degree he was invited to London to serve for two months the cure of a friend. While in London he received letters from the Wesleys, who were in Georgia, "which made him long to go and help them but not seeing his way clear then he returned to Oxford." From there he was called to Dummer but his mind, as Wesley put it, "still ran on going to America."

In the next two years, through his preaching in London, Bath, Bristol, and elsewhere, he became widely known throughout the Kingdom. At length on December 30, 1737, he went on board ship bound for America. After a month's delay and a stop at Gilbralter, where he ministered to all classes of people, he proceeded on what proved the first of thirteen passages across the Atlantic. On May 7 he reached Georgia where he remained until August, 1738.

In his autobiography Benjamin Franklin says, "The settlement of that province [Georgia] had lately been begun but instead of being made with hardy, industrious husbandmen, accustomed to labor, the only fit for such an enterprise, it was with families of broken shopkeepers and insolvent debtors, many of indolent and idle habits, taken out of the jails, who being set down in the woods, unqualified for clearing land, and unable to endure the hardships of a new settlement, perished in large numbers leaving many helpless children unprovided for. The sight of their miserable situation inspired the benevolent heart of Mr. Whitefield with the idea of building an orphan house there, in which they might be supported and educated."

Wesley, speaking of the first visit of Whitefield to America, says: "It was now that he observed the deplorable condition of many children there that God put into his heart the first thought of founding an orphan house for which he determined to raise contributions in England."

Having returned to England, on January 14, 1739 Whitefield was ordained priest at Christ Church, Oxford.

After many delays, during which he went from place to place raising money for his Orphan House and for which the Trustees of Georgia had granted him a commission (May 16, 1739) and 500 acres of land (June 2, 1739), eventually on August 14, 1739, he embarked again for America.

On board ship Whitefield wrote "A Short Account of God's Dealings with the Reverend Mr. George Whitefield, A.B., late of Pembroke College, Oxford, from His Infancy to the time of his entering Holy Orders." The manuscript he sent over from Philadelphia to London to be published for the benefit of the Orphan House.

On his return to England from America in 1741, Whitefield was married in Wales to a widow. A son, John, born to the union, died at the age of four months. The domestic relations of Whitefield, like those of John Wesley, were not pleasant, due, it is thought, to his frequent and often lengthy absences. Mrs. Whitefield died on August 9, 1765, Whitefield, himself, preaching her funeral sermon four days later.

In 1770 Whitefield came to America for the last time. After five months at Savannah he proceeded to Philadelphia, thence to New York via Bristol and Burlington. From New York he sets out for Boston. On September 23 we find him at Portsmouth, N. H.; then, Kittery, Maine; York, Maine; Portsmouth again, and Exeter, where he preached September 29 for Dr. Daniel Rogers, his last sermon.

From Exeter Whitefield rode to Newbury, accompanied by the Rev. Moses Parsons, at whose home he died September 30, 1770. According to Belcher, "Dr. Hallock, who visited Newburyport and the tomb of Whitefield in 1822, was then told by persons he considered reliable that when Whitefield was retiring to his chamber on the last evening of his life, many were so desirous to see and hear him that he stood on the stairs with a lamp in his hand and gave them a tender spiritual address." At his own request he was buried in a crypt under the pulpit of Old South Church, Newburyport, Mass.

The zeal of Whitefield for souls is revealed in a measure in Franklin's letter to him dated at Philadelphia June 19, 1764. "Your frequently repeated wishes for my eternal as well as temporal happiness are very obliging and I can only thank you for them and offer mine in return. I have myself no doubt that I shall enjoy as much of both as is proper for me. That Being who gave me existence and through almost three score years has been continually showering his favors upon me, whose very chastisements have been blessings to me; can I doubt that he loves me? And if he loves me, can I doubt that he will go on to take care of me, not only here but hereafter? This to some may seem presumptuous; to me it appears but grounded hope; hope of the future built on experience of past."

That Whitefield was severely criticized, condemned, and even his character attacked is commonly known. "Many condemn," said Joseph Pilmoor, but he adds, "few are either able or willing to imitate him."

"His writing and printing," said Franklin, "from time to time gave great advantage to his enemies; unguarded expressions and erroneous opinions, delivered in preaching, might have afterwards been explained or qualified by supposing others that might have accompanied them, or they might have been denied, but *littera scripta manet*. Critics attacked his writings violently and with so much appearance of reason as to diminish the number of his votaries and prevent their increase; so that I am of the opinion if he had never written anything he would have left behind him a much more numerous and important sect, and his reputation might in that case have been still growing after his death, as, there being nothing of his writing on which to found a censure and give him a lower character, his proselytes would be left at liberty to feign for him as great variety of excellencies as their enthusiastic admiration might wish him to have possessed."

Again, Franklin said, "I, who was intimately acquainted with him (being employed in printing his sermons and Journals, etc.) never had the least suspicion of his integrity, but am to this day decidedly of the opinion that he was in all his conduct a perfectly honest man; and methinks my testimony in his favor ought to have more weight, as we had no religious connection. He used indeed, sometimes to pray for my conversion, but never had the satisfaction of believing that his prayers were heard. Ours was a mere civil friendship, sincere on both sides and lasted to his death."

On learning from his wife that his character had been aspersed by a certain clergyman, Whitefield said, "I am content to wait till the day of judgment for the clearing up of my character; and after I am dead, I desire no other epitaph than this, 'Here lies George Whitefield. What sort of man he was the great day will discover.' "

CHAPTER II

Laying the Foundations

In December, 1736, after about six months' stay in America, Charles Wesley returns to England where on the twenty-first day of May he was converted. On February 1, 1738, John Wesley, after an absence of almost two years and four months, landed at Deal. The first and only visit of the brothers to America has been completed.

Tuesday, February 7, 1738, John Wesley writes in his Journal, "(A day much to be remembered.) At the house of Mr. Weinantz, a Dutch merchant, I met Peter Bohler, Schulius Richter and Wensel Neiser, just landed from Germany."

On February 17, 1738, Wesley, in company with Peter Bohler, went to Oxford. "By him," says he, "(in the hand of a great God) I was, on Sunday, the 5th (March) clearly convinced of unbelief, of the want of that faith whereby alone we are saved." Wesley saw Bohler had "an inner peace, a vivid consciousness of salvation" he himself did not possess. He decided to quit preaching but Bohler urged him to continue. "But what can I preach?" asked he. "Preach faith till you have it," was the answer, "and then because you have it, you will preach faith." Being convinced that Bohler's views on faith were scriptural, Wesley strove earnestly to possess it.

On May 1, 1738, John Wesley was recalled from Oxford by his brother's illness. Charles was at the home of James Hutton in Aldersgate Street near Temple Bar. Here on the evening of his arrival, writes Wesley, "The little society began, which after met in Fetter Lane. Our fundamental rules were as follows: In obedience to the command of God by St. James and by the advice of Peter Bohler, it is agreed by us." Then followed eleven rules, the substance of which were that the group meet weekly; form themselves into bands of five and ten; speak freely to one another about their religious life; have a general meeting every Wednesday evening and a love feast once a month on Sunday night from seven to ten;

that admission to the society should be, if no objection, after two months' trial, and that any member who acts contrary to order of the society, not conforming after being thrice admonished was not any longer to be esteemed a member.

From the rules it would appear that this society was the pattern after which later the Methodist Society was fashioned.

In the group who met at the time were the Wesleys, Hutton, Bohler, Bray, and later Whitefield, Delamotte, Ingham, and others.

On May 22-24, 1738, Wesley writes: "All the time I was at Savannah I was thus beating the air. Being ignorant of the righteousness of Christ, which by saving faith in him, brought salvation 'to every one that believeth.' I sought to establish my own righteousness, and so labored in the fire all my days. In the evening (twenty-fourth) I went very unwillingly to a society [above referred to] in Aldersgate Street where one was reading Luther's Preface to the Epistle to the Romans. About quarter before nine, while he was describing the change which God works in the heart through faith in Christ, I felt my heart strangely warmed; I felt I did trust in Christ, Christ alone, for salvation, and an assurance was given me that He had taken away my sins, even mine, and saved me from the law of sin and death. I began to pray with all my might for all those who had in an especial manner despitefully used and persecuted me. I then testified openly to all what I now felt in my heart. But it was not long before the enemy suggested, 'This cannot be faith, for where is the joy?' Then was I taught that peace and victory over sin are essential to faith in the Captain of our salvation; but that as to the transports of joy that usually attend the beginning of it, especially in those that have mourned deeply, God sometimes giveth, sometimes withholdeth them, according to the counsels of his own will."

In his Journal (February 9, 1736) Wesley quotes Spankenberg as saying that the village of Hernhuth, thirty miles from Dresden on the Bohemian border, contained "about a thousand souls, gathered out of many nations," and that they "hold fast the discipline as well as the faith and practice of the apostolical church." On June 7, 1738, Wesley writes of his determination "to retire for a short time into Germany" to this

Moravian settlement, which he had proposed to do before he left Georgia. He hoped that "conversing with those holy men who were living witnesses of the full power of faith and yet able to bear with those that are weak, would be the means under God of so establishing" his own soul that he "might go from faith to faith and from strength to strength."

On August 1, 1738, Wesley arrives at the settlement. On September 16 we find him back again in London. From that date until the spring of 1739 he divides his time largely between London and Oxford.

In November, 1738, several persons came to Wesley desiring him to advise and pray with them. He agreed to meet them on Thursday nights at the Foundry in London. Their numbers increased and in 1739 the first Methodist Society was organized. Later other Societies were organized in Bristol, Kingswood, New Castle, and in many parts of England, Scotland, and Ireland.

Continuing his account of the request for advice and prayer, Wesley makes this significant statement—for let it be remembered, it was after his heart-warming experience of May 24— "It may be observed, the desire was on *their* part, *not mine*, my desire was to live and die in retirement. But I did not see that I could refuse them my help and be guiltless before God."

Leaving Wesley for the time, let us turn now to George Whitefield, who during Wesley's absence in America, preached in London and elsewhere in the Kingdom. Of his London ministry he later wrote, "Many were awakened by my preaching."

While in London, as we have related, Whitefield received letters from the Wesleys, then in Georgia, that awakened in him a desire to join them. At length, on December 30, 1737, he boarded the ship "Whitaker," which after a month's delay, set sail, by way of Gilbralter, for America.

A short time after Whitefield sailed for Georgia his vessel passed the one on which Wesley was returning from that colony. On January 29, 1738, Wesley writes in his Journal: "Toward evening was calm; but in the night a strong wind brought us safe into the Downs. The day before, Mr. Whitefield had sailed but neither of us then knowing anything of the other." When Wesley landed and learned of Whitefield's departure and found it possible to communicate with him, he wrote: "When I saw God by the wind which was carrying you out brought me in, I asked counsel of God, his answer you have enclosed." The enclosed was a slip of paper upon which were written: "Let him return to London." This instruction, it is supposed, Wesley in some way obtained by lot, to which he frequently had recourse. Whitefield prayed for direction and then resumed his voyage.

It is said that "the first voyage of Whitefield to America was invested with scenes of far more than common interest. He was a stripling in his twenty-third year and yet in his hands all on board became as pliable as willow. He converted the chief cabin into a cloister, the deck into a church and the steerage into a schoolroom."

On May 7, 1738, Whitefield arrived at Savannah. On June 11 he opened a girls' school. After visiting Fredericka, Thunderbolt, Highgate, Ebenezer, and Charleston he left for England September 9, 1738, for the purpose of obtaining priest's orders and to raise money to erect an orphanage at Savannah.

Reaching London December 8, Whitefield, in his Journal says, "In the evening I went to a truly Christian society in Fetter Lane, and perceived God had greatly watered the seed sown by my ministry when last in London." On December 10 he writes, "Here seems to be a great pouring out of the Spirit and many who were awakened by my preaching a year ago are now grown strong men in Christ by the ministry of my dear friends and fellow-laborers, John and Charles Wesley."

On his return from America, "Whitefield found," says another, "that the unpopularity of the Wesleys soon began to extend itself to him." December 10 he writes, "Five churches have been already denied me, and some of the clergy, if possible would oblige me to depart out of these coasts but I rejoice in this opposition, it being a certain sign that a more effectual door will be opened, since there are so many adversaries. However, I had an opportunity of preaching at St. Helen's and at Islington in the afternoon, to a large congregation indeed, with great demonstration of the spirit, and with power. In the evening I went to Fetter Lane Society where we had what might not be improperly called a love feast. Sunday, December 24, preached twice and went in the evening to the Crooked Lane Society."

In the course of time we find Whitefield in Bristol. "Thursday, February 15, I went . . . . to the reverend Mr. G——s, minister of St. Mary, Ratcliffe who, as I was informed, had promised to lend me his church to preach in for the orphan house. But he, in effect, gave me a refusal telling me he could not lend me his church without a special order from the chancellor."

While in Bristol collecting money for his orphanage it was "tauntingly" said of Whitefield wrote Wesley, "If he will convert heathen why does he not go to the colliers of Kingswood?" This made a deep impression upon him and being denied access to the pulpits he turned, February 16, 1739, to open air preaching. Taking his stand under an old sycamore tree on Hanham Mount he preached to about two hundred colliers. Five days later he preached to five thousand people; on February 23 to ten thousand "with tears streaming down their cheeks." At Rose Green he preached to fourteen thousand at one time and twenty thousand at another. "March 25 he preached at Hanham to a larger congregation than ever—twenty-three thousand." Gradually his circle extended from Bath to Newport and Cardiff.

Being impressed with the magnitude of the work about Bristol and feeling called to return to America, Whitefield sent for Wesley.

Thursday, March 15, 1739, Wesley writes in his Journal, "I had no thought of leaving London, when I received a letter from Mr. Whitefield and another from Mr. Seward, intreating me, in the most pressing manner, to come to Bristol without delay. This I was not at all forward to do, and perhaps a little less inclined to it because of the remarkable scriptures which offered as often as we inquired touching the consequences of this removal." Wesley, it seems, had gone to the Society, now in Fetter Lane, to consult the brethren. It was suggested that they open their Bible at random and be guided by the texts to which they opened. These texts (Deut. 32: 49, 50; 34: 8; Acts 9: 16; 8: 2) were not very encouraging to take the trip. Lots were then drawn and the answer was "go." Accordingly, on Thursday, March 29, Wesley left London for Bristol. In the evening of the thirty-first he arrived at his destination.

"Saturday, March 31 at my return home," says Whitefield, "I was much refreshed with the sight of my honored friend, Mr. John Wesley, whom God's providence has sent to Bristol. Lord now lettest thy servant depart in peace." Wesley's hostess at Bristol was Mrs. Grevil, Whitefield's sister. It was in her home in Wine Street that the two met.

On the very night of his arrival Wesley went with Whitefield to a meeting at Weaver's Hall, "one of the early meeting places," says Dr. Frederick Platt, "of the Religious Societies which had so intimate association with the work of God in those earliest weeks of the Revival."

On Sunday, April 1, Whitefield set Wesley the example of preaching in the open. Commenting on it Wesley says, "I could scarce reconcile myself at first to this strange way of preaching in the fields of which he set me an example on Sunday." On the same day Wesley addressed a religious group meeting in Nicholas Street while Whitefield addressed another in Baldwin Street. The rapid growth of these groups doubtless led to the building of the first chapel, "The New Room" in the Horse Fair. Wednesday, May 9, Wesley writes, "We took possession of a piece of ground near St. James church yard, in the Horse Fair where it was designed to build a room large enough to contain both the societies of Nicholas and Baldwin Streets."

Monday, April 2, Wesley takes the momentous step and preaches in the open. "I submitted," writes he, "to be more vile and preached in the highways the glad tidings of salvation, speaking from an eminence in a ground (brickyard) adjoining the city to about three thousand people."

On June 11 he receives "a pressing letter from London to come thither as soon as possible" as his brethren in Fetter Lane "were in great confusion for want of his presence and advice." Two days later he hastens to London and at six o'clock in the evening "knowing how they had been lately shaken" he warned the women "not to believe every spirit but to try the spirits whether they be of God." At eight o'clock he met the brethren when "it pleased God," writes he, "to remove many misunderstandings and offences that had crept in among them and to restore in good measure 'the spirit of love and of a sound mind.'"

Peace at Fetter Lane was, however, only temporary. Grave disorders and disputings arose about the ordinances, over doctrine and because of claims, concerning themselves and concerning the Moravian Church, made by certain ministers. After many times healing their divisions, finally on July 16, 1740, Wesley's usefulness came to an end. In answer to the question whether they would suffer him to preach at Fetter Lane and after a short debate, it was answered, "No; this place is taken for the Germans."

At the close of the meeting at Fetter Lane on the following Sunday, Wesley read a paper in which he said, "I have warned you hereof again and again and besought you to turn back to the law and the testimony. I have borne with you long, hoping you would turn. But as I find you more and more confirmed in the error of your ways, nothing now remains but that I should give you up to God. You that are of the same judgment, follow me." "I then," says Wesley, "without saying anything more, withdrew, as did eighteen or nineteen of the society."

Wesley's "attempt at field preaching," as another has well said, "was the precursor of a lifelong practice of his up and down the country despite his acknowledged greater love of the reverence and quietness of indoor services." Declaring the world his parish, he rode for half a century throughout Britain, averaging 4,000 miles a year and visiting practically every town and village. Beginning his labors at four or five o'clock in the morning and preaching on the average of fifteen sermons a week and no less than 40,000 during his ministry.

Relieved of the work at Bristol, Whitefield almost immediately, on Wesley's arrival, prepared to leave.

Writing of his leave taking, Monday, April 2, Whitefield

IN ENGLAND AND IN AMERICA

says: "Crowds were waiting at the door to give me a last farewell, and nearly twenty friends accompanied me on horseback. . . . . Many sinners, I believe have been effectually converted . . . . numbers have come to me under conviction and all the children of God have been exceedingly comforted. And what gives me the greater comfort is the consideration that my dear and honored friend, Mr. Wesley, is left behind to confirm those that are awakened; so that when I return from Georgia, I hope to see many bold soldiers of Jesus Christ."

From Bristol Whitefield crossed to Wales, preaching there on walls, on tombstones, and in the fields. Returning to England he visited his native town of Gloucester, Cheltenham, Oxford, and London where he found but one pulpit open to him. That soon closing, he preached in the church yard of Islington, Moorfields, and on the Kennington Common. On August 14, 1739, with a thousand pounds in his possession for the erection of the orphanage in Savannah and accompanied by William Seward, of London, eight men, a boy, and two children, whom he called his "family," he sailed for the second time to America.

In America, where he preceded Whitefield by nearly two years, Wesley's labors were confined largely to Georgia and carried on over the period just mentioned on his first and only visit. That he considered another trip to this country seems clear from his last words on leaving America (December 22, 1737) and from his correspondence. Writing to Whitefield, then on his last visit here, Wesley said: "I trust our Lord has more work for you to do in Europe as well as in America. And who knows, but before your return to England I may pay another visit to the new world! I have been strongly solicited by several of our friends in New York and Philadelphia."

In a letter to Rev. Walter Sellon, dated London, December 30, 1769, Wesley writes: "My dear Brother: It is not determined whether I should go to America or not. I have been importuned for some time; but *nil sat firmi video*. I must have a clear call before I am at liberty to leave Europe."

On December 14, 1770, he writes to a Mrs. Marston of Worcester.

"My dear Sister: If I live till spring and should have a clear, pressing call, I am as ready to embark for America as for Iceland. All places are alike to me. I am attached to none in particular. Wherever the work of the Lord is to be carried on, *that* is my place for today. And we live for today; it is not our part to take thought for tomorrow.

"I am, my dear Mollie, your affectionate Brother,

John Wesley."

Referring to rumors that he was going to America, on February 1, 1772, he wrote to Sellon:

"Dear Walter: You do not understand your information right. Observe, 'I am going to America to turn bishop.' You are to understand it is *in sensu composito*. I am not to be bishop until I am in America. While I am in Europe, therefore, you have nothing to fear; but as soon as ever you hear of my being landed in Philadelphia, it will be time for your apprehensions to revive. It is true some of our preachers would not have me stay so long, but I keep my old rule, *Festina lente*.

"I am, dear Walter, your affectionate Brother,

John Wesley."

In spite of his invitations, his inclinations, and the rumors Wesley never made the second visit to America. It is thought that in his later years at least he was deterred by the fact that there was no one to take his place as head of the Societies and his feeling that his people would object strongly to his going.

Before and After the Revival

Before the Methodist Revival, England had sunk in some respects to the lowest depths of degradation. "Walpole's period of Supremacy," it is said, "had given England peace and plenty, but his rule was not an inspiring one. 'Soul extinct, stomach well alive' might have been the motto for the period." Gambling, sports of the cruelest kind, drunkenness and profligacy were rife and the Church was without inspiration or leadership.

"The outward state of things," said Bishop Burnett, "is bad

enough but that which heightens my fears arises chiefly from the inward state into which unhappily we are fallen."

"Both among dissenters and churchmen," said Watts, "there was a general decay of religion in the hearts and lives of men."

"The very devil of sensual impiety and heartless irreligion," declared Brewster, "pervaded all walks of life. Christianity was not believed in. The chief ministers of the Church often stained with sin and puffed up with pride, delivered over to underlings the people they were deputed to guide and save."

"Is there a nation under the sun," asks Wesley (1744), "which is so deeply fallen from the first principles of all religion? Where is the country in which is found so utter disregard to even heathen morality; such as a thorough contempt of justice and truth, and all that should be dear and honorable to rational creatures.

"What species of vice that can possibly be named, even of those that nature abhors, of which we have not had for many years a plentiful and still increasing harvest. What sin remains, either in Rome or Constantinople, which we have not imported long ago (if it was not of our own native growth) and improved upon ever since?

"Such a complication of villainies of every kind . . . . such a scorn of whatever bears the face of virtue, such injustice, fraud, falsehood, perjury . . . . and such a method of law we may defy the world to produce.

"What multitudes . . . . who do not profess any religion at all! What numbers that profess much confute their profession by their practice! Yea, and perhaps by their exorbitant pride, vanity, covetousness, rapaciousness or oppression cause the very name of religion to stink in the nostrils of many (otherwise) reasonable men."

In America conditions were quite similar to those in England. For example in Philadelphia, the metropolis of America, drunkenness, Sabbath desecration, ruffianism, dissipation, immorality, murder, and gambling were all too common. Much of the existing evil was traceable to lotteries resorted to for every conceivable purpose and by all classes of people. The erection of public baths and pleasure grounds, the paving of streets and even the building and finishing of churches were accomplished by lottery, apparently without conscience or compunction.

Through the preaching of Wesley and Whitefield, a moral and spiritual revolution broke out among all classes. All England, and without doubt, in only a slighter degree, America were regenerated. "What a change," wrote Rev. John Newton in 1770, "has taken place throughout the land within little more than thirty years, that is, since the first set of despised ministers came to Oxford. And how much of this change has been owing to God's blessing on Mr. Whitefield's labors, is well known to many who have lived through this period, and can hardly be denied by those least willing to allow it."

Whitefield seemed to have "bulked larger," as another has expressed it, among contemporaries than either John or Charles Wesley. The following sarcastic article in *Lloyd's Evening Post* (May 26, 1769) would seem to support this opinion. "The public were informed that the following promotions in the Church were about to be declared: The Rev. G. Whitefield, Archbishop of Boston; Rev. W. Romaine, Bishop of New York; Rev. J. Wesley, Bishop of Pennsylvania; Rev. M. Maxam, Bishop of the Carolinas; Rev. W. Shirley, Bishop of Virginia and the Rev. C. Wesley, Bishop of Nova Scotia."

Comparing Whitefield and Wesley a writer in the *North Bristol Review* said: "Few characters could be more completely converse and in the Church's exigencies, more happily the supplement of one another than were those of George Whitefield and John Wesley.

"Whitefield was soul, Wesley was system. Whitefield was a summer cloud which burst at morning or noon a fragrant exhalation over an ample track, and took the rest of the day to gather again; Wesley was the polished conduit in the midst of the garden through which the living water glided in pearly brightness and perennial music, the same vivid stream from day to day.

"A master of assemblies, Whitefield was no match for the isolated man. Wesley could conquer any number one by one. All force and impetus, Whitefield was the powder blast in the quarry and by one explosive sermon would shake a district and detach materials for other men's long work. Wesley loved to split and turn each fragment into uniform plinths and polished stones. Whitefield was the bargeman or wagoner who brought the timber of the house, Wesley was the architect that set it up."

Again says the writer in the *Review*, "Wesley was always constructing societies and with a king-like craft of ruling was most at home presiding over a class or conference." It was souls, not societies, Whitefield was most interested in. "He had no patience for ecclesiastical polity, no aptitude for pastoral details." These were the things he left to Wesley and to those who were commissioned and trained by him. Moreover, he rejoiced in the fact that Wesley faithfully shepherded those he was instrumental in winning for Christ.

"Whitefield and Wesley," said William Blake—painter-seer, "were Miracles of the 18th Century. God sent his two servants Whitefield and Wesley; were they prophets, or were they idiots and madmen? Show us miracles? Can you have greater miracles than these? Men who devote their whole comforts to entire scorn, injury and death?"

Chapter III

Rise of the Society, Class, Itinerant, Conference, etc.

The first step, referred to elsewhere, leading to the organization of Methodism seems to have been taken by Wesley in November, 1738. While Wesley is quoted as saying "In the latter end of 1739, etc.," it is evident that 1738 and not 1739 is meant. 1739 does not dovetail with other dates and facts nor does it agree with the British Conference Minutes of 1766 (Vol. I, page 60) which give 1738.

The First Society—"In November, 1738," says Wesley, "two or three persons who desired to flee the wrath to come, and then seven or eight more, came to me in London and desired me to advise and pray with them. I said if you will meet on Thursday night, I will help you as well as I can! More and more then desired to meet with them till they increased by many hundreds."

"Thus arose, without any previous design on either side what was afterward called *a Society;* a very innocent name, and very common in London, for any number of people associating themselves together. The thing proposed in their associating themselves together was very obvious to every one. They wanted to 'flee the wrath to come,' and to assist each other in so doing. They therefore united themselves "in order to pray together, to receive the word of exhortation, and to watch over one another in love, that they might help each other to work out their salvation.'" (Plain Acct. Etc.)

"This (then) was the rise of the Methodist Society, first in London, afterward in Bristol, New Castle, and other parts of England, Scotland and Ireland" and eventually in America.

We have seen in the second chapter that when on Sunday, July 20, 1740, Wesley left the Fetter Lane Society, eighteen or nineteen followed him. These met with him and the others already meeting there at the Foundry. "About twenty-five of our brethren, God has given to us already," says he, July 23, "all of whom think and speak the same thing; seven or eight and forty likewise, of the fifty women who were in band, desired to cast in their lot with us."

By 1743 the Fetter Lane Society, which had become purely Moravian, numbered but seventy-two, while the London Methodists numbered nearly two thousand.

On December 25, 1738, a set of Rules were drawn up for the guidance of the members in the Societies. On May 1, 1743, at New Castle, John and Charles Wesley framed a set of General Rules for the guidance of the United Societies. These Rules define a Society, state its purpose, and lay down the one condition of membership and how it is met and manifested.

Officers of a Society—The officers of a Society consisted of "the Minister, the Assistant, Stewards, Leaders, Visitors of the Sick, School Masters, and Housekeepers."

The "Housekeeper" in some of Wesley's Societies resided in the houses built in several of the large towns where both he and the preachers abode during their stay. "They were," says Watson, "elderly and pious women, who, being once invested with an official character, extended it *from the house to the church*, to the occasional annoyance of the preachers. As married preachers began to occupy the house, the housekeepers were at length dispensed with."

Stewards—To accommodate the little group that met for prayer and advice, Wesley leased an abandoned government cannon foundry. "In a few days," says he, "some of them said, 'Sir, we will not sit under you for nothing. We will subscribe quarterly.' I said, 'I will have nothing for I want nothing. My Fellowship supplies me with all and more than I want.' One replied, 'Nay but you want £115 to pay for the lease of the foundry, and likewise a large sum of money will be wanting to put it in repair.' On this consideration, I suffered them to subscribe. And when the Society met, I asked, 'Who will take the trouble of receiving this money and paying it where it is needful?' One said, 'I will do it and keep the account for you.' So here was the first Steward. Afterward I desired one or two more to help me as Stewards, and in process of time a greater number.

"Let it be remarked, it was I myself, not the people who

chose these Stewards and appointed to each the distinct work wherein he was to help me as long as I desired. And herein I began to exercise another sort of power; namely, that of appointing and removing Stewards."

Assistants, Helpers—After a time young men (Thomas Maxfield, one of Wesley's first converts in Nicholas St. Bristol, May 1, 1739, Thomas Richards and Thomas Westall were the first three) came to Wesley desiring to help him, laboring when and where he should direct. Those accepted were "appointed" as Wesley's "assistants." Wesley says, "Here commenced my power to appoint preachers when and where and how each should help me and of desiring any of them to meet me when I saw good while he chose to continue with me—for each had the power to go away when he pleased." The term "assistant" was eventually applied to one in charge of preachers on a Circuit. All traveling preachers or itinerants were called "helpers"—that is helpers of Wesley.

In 1784 the "helper" or traveling preacher was called upon to "Observe, you are not to ramble up and down but to go where the Assistant directs, and there only."

Maxfield, probably too quick to exercise his gifts, while Wesley was away, began to preach in London. Wesley on returning was about to prohibit him from further preaching. Mrs. Wesley, however, had heard him preach and she remonstrated with her son, saying, "Be careful what you do with respect to the young man for he is as surely called of God to preach as you are. Examine what have been the fruits of his preaching and hear him for yourself."

The First Chapel—Methodists and Dissenters in England spoke and still speak of their houses of worship as chapels. The first place of Methodist worship to be called a church was St. George's, Philadelphia.

The foundation stone for the first Methodist chapel was laid at Bristol, May 12, 1739, by Wesley. The first sermon was preached by him at the opening service on June 3 of that year in "the shell" of the new Society room. About 2,000 people, it is said, were present in the surrounding garden. The Room, or "New Room," as it is called, seems to have been a long building divided into a Society room and school, with a smaller room in which Wesley spoke with those who came to him, and a garret in which he slept.

In 1792 Portland Chapel was built largely through the efforts of Captain Webb, whose body is buried in one of its vaults. After the erection of this Chapel the "uses of the 'New Room' declined." For a time it seems to have been abandoned and in 1808 was sold to the Welsh Calvinistic Methodists. In 1930 it was repurchased and presented to the Wesleyan Methodist Conference.

Dr. Platt gives the following interesting account of the decline of the "New Room." "At the opening services of Portland Chapel, Samuel Bradburn and Thomas Roberts, at the request of the trustees, wore gown and bands and read the liturgy in surplices. Later on the Lord's Supper was administered in the chapel when Henry Moore, one of the preachers whom Wesley had ordained, took part. The trustees of the 'New Room' promptly disavowed these actions and served Moore with a legal notice forbidding him to preach in the 'New Room.'"

This action on the part of the trustees of the "New Room" was a distinct violation of the provisions of the "Poll Deed" enrolled by Wesley in Chancery in 1784.

Dr. Platt continues: "As there was a growing desire throughout Methodism to have the sacraments administered in Methodist chapels and by Methodist preachers, the Bristol controversy threatend to divide the whole Connexion. Conference was appealed to, but hesitated to give judgment for fear of a disastrous schism. Again Bristol became the sphere of a new and momentous departure in the history of Methodism. Early in 1795 Benson and Moore, the opposing leaders in the controversy, met in Bristol, and, with the help of Dr. Coke and Samuel Bradburn, sketched the scheme of compromise which took shape at the ensuing Conference as the famous *Plan of Pacification*.' This became a sort of Magna Charta for the Methodist preachers. It decreed that with the consent of the majority of the trustees, leaders and stewards, the Sacrament of the Lord's Supper could henceforth be administered in any chapel by Methodist preachers. The Portland trustees had won the battle for the whole Connexion; the administration soon became general. Henry Moore took charge of Portland, leaving the 'New Room' under the care of Joseph Benson. Soon Benson's people were reduced to a handful, when Old King Street chapel was opened; and the glory of the oldest Methodist shrine was eclipsed for more than a century."

In 1748, when, as Wesley writes, "there was no small danger of the room falling upon our heads," the building was enlarged to about twice its size.

The First Local Preacher—Wesley's ministers from the beginning were laymen. He called them at first his "assistants." In 1740 at Kingswood he authorized John Cennick, the first "local preacher," and the first of that band of faithful laymen from whose ranks the itinerant was recruited and who aided greatly in the expansion of Methodism.

Cennick, by his Calvinistic teaching, became the center and source of the first Methodist controversy, divided the Kingswood Society, separated from Wesley, and in 1742 formed the first Moravian Society in Kingswood.

Cennick was the author of a number of hymns, three of which are very familiar—"Jesus, my all to heaven is gone," "Thou dear Redeemer, dying Lamb," and "Children of the Heavenly King." He was author of two "graces," also, the more familiar of which is "Be present at our table, Lord," often referred to as "Wesley's grace."

The First School—In June, 1739, the foundations of the first Methodist School were laid at Kingswood by John Wesley and George Whitefield. John Cennick was the first Master of Kingswood. The purpose of the School was to educate coal miners' children at a time when there was no provision for the instruction of the children of the poor. The School was the forerunner of the New Kingswood School at Bath for preachers' sons.

The Watch Night Service—The first notice we find of this service is in Wesley's Journal, Friday, April 9, 1742, as follows: "We had the first watch-night in London. We commonly choose for this solemn service the Friday night nearest the full moon, either before or after, that those of the congregation who live at a distance may have light to their several homes. The service begins at half an hour past eight, and continues a little after midnight. We have often found a peculiar blessing at these seasons. There is generally a deep awe upon the congregation, perhaps in some measure owing to the silence of the night, particularly in singing the hymn, with which we conclude—

" 'Hearken to the solemn voice, the awful midnight cry!
Waiting souls, rejoice, rejoice, and feel the Bridegroom nigh.' "

The following is Wesley's own account of the origin of this service. "I was informed that several persons in Kingswood frequently met together at the School and (when they could spare the time) spent the greater part of the night in prayer and praise and thanksgiving. Some advised me to put an end to this; but upon weighing the thing thoroughly and comparing it with the practice of the early Christians (Wesley probably refers to the Vigiliae held in connection with the Agapae), I could see no cause to forbid it. Rather I believed it could be made of more general use. So I sent them word I designed to watch with them on Friday nearest the full moon, that we might have light thither and back again. I gave public notice of this the Sunday before, and withal that I intended to preach; desiring they, and they only, would meet me there who could do it without prejudice to their business or families. On Friday abundance of people came. I began preaching between eight and nine and we continued a little beyond the noon of the night, singing, praying, and praising God."

In 1789 it was enjoined that "every watch-night should be held till midnight."

The Class Meeting—On February 15, 1742, there came into existence what was for years a characteristic feature of Methodism—the Class Meeting. This arose primarily out of the necessity of paying the debt on Bristol Chapel. Captain Foy proposed that every member of the Society should pay one penny a week. Someone then suggested that perhaps there were some too poor to afford it. To this Captain Foy replied, "Put eleven of the poorest with me, and if they can give nothing, I will give for each of them as well as for myself, and each of you call on eleven weekly, receive what they can afford and make up the difference." The members were then divided into groups of twelve, a leader being appointed to collect a penny weekly from his fellows. To this was added later the "ticket money" of a shilling a quarter.

It would seem that the Class originally did not meet together at any particular time or place but was simply a group of members, from whom one of their number, "the leader," was to collect a penny a week on the debt incurred for the repair of the Chapel.

After making their visitations some of the leaders informed Wesley that they found certain ones who did not live as they might. "It struck me immediately," said he, "this is the very thing we have wanted so long. I then called together all the leaders of the classes and desired that each would make a particular inquiry into the behavior of those he saw weekly. They did so. Many disorderly walkers were detected. Some turned from the error of their ways. Some were put away from us. Many saw it with fear and rejoiced unto God with reverence."

It became the duty of the leader (1) to see each person in his Class at least once a week, "to inquire how their souls prospered, to advise, reprove, comfort, exhort, and to receive what they were willing to give"—at first the penny a week to the Chapel debt, later toward the relief of the poor.

2. The leader was to meet the minister of the Society, in order to inform him of any sick or of any disorderly who would not be reproved.

3. To meet the stewards and pay what they had received from their Classes in the week preceding.

In the beginning each person was visited in his own home, but this was soon found inexpedient as it took up more time than the leaders could spare. Then, too, many lived with relatives or as servants, whose employees would not permit them to be visited. Where visiting was permissible, little or no opportunity was afforded to converse alone and thus "exhort, comfort, or reprove."

"It frequently happened," said Wesley, "that one affirmed

The Foundry, Moorfield, London

what another denied and the matter couldn't be cleared up without seeing them together. Little misunderstandings and quarrels of various kinds arose among neighbors and relatives and effectually to remove which, it was necessary to see them all face to face." For these reasons it was found expedient to meet together "in Class." This they eventually did.

In spite of the apparent advantages of meeting together some objected—"There were no such meetings when I came into the society first; and why should there be now?" The answer was, "It is a pity but they had been at first. But we knew not then either the need or the benefit of them."

Again it was said, "There is no Scripture for Classes, etc." "No," answered Wesley, "and there is no Scripture against it, but much Scripture for it in those texts that enjoin the substance of the various duties performed. Scripture in most points gives only general rules and leaves the particular circumstances to be adjusted by the common sense of mankind."

And still again it was objected—"These are all men's inventions." Wesley answered, "They are methods which men have found by reason and common sense for the more effectually applying several Scripture rules couched in general terms to particular occasions."

Objections were made to the leaders also. They were said to be insufficient and without gifts or graces for the work. The reply was, "Such as they are it is plain God has blessed their labors."

In spite of objection and opposition, the Class Meeting spread throughout the Connexion and in many instances antedated and became the nucleus of a Society.

When on May 1, 1743, John and Charles Wesley drew up the Rules of the Methodist Society, the practice of the Bristol Society was made general and permanent.

Bands—Among the members of the Class, the more spiritually minded "wanted," says Wesley, "some means of closer union; they wanted to pour out their hearts without reserve, particularly with regard to the sin that did so easily beset them and the temptations which were most apt to prevail over them." On December 25, 1744, Wesley, therefore, drew up directions for smaller companies called "Bands." These Bands, having their own Leaders, were composed of all classes but meeting separately—male or female, married or single as the case might be. This separation was due to the fact that they obeyed St. James' injunction to "Confess your faults one to another."

In 1768 the preachers were instructed "As soon as there are four men or women believers in any place, put them into a Band."

The "ticket" was probably introduced first in the Band. Probably the love feast, also, was at first open only to Band members.

Tickets—Wesley says, "As the Societies increased, I found it required still greater care to separate the precious from the vile." In order to do this he met every member personally once in three months. "To each of those whose seriousness and good conversation I found no reason to doubt, I gave," says he, "testimony under my own hand and writing their name on a ticket prepared for that purpose, every ticket implying a strong recommendation of the person to whom it was given."

These tickets as Wesley pointed out supplied a quiet and inoffensive method of removing any disorderly persons. "If such a one had no ticket at the quarterly visitation (for so often the tickets were changed) it was immediately known that he was no longer of the society."

The tickets admitted, also, the holder to the social services of the society, particularly to the love feasts, for which reason, in time, they came to be improperly called love-feast tickets.

In 1758 the question was asked, "Ought any tickets be given to children?" The answer was, "Not to the unawakened. It makes them too cheap."

At the Wesleyan Conference of 1782, it was ordered that every Assistant ask every person changing his ticket, "Can you afford to observe our rule? (i.e., paying one penny a week or one shilling a quarter), unless in extreme poverty and receive what he is able to give."

In time the membership ticket, for such it was, bore beside the date, a verse of Scripture, the name of the member, and the name also of the assistant or minister who issued it as it had borne originally that of John Wesley.

Information relative to tickets of the American Societies will be found elsewhere.

The Conferences—Wesley invited a number of clergymen and all who served him as "Assistants" to meet and advise him concerning the best method of carrying on the work of the Gospel. The first Conference or "Conversation," as they were then called, met at the Foundry, June 25-29, 1744. Six clergy began the Conference. By agreement four Lay Preachers joined the group. Ten preachers in all—the same number as composed the First Conference of American Methodism.

As the numbers of preachers increased, Wesley invited those with whom he desired to confer to meet him at a place appointed. Finally he gave general permission that all who desired might come, making it clear that they came on his invitation "to advise," and "not to govern" him. Matters were not determined by vote until after the death of Wesley in 1791. In the Conferences, during the life of Wesley, the Doctrines, Discipline, and Practices of Methodism "were agreed" upon.

The Prayer Meeting as an institution seems to have resulted, first, from the observance of the National "fast day" of Great Britain and, later, from what was called "the intercession" of the early Methodists. Weekly fasts were prescribed by the Church of England and for many years Friday was a National day of fast and prayer. There is no mention by Wesley of the "Prayer Meeting" but throughout his Journal he refers to "fasting and prayer." His first reference is of February 17, 1744. "We observed a day of solemn fast and prayer." From then till 1789 Wesley speaks frequently of calling on the Methodists to observe and observing with them "The National fast."

In the Conferences, General fast days were called for from time to time by "all the Societies" on the last Friday in September; on the "first Friday after Christmas day," "after New Year's day," "after Lady day," "after Midsummer day," and "after Michaelmas day." Quarterly fasts were to be observed on the first Friday in August, November, February, and May.

Fasting and prayer are always connected. Prayer was made for "the King," "for Country," "in the confused state of public affairs" in the "want of trade" in face of "scarity of provisions," for "the success of the Gospel" and "the increase of the work of God." These "fast and prayer" day services were held by the Methodists at all hours, 5-7-9-10 in the morning, at 1 and 5 in the afternoon and in the evening. They were often closed with a "Watch Night" or a "Love Feast." Only occasionally were they held on other than a Friday, then on Wednesday.

The Minutes of 1765 make the last reference, before the death of Wesley, to the fast day. The same minutes make first mention of "the intercession" in this significant or suggestive way—"Have the Preachers observed the rules? Answer, Not exactly. For the time to come let them take care. 5. Use intercession *on Friday*, and *recommend fasting* both by precept and example."

In 1766 Wesley says, "I therefore, have over and over again advised, use no long prayer either before or after a sermon. Therefore, I myself frequently use only the collect, and never enlarge in prayer unless at intercession, or on a watch night or on some extra occasion."

There seems, now, some warrant for concluding that the old service of "fasting and prayer" on fast day had become "the intercession,"—a change of name but with the same purpose and characteristics. In the course of time "the intercession" seems to have given place to "the Prayer Meeting." In the Wesleyan Form of Discipline, 1797, Sec. 29, Art, 32, it is stated "Prayer Meetings have been found exceedingly useful, therefore let us appoint them whenever we can make it convenient." This is the first reference to the "Prayer Meeting" as an institution. No further reference is made to "the intercession." The name, although not the purpose or the characteristics of the service, has again been changed.

It would seem, therefore, from the above that the Prayer Meeting is the successor of the old Friday "fast and prayer service" and the later "Intercession" of the Methodists. This opinion is supported, as we shall see, by the history of the "Intercession" and the "Prayer Meeting" in America.

The Love Feast—The "Lord's Supper," as it has come to be called, was instituted in connection with and at the close of the Passover Feast. It was continued and commemorated by the early Christians in connection with a feast they called the Agapae (or Love Feast) held in different places, often in private homes, first at midnight (probably their "Vigiliae" or "watch-night"), then early in the morning and on the first day of the week. The meal was provided either out of common funds or through the generosity of some individual.

Pliny, the younger (61-62 A.D.), Propraetor of Bithynia, where Paul labored, writing about 110 to Emperor Trajan, said, "They" (the Christians) "were in the habit of meeting on a certain fixed day before dawn, when they sang a song in alternate verses, a hymn to Christ as to God, and they bound themselves by an oath to do no wicked deeds, to commit no fraud, no theft, no adultery, and never to falsify their word, and where anything is intrusted to their care to deliver it faithfully. After this it is their custom to separate and then to reassemble to partake of food of an ordinary kind."

At some time during, perhaps, but in all probability after the meal, as originally, the Lord's Supper was observed; the bread and wine being passed, after a blessing, by an apostle, or an elder representing him (I Cor. 10: 15). In administering the elements the identical words employed by the Master were used. Unlike that used at the Passover, the bread used was of that brought (leavened) to the feast. Some think that the food partaken at the Agapae was done in the "Eucharistic fashion" (Acts 27: 35).

In time grave abuses in connection with the feast crept in. Some early Christians, apparently, forgot (I Cor. 11: 27, 28) the real purpose of their fellowship or communion. They lost sight of the Lord's Memorial in their anxiety to partake of the food provided. They began to come for what they could get. They came hungry and, without waiting for others, began to satisfy their hunger (I Cor. 11: 33, 34). In a word, they now emphasized the material rather than the spiritual significance of their coming together. "They did not observe," as Paul puts it, "the Lord's body." As a result many became "weak," "sickly," and "slept."

From the following words of Tertulian (160 A.D.) the abuses complained of by Paul persisted: "The nature of our coena may be gathered from its name. It is the Greek term for love. However much it may cost us, it is real gain to incur such expenses in the cause of piety, for we aid the poor in the refreshment. We do not sit down to eat until we have first tasted of prayer to God; we eat to satisfy our hunger; we drink no more than benefits the temperate; we feast as those who recollect that they are to spend the night in devotion; we converse as those that know that the Lord is a near witness. After water for washing hands and mouths has been brought in, every one is required to sing something to the praise of God, either from the scripture or from his own thoughts. By this means if anyone has indulged to excess he is detected. The feast is closed with prayer. Contributions for the poor were frequently made on such occasions."

Eventually the two features, the feast and the commemoration of Christ's death, were separated. The latter persisting in "The Lord's Supper," the former, being for a time abandoned, was revived in a modified and semi-religious form, particularly by the Moravians. Both Wesley and Whitefield participated with the Moravians in the observance of these revived "Love Feasts." At the organization of the Aldersgate Street Society, May 1, 1738, at the home of James Hutton, it was provided that a "Love Feast" should be held monthly. Later Wesley introduced these feasts in the economy of Methodism. The feast, held quarterly, "was begun," says Wesley, "and ended with thanksgiving and prayer, and celebrated in so solemn a manner that the Christians of the Apostolic Age would have allowed it to be worthy of the churches of the earliest days."

In 1765 the Feast was limited to one and a half hours. "Every one should be home by nine."

In the Moravian Church the people do not drink from the same cup nor do they "break each other's cake" or bread. Tea, coffee, or some other beverage is drunk according to the habit of the country.

Very early, however, some Methodists under James Wheatley, began the custom, which Wesley disapproved and prohibited in 1765, of "breaking each other's bread" and, perhaps, drinking out of the same cup. Wesley called the custon "silly" and said it tended to confusion. However, it persisted and was adopted in America where buns or bread and water are used.

The Communion Table—In the Feasts of the early Christians where the Master's Memorial was observed, the bread and wine to be used for the purpose were kept separate on a special table called "The Lord's Table," later taking the name from the gathering and their participation in the Memorial, "the Communion Table." The "Cup of the Lord" and "the bread of the Lord" were therefore set apart and distinguished from those used in the rest of the meal.

The Lord's Table, hence the Communion Table, was in a sense synonymous with and figuratively served the same purpose as the altar. On the altar were placed the sacrifices that were to be offered up; on the table were placed the elements symbolical of the shed blood and broken body of Christ offered for the redemptionn of the world.

A table, instead of an altar, is used today by many Protestant and most Methodist Churches, on which to place the elements when administering the Lord's Supper. Where both the altar and the table are present, the table, which is placed before the altar, is used rather than the altar. Wesley very early installed a Communion Table in the "New Room," Bristol Chapel.

The Circuit—At the Bristol Conference in 1746, the Circuit System was introduced. Circuits, seven in number, comprising one or more Societies, were organized. In this way Methodism became a Connexion. In 1749, Wesley divided his Societies into nine Circuits.

In 1770 there were sixty Circuits, America being included as one of them.

The Model Deed

In 1750 Mr. Wesley framed and published a model deed for the settlement of the ownership of chapels. It provided "that the trustees in whom the legal title to the property was placed, should permit Mr. Wesley himself and such persons as he might appoint, to have the full use of such premises and preach therein. In case of his death, his brother Charles should have such power, and after him, Mr. Grimshaw should succeed. After the death of all, they were to be held in trust for such persons as were appointed by the *yearly Conference of the people called Methodists,* provided that they preached no other doctrines than those contained in Wesley's Notes on the New Testament and his four volumes of sermons."

This mode of deed was not satisfactory to many of the preachers, who felt that the purpose intended by the original builders of the chapels was not fully preserved.

The term Conference as used in the Model Deed, it was felt, also, "was a loose one" and needed to be defined. It was likewise contended that the Conference meant not simply "an assembly for discussion," as it was apt to be construed, but *The persons* composing the association or conference.

A case arose at Birstal which brought matters to a head. Here a deed, for a new preaching-house, was prepared "which gave a few persons the power of placing and displacing preachers at their pleasure."

At the Conference in 1782 the following question was raised: "What can be done with regard to the preaching house at Birstal?" The answer was: "If the trustees still refuse to settle it on the Methodist plan: 1. Let a plain statement of the case be drawn up; 2. Let a collection be made throughout all England in order to purchase ground and to build another preaching house as near the present one as can be."

In answer to the question "Why should not the Birstal preaching-house or any other be settled according to that deed" Wesley said, "I answer, because, whenever the trustees exert their power of placing and displacing preachers then, I. Itinerant preaching is no more. When the trustee had found and fixed a preacher they liked the rotation of preachers is at an end; at least till they are tired of their favorite preacher, and so turn him out. 2. While he stays, is not the bridle in his mouth? How dare he speak the full and whole truth, since whenever he displeases the trustees he is liable to lose his bread? How much less will he dare to put a trustee, be he ever so ungodly, out of society?

"No Methodist trustee, if I can help it, shall after my death, any more than while I live, have the power of placing and displacing preachers."

The "Poll-Deed" and Legal Hundred

In the Conference of 1782 the question was definitely asked, "What is a Conference of the people called Methodists?" Dr. Coke who had recognized the looseness of the deeds drawn in favor of the Conference unless the meaning thereof was expressed in legal terms, apparently acted on the matter. "In the Conference held in the year 1782," says he in an address to the Methodist Societies in Great Britain and Ireland on the Settlement of Preaching-houses, "several complaints were made in respect to the danger in which we were situated, from want of specifying in distinct and legal terms what was meant by the term 'The Conference of the people called Methodists!' Indeed the preachers seemed universally alarmed and many expressed their fears that division would take place among us after the death of Mr. Wesley on this account and the whole body of preachers present seemed to wish that some methods might be taken to remove this danger, which appeared to be pregnant with evil of the first magnitude. In consequence of this (the subject lying heavy on my heart) I desired Mr. Clulow of Chancery Lane, London, to draw up a case as I judged sufficient for the purpose and then to present it to that eminent counsellor, Mr. Maddox, for his opinion. This was accordingly done and Mr. Maddox informed us in his answer that *The Deeds of our preaching-houses were in the situation we dreaded*, that the law would not recognize the Conference in the state in which it stood at that time and consequently that there was no central point which might preserve the connexion from splitting into a thousand pieces after the death of Mr. Wesley. To prevent this he observed that Mr. Wesley should enroll a Deed in Chancery, *which Deed should specify the persons by name who composed the Conference* together with the mode of succession for its perpetuity, and at the same time such regulations be established by the Deed as Mr. Wesley would wish the Conference should be governed by after his death."

Coke read the opinion of Mr. Maddox to the Conference of 1783 and the Conference expressed the wish that such a Deed might be drawn up and executed by Wesley. After the Conference Wesley authorized Coke to draw up, with the assistance of Mr. Clulow, the main parts of a Deed that should answer the purpose desired. This was done and the Deed was submitted to Mr. Wesley for his approval. There remained nothing but the insertion of the names of those who were to constitute the Conference and the enrollment of the Deed in Chancery.

Wesley first thought of naming only ten or twelve. Finally he decided he would limit the number of names to a hundred. This was contrary to the opinion of Coke, who felt that every member in full connection should be named. Referring to this seeming arbitrariness of his choice of the hundred Wesley said, "If I had thought as well of them as they did themselves I might have named other preachers than those I did."

Naturally opposition developed among those whose names were omitted. Among these were Joseph Pilmoor, John Atlay, William Eels, and the John Hamptons, father and son.

The deed called the "Poll Deed" and generally known as the "Deed of Declaration" was signed and sealed by Wesley, signed by two witnesses and enrolled in Chancery, February 28, 1784.

By this deed the property belonging to the entire connexion was morally and legally vested in the Conference, i.e., in the legal hundred persons who were assumed to be or were designated as composing, the Conference.

On July 30, 1785, at London, those whose names were underwritten who were present at the Bristol Conference declared that Mr. Wesley was desired at that Conference to draw up a deed that should give legal specification of the phrase, "The Conference of the People called Methodists," that the mode of doing it was left entirely to his judgment and discretion and that they approved of the substance and design of the deed Mr. Wesley had executed and enrolled.

At the same Conference those whose names were underwritten but who were not present at Bristol, declared their approval of the substance and design of the deed lately executed and enrolled.

After February 24, 1784, the following was inserted, in deeds of preaching-houses and chapels, after London, Bristol, Leeds, Manchester—or "elsewhere, specified by name in a deed enrolled in Chancery, under the hand and seal of the Rev. John Wesley and bearing the date of the 28th day of February, 1784, and no others, to have and enjoy the said premises in order that they may herein preach and expound God's holy word, and perform all other acts of religious worship, provided that the persons so appointed preach no other doctrines, etc."

The Poll Deed has been called Methodism's Magna Charta. Without it organized Methodism might not have survived after Wesley's death or perhaps would not have had an itinerant system.

The Foundry

The Foundry where organized Methodism began was located in London.

At the begininng of the eighteenth century the British Government had a gun factory opposite the Artillery Barracks at the end of Moorfields. In 1716 an explosion "shattered the building" and it remained empty until 1738. In November of that year, Wesley leased (or purchased) it for £115 to hold the prayer meetings which resulted in the organization there of the first or "Mother Society." The building was put in repair and remodelled at a cost of approximately £700 or more. Provision was made for a chapel seating 1,500, a dispensary, book room, living quarters for Wesley and a stable for his horses. It was formally opened, July 23, 1740; the society at that time numbering 70 members.

In the Foundry, as we have seen, not only was the first society organized, the first steward appointed, and the first Conference held but the first Methodist dispensary set up, the first book room opened and the first "loan fund to assist the poor and prevent them from pawning their goods and paying exhorbitant interest."

The Foundry was Wesley's home and preaching place

when in London, for years. Here, in 1742, his mother died. After forty years of occupancy the Foundry was abandoned. "August 8, 1779," Wesley writes, "This was the last night which I spent at the Foundry. What hath God wrought there in 40 years!"

City Road Chapel

City Road Chapel, successor to the Foundry, was opened on November 1, 1778. Concerning it Wesley wrote, "It is perfectly neat but not fine and contains far more people than the Foundry." Here he continued to administer the affairs of the United Societies and to preach when in London. In the front of the Chapel a monument has been erected to his memory. In the rear there is a graveyard where Wesley was buried, as are also, some of his well-known associate preachers including Thomas Rankin, the convener of the First Conference of American Methodism held in St. George's, Philadelphia, July 14, 15, 1773.

Chapter IV

Whitefield and Early American Methodism

While Wesley was itinerating and organizing in Great Britain, Whitefield was crossing and recrossing the Atlantic and in the intervals preaching in America from Maine to Georgia and in England, Ireland, Scotland, and Wales. In 1750, he wrote at London: "Ranging seems my province; and methinks I hear a voice behind me saying, 'This is the way, walk in it.' My heart echoes back, 'Lord, let thy presence go with me, and then send me where thou pleasest.' In the midst of all, America, dear America is not forgotten. I begin to count the days and to say to the months, 'Fly fast away that I may spread the gospel net once more in dear America.' "

It is difficult to estimate how many miles Whitefield covered in the course of his ministry. On one occasion, however, he speaks of traveling a 150-mile circuit and preaching every day. On another, in July, 1769, he covered a 500-mile circuit and was "enabled to preach and travel through the heat every day." "No preacher," says another, "whose history is on record, has trod so wide a field as did Whitefield or has trod it so often." It is estimated that he preached more than 18,000 times.

"Although," as Flangen puts it, "it is historically stated that Methodism was introduced into New York and Maryland (about 1763 to 1766) and gradually spread along the coast, it may, nevertheless, be fairly claimed that Philadelphia is the birthplace of American Methodism.

"For many years," prior to Methodism's organization, "the 'Quaker City' was the fountain from which flowed the streamlet which in after times grew to be swollen rivers of gospel truth and vital Christianity." Here, as early as 1739, Methodism began in America with the intensive and extensive activities of one of its three outstanding leaders—George Whitefield.

That certain historians have stated and others have implied that *Methodism* began in New York in 1766 is due in most instances to their failure to distinguish between Methodism as a movement and organized Methodism. To them, apparently, there was no Methodism in America until it was organized. Yet in England, Methodism as a movement, was recognized for at least ten years prior to the organization of the first Society.

Again, those, who would ordinarily distinguish between the two phases of Methodism, have been led to copy without investigation statements that to say the least are questionable.

The history, character, and results of Whitefield's activities while perhaps strangely unknown to some have been deliberately ignored or discounted by others. Even some of his own biographers seem not to have been aware of the important part he played in the founding of American Methodism.

On August 14, 1739, Whitefield, as we have seen set sail the second time for America.

On Tuesday, October 30, he informs us, his ship arrived at "Cape-Lopen" (Henlopen). A pilot having come on board Whitefield, Mr. Seward, and another returned with him in his boat to Lewis Town (Lewes) Del., in order to go to Philadelphia by land and get a house in readiness for his family "before the ship arrived at that place."

At five o'clock in the evening landing was made at Lewis Town. "We had not been long in the inn," writes Whitefield, "before God showed us He had prepared our way; for news had been brought a fortnight ago of my coming hither, and two or three of the chief inhabitants being apprized of my arrival came and spent the evening with us, and desired me to give them a sermon on the morrow, which I promised to do."

"Next day (Wednesday, October 31) I preached at two in the afternoon to a serious and attentive congregation." At five in the evening Whitefield left Lewis Town and, having ridden twenty-seven miles through the woods, stopped overnight at "what they call a tavern." Thursday at eight o'clock he set out and, having dined at Dover, proceeded fifty miles further to an inn at which he stopped for the night. Friday, November 2, he rode nearly sixty miles further "without fatigue" and reached Philadelphia before eleven at night. On the following day he delivered letters committed to his care and visited his family on board the "Elizabeth" which, also, arrived the night before.

Philadelphia immediately became both the scene and the center of intensive and extensive evangelistic labors on the part of Whitefield.

He preached at first in the church (presumably Christ Anglican), but "the inhabitants were very solicitous" for him to preach in another place beside the church. Franklin, in his autobiography, says, "He was at first permitted to preach in some of the churches; but the clergy, taking a dislike to him, soon refused him their pulpits, and he was obliged to preach in the fields." Whitefield therefore preached at various outdoor places, the Court House steps being the first and a favorite stand. In a letter to a friend dated November 11, 1739, James Pemberton says, "He preached three nights successively upon our Court House steps where he exceedingly takes with the people."

"He preached one evening," writes Benjamin Franklin, "from the top of the Court-house steps, which are in the middle of Market Street and on the west side of Second Street, which crosses it at right angles. Both streets were filled with his hearers to a considerable distance. I had the curiosity to learn how far he could be heard, by retiring backwards down the street toward the river, and I found his voice distinct till I came near Front Street, when some noise in that street obscured it. Imagining then a semi-circle, of which my distance should be the radius, and that it was filled with auditors, to each of whom I allowed two square feet, I computed that he might well be heard by more than thirty-thousand."

At No. 177 South 2nd Street, at the junction of Little Dock and 2nd Street, according to Watson's "Annals of Philadelphia and Pennsylvania," was a two-story frame house of singular construction, owned by a Benjamin Loxley. On the front of the second floor of this building was a porch or gallery from which Whitefield frequently preached, "his audience occupying the street (then out of town) and the opposite hill at the margin of a stream called 'Bathsheba's Bath and Bower.'" Samuel Coates says that when a lad he had seen Whitefield from a gallery, and that "his audience, like a rising amphitheatre, surrounded the site of the bath and bower on the western side of 2nd Street."

According to the *Philadelphia Gazette* Whitefield preached to fifteen thousand people on what was called "Society Hill."

Writing in his Journal, November 12, 1739, Whitefield informs us that on his arrival at Philadelphia he received a letter with a very pressing invitation to come to New York, from a Mr. Abel Nobel, who seems to have been an itinerant preacher and had himself preached as early as 1736 from the Court House steps. On the ninth of the month another letter from Nobel arrived. On the twelfth Whitefield set out for New York via Burlington, Trenon, New Brunswick, and Elizabeth Town—preaching along the way. At Elizabeth Town he takes a boat for New York, arriving there on the fourteenth.

Owing to some difficulty with the clergy over his credentials, license, etc., he preached in the fields, in private homes, in the Dutch Calvinistic Meeting House, and at the Old City Exchange.

Leaving New York Sunday night, November 18, he returns to Philadelphia, stopping at Neshaminy, Abingdon, and Germantown.

Franklin endeavored to persuade Whitefield to build his orphanage in Philadelphia but without success. "I did not disapprove of the design," says he, "but, as Georgia was then destitute of materials and workman, and it was proposed to send them from Philadelphia at a great expense, I thought it would have been better to have built the house here and brought the children to it. This I advised; but he was resolute in his project, rejected my counsel and I therefore refused to contribute. I happened soon after to attend one of his sermons, in the course of which I perceived he intended to finish with a collection and I silently resolved he should get nothing from me. I had in my pocket a handful of copper money, three or four silver dollars and five pistoles of gold. I determined to give the copper. Another stroke of his oratory made me ashamed of that and determined me to give the silver, and he finished so admirably that I emptied my pockets wholly into the collection.

"At this sermon there was one of our club, who being of my sentiments respecting the building in Georgia, and suspecting a collection might be intended had, by precaution, emptied his pockets before he came from home. Toward the conclusion of the discourse, however, he felt a strong desire to give and applied to a neighbor, who stood near, to borrow some money for the purpose. The application was unfortunately made to perhaps the only man in the company who had firmness not to be affected by the preacher. His answer was, 'At any other time, Friend Hopkinson, I would lend to thee freely; but not now, for thee seems to be out of thy right senses.'"

At this time Andrew and Bradford, Philadelphia printers, reprinted John and Charles Wesley's "Hymns and Sacred Poems," published by them in 1739. This reprint was doubtless made for George Whitefield and was sold by him for the "Benefit of the Poor in Georgia."

The time came when Whitefield, brushing aside all inducements, felt he must proceed to Savannah.

Thursday, November 29, he tells us that a sloop which Mr. Seward named the "Savannah," was loaned to him. Having seen his family and the supplies for Georgia safely aboard he sets out for Savannah by land.

So great was his popularity that when he left Philadelphia twenty gentlemen on horse accompanied him. Seven miles off another company awaited him. Eventually about two hundred were in his escort and hundreds more traveled on foot the distance of fifteen miles to Chester to hear him preach.

His itinerary lay through Chester, Wilmington, White Clay Creek, and New Castle, into Maryland, Virginia, North Carolina, and South Carolina. On January 11, he reached Savannah. On March 25, 1740, he laid the first brick for his Orphan House.

On April 1 Whitefield left Charleston in his sloop for New Castle, Delaware. Arriving there on the tenth, he preached morning and evening. The next day, Monday, he preached at Wilmington to about three thousand people, leaving for and arriving at Philadelphia in the evening. On Tuesday evening he preached to about eight thousand on Society Hill, and at the same place the following morning and evening. From then on he preached at Whitemarsh, Germantown, again in Philadelphia, thence to Salem, New Jersey, at Neshaminy, Skippack, Frederick township, Amwell, New Brunswick, Elizabeth Town, and New York.

When Whitefield preached at Skippack, Peter Bohler also preached—preaching in Dutch to those who did not understand English.

On April 25, 1740, Whitefield purchased from a William Allen 5,000 acres of land near "the forks of the Delaware and Lehigh Rivers" at a place now called Nazareth. It was his intention to build a school for Negroes.

On his return to Philadelphia he had brought with him Peter Bohler and the remnant of the Moravians who had settled in Georgia in 1735. Many of these Moravians were carpenters with whom he entered into an agreemeent to go to Nazareth and erect the proposed school building. Before the building was completed, however, argument arose with Bohler with the result that Whitefield ordered the Moravians to leave Nazareth. It being winter appeal was made to Allen and the Moravians were permitted to remain until spring when they moved to Bethlehem. The building was later sold to and finished by them. It is now known as the "Whitefield House" and is used for a home for Moravian Missionaries.

On Sunday, May 11, Whitefield preached to vast audiences in Philadelphia and then prepared to leave again for the South. He proceeded to Darby, Chester, Wilmington, White Clay Creek, Nottingham, Fogg's Manor, and New Castle, preaching at every place. At New Castle he boarded his sloop for Savannah, arriving there on June 5.

While in Charleston Whitefield was urgently invited to visit New England. Writing in his Journal he says, "Arrived (Sunday September 14) at Newport, R. I., just after the beginning of evening service. We came purposely thither first with our sloop. In the evening in company with a Mr. Clap, an old dissenting minister, he visited the minister of the Church of England and finally secured consent to preach in the church on week days.

IN ENGLAND AND IN AMERICA

From New England Whitefield proceeded to New York and then to Philadelphia.

"It being found inconvenient," writes Franklin, "to assemble in the open air, subject to inclemencies, the building of a house to meet in was no sooner proposed, and persons appointed to receive contributions, but sufficient sums were soon received to procure the ground and erect the building, which was 100 feet long and 70 feet broad, about the size of Westminster Hall; and the work was carried on with such spirit as to be finished in much shorter time than could have been expected. Both house and ground were invested in trustees, expressly for the use of any preacher who might desire to say something to the people of Philadelphia; the design in building not being to accommodate any particular sect but the inhabitants in general."

The Deed recited that "a considerable number of persons of different denominations united to erect a large building on the land intending it should be appointed for use of a charity school for the instruction of poor children, gratis, in useful literature and in the Christian religion" and directed that "it should be used as a house of public worship and its use should be under the direction of certain trustees."

The trustees had the power to introduce such Protestant ministers to preach the Gospel who "were sound in principles, zealous and faithful in the discharge of their duties, acquainted with the religion of the heart and experimental piety without to distinction or different sentiment in lesser matters." (Hazzard, Annals, Philadelphia and Pennsylvania, 1857.)

On November 14, 1740, "the lot was conveyed" to George Whitefield of the Province of Georgia, clerk; William Seward of London, England; John Benezet, merchant; Thomas Noble, of the city of New York, merchant; Robert Eastbourne of Philadelphia, blacksmith; James Read of Philadelphia, gentleman; Edward Evans of Philadelphia, cordwainer; Charles Brocken of Philadelphia, gentleman; and Samuel Hazard of the city of New York, merchant.

In time Benjamin Franklin became a trustee of the building and its grounds.

Concerning this building Whitefield writes (November 7,

1740),."It is one hundred feet long and seventy feet broad. A large gallery is to be erected all around in it. Many footsteps of Providence have been visible in the beginning and carrying it on. Both in the morning and evening God's glory filled the house, for there was great power in the congregation. The roof is not yet up, but the people raised a convenient pulpit and boarded the bottom. The joy of most of the hearers when they saw me was inexpressible."

Watson in his "Annals" says the amount subscribed toward the enterprise was £2,500. The building was not completed until 1744.

In this building the celebrated Gilbert Tennant preached for many years. In 1801 a group of Methodists from Old St. George's bought the south end of the building, called at that time the "Academy," for $8,000 and worshiped in it for many years.

But the fame of the building rests largely on the fact that it was the birthplace of the Univeristy of Pennsylvania.

In 1749 Franklin "set on foot a subscription for the opening and supporting an academy; it was to be paid in quotas yearly for five years. The subscribers to carry the project into immediate execution, chose out of their number twenty-four trustees, and appointed Mr. Francis, then attorney-general, and myself (Franklin) to draw up constitutions for the government of the academy; which being done and signed, a house was hired, masters engaged, and the schools opened in the same year.

"The scholars increased fast, the house was soon found too small and we were out looking for a piece of ground, properly situated with the intention to build, when Providence threw into our way a large house already built which, with a few alterations, might well serve our purpose." This was the building erected for George Whitefield.

Franklin, as trustee of both this building and the Academy he was instrumental in founding, procured the purchase of the structure for £777 for the accommodation of the Academy. The building, therefore, came to be called the "Academy."

No. 62 North 4th Street bears a bronze tablet on which is the following inscription:

"On this site stood the 'New Building' erected in 1740 for George Whitefield and for a Charity School—subsequently used until 1812 by the School, Academy, College (1753) and University of Pennsylvania (1779) successively."

On Whitefield's monument at the University is this inscription:

"The University of Pennsylvania held its first sessions in a building erected for his congregations and was aided by his collections, guided by his counsel, inspired by his life."

Of Whitefield's influence in Philadelphia and the character and results of his labors, abundant testimony is borne. Franklin says, "The multitudes of all sects and denominations that attended his sermons were enormous; and it was a matter of speculation with me to observe the influence of his oratory on his hearers and how much they admired and respected him, notwithstanding his common abuse of them, by assuring them that they were naturally half beasts and half devils. It was wonderful to see the change soon made in the manners of our inhabitants. From being thoughtless and indifferent about religion, it seemed as if all the world was growing religious; so that one could not make through the town in the evening without hearing psalms sung in different families in every street."

Another says, "No man since the Apostolic Age preached oftener or with better success. His sermons in the open air lasted one and a half hours."

"Since his preaching among us," said the *Philadelphia Gazette* of the time, "the dancing room, assembly and concert room have been shut as inconsistent with the Gospel; and although the men concerned broke open the doors no company went the last night. The change to religion here is altogether surprising through the influence of Whitefield."

In his biography of Whitefield, Belcher says, "An aged man who was living in 1806 and who well remembered the scene he witnessed, bore testimony that after the first visit of the great evangelist, public worship was regularly celebrated in Philadelphia twice a day for a whole year and that on the

Lord's day it was frequently celebrated three and four times in each church. He said there were not less than twenty-six societies regularly held for prayer and Christian conference.

"Such was the influence of Whitefield not only in Philadelphia but throughout the colony of Pennsylvania, that in the city attention to commerce was suspended and in the country the cultivation of the land for the time being was abandoned, that the people might hear him proclaim the gospel of the Lord Jesus."

On Monday, November 17, 1740, he left Philadelphia, thence to Jersey, Maryland, and Charleston, from which he sailed for England, February 1, 1741, landing at Falmouth, March 11, 1741, after his second and eventful visit to America.

In 1744 Whitefield made his third visit to America, this time landing October 19, at York, Maine.

When he arrived in sight of York, in order to land a few hours earlier, he boarded a fishing smack, but the darkness coming on, she missed her course and was tossed about all night. "Hungry, so hungry," says Whitefield, "I could have gnawed the boards. Sick and discouraged, I lay in the cabin, when a man lying at my elbow began to talk of one Mr. Whitefield, for whose arrival the 'New Lights' in New England were watching and praying. This made me take courage. I continued undiscovered; and in a few hours, in answer, I trust, to *new light* prayers, we arrived safe."

After visiting Portsmouth, Newburyport, Boston, New Haven, New York, and New Jersey, we find Whitefield in Philadelphia again. Here, we are told, "A flattering reception awaited him. The people were anxious to retain him and made him tempting offers, which he refused." "He was delighted to find," says another, "that the interest in divine things during his first visit had been steadily maintained."

In 1746 while in Maryland, he writes, "I trust the time for favoring this and the neighboring southern provinces is come. Everywhere, almost, the door is opening for preaching, great numbers flock to hear, and the power of an ascended Saviour attends the world. Lately I have been in seven counties in Maryland and preached with abundant success."

January, 1747, at Charleston, S. C., he writes, "The Lord

Jesus is pleased to give me great access to multitudes of souls."
In April Whitefield is again in Maryland, writing on the twenty-fifth from Bohemia.

After short trips to New York, Newport, Portsmouth, and Boston he is back again in Philadelphia and Maryland, thence to North Carolina where he writes, "I am here, hunting in the woods, these *ungospelized* wilds, for sinners."

In May, 1747, Whitefield tells us "Maryland is yielding converts to the blessed Jesus. The gospel seems to be moving southward. The harvest is promising. The time of singing of birds is come."

In June at Philadelphia—"At present I have full work here. The congregations yesterday were large and for this month past I have been preaching to thousands in different places."

Due to impared health and on the advice of his physicians to try a change of climate, he sets sail for Bermuda, arriving there on March 15, 1748. After preaching from one end of Bermuda to the other he embarks for England, landing in July, 1748.

Whitefield's next visit to America is in May, 1754. This time he lands at South Carolina. The following July we find him in New York and Philadelphia, dividing his time for two months between these cities. "Everywhere," writes he, "a divine power accompanies the word, prejudices were removed, and a more effectual door opened than ever for preaching the gospel."

After a visit to New Jersey, on October 1 he sets out for Boston, arriving on October 9. From Boston he turns south to Virginia, going either by boat from Rhode Island to Maryland or overland via New York, New Jersey, and Philadelphia.

In his letter to Wesley urging preachers to be sent to America, Thomas Taylor, a member of the John St. Society, recognizes Whitefield as a factor in the religious life of America and bears testimony to the "fruit of his labors" particularly in New York and during the period from 1754 on.

"NEW YORK, April 11, 1768.

"REV. AND VERY DEAR SIR: I intended writing to you for several weeks past; but a few of us had a very material transaction in view. I therefore postponed writing until I could give you a particular account thereof; this was the purchasing of ground for building a preaching-house upon, which, by the blessing of God, we have now concluded.

"Before I proceed I shall give you a short account of the state of religion in this city. By the best intelligence I can collect, there was little either of the form or power of it until Mr. Whitefield came over, thirty years ago; and even after his first and second visits there appeared but little fruit of his labors. But during his visit fourteen or fifteen years ago there was a considerable shaking among the dry bones. Divers were savingly converted; and this work was much increased in his last journey, about four years since, when his words were really like a hammer and like a fire. Most part of the adults were stirred up; great numbers pricked to the heart, and, by a judgment of charity, several found peace and joy in believing. The consequence of this work was, churches were crowded, and subscriptions raised for building new ones. Mr. Whitefield's example provoked most of the ministers to a much greater degree of earnestness. And by the multitudes of people, old and young, rich and poor, flocking to the churches, religion became an honorable profession. There was now no outward cross to be taken up therein. Nay, a person who could not speak about the grace of God, and the new birth, was esteemed unfit for genteel company."

In August, 1763, Whitefield arrives for the sixth time in America at Rappahannock, Virginia. The months of September, October, and November are spent in Philadelphia. "Here," he says, "are some bright young witnesses rising up in the church. Perhaps I have already conversed with forty new creature ministers of various denominations. Sixteen popular students, I am creditably informed, were converted in the New Jersey College last year."

After visits to New Jersey and New York Whitefield proceeded to Boston where he arrived at the end of February, 1764. Here the thanks of the town were voted to him for collecting money in Great Britain for the sufferers of the Boston fire of 1760.

On his way back to Philadelphia in September, Whitefield preached at the Princeton Commencement. Leaving Philadelphia he sets out for Virginia and South Carolina. In March, 1765, he leaves for Philadelphia. "All the way," says he, "from Charleston to this place the cry is 'For Christ's sake, stay and preach to us.' Oh for a thousand tongues to speak for Jesus."

On July 5, 1765, after a passage of twenty-eight days, Whitefield once more is in England.

Writing to Captain Joss, Whitefield says, "Last night (August 8, 1769) I went on board the 'Friendship.' The Captain is to dine with me tomorrow. I expect to sail the first week in September." Ten days later he wrote to a Mr. Adams: "My dear Tommy, talk not of taking a personal leave. You know my make. Paul could stand a whipping, but not a weeping farewell." In his last sermon in Tottenham Court Road Whitefield said: "It is now high time for me to preach my own funeral sermon. I am going for the thirteenth time to cross the Atlantic."

In September Whitefield embarked for the last time for America leaving behind him an affectionate farewell letter to Wesley.

On November 30, he landed at Charleston. Without loss of time he proceeded to Georgia and his "beloved Bethesda." After five months in the South, "We are not surprised," says Belcher, "to find that applications poured in from every part of the North entreating Whitefield to visit the scenes of other years. After some hesitation as to where he should go first, he set out in March for Philadelphia," arriving on May 6, 1770.

On the evening of the seventh, "I was enabled," he writes, "to preach to a large auditory and have to repeat the delightful task this (9th) evening. Pulpits, hearts and affections seem to be as open and enlarged to me as ever." On May 24, he writes, "A wide and effectual door, I trust, has been opened in this city. People of all ranks flock as much as ever. Impressions are made on many, and I trust they will abide. To all Episcopal churches as well as most of the other places of worship, I have free access." Here he met Boardman, at the time stationed at Philadelphia.

Late in the summer Whitefield left Philadelphia for Boston via Bristol, Burlington, and New York.

At New York, Saturday, June 25, Pilmoor writes, "I had the honor to wait on the Rev. Mr. Whitefield and congratulate him on his safe arrival. He was remarkably loving and affectionate and desired me to be free and frequently call on him."

Leaving New York, Whitefield proceeded to Albany, thence to Boston and eventually to Newbury, Mass., where, as we have seen, he passed away September 30, 1770.

Whitefield "The Advance Courier"

It seems to be generally agreed that though Whitefield formed no Societies he did prepare the way for those who did later in the name and under the authority of Wesley.

There is abundant evidence, however, that societies for religious purposes such as those that sprang up in England and were in many instances absorbed by the organizations of Wesley, sprang up everywhere in America—in New York, Philadelphia, Maryland, Virginia, and New England.

We have already quoted Belcher's informant to the effect that after Whitefield's first visit to Philadelphia in 1739 "no less than twenty-six societies were regularly held for prayer and Christian conference."

In 1740, in New Brunswick he met Mr. Noble who according to Seward's Journal told him "their Society at New York was enlarged from seventy to one hundred and seventy."

In 1741, while in Philadelphia, Whitefield says, "It would be almost endless to recount all particular instances of God's grace which I have seen this week past. Many that were before only convicted now plainly proved that they were converted and had a clear evidence of it within themselves. *Several societies* are now in town, not only of men and women but of little boys and girls. Being so engaged, I could not visit them as I should but I hope the Lord will raise up some fellow laborers and that elders will be ordained in every place."

In 1744 at York, Maine, as we have seen the "New Lights" were watching and praying for Whitefield. Leaving Philadelphia in 1765, he went through Virginia where he says, "in places as unlikely as Rome itself, I found societies of Christians, formed and led on by a wealthy planter." He tells us they met him in a body, wishing publicly to identify themselves with him. "At Newbern (Virginia), November 22, 1765, I have met," says Whitefield, "with what they call 'New Lights' in every place and have the names of several of their preachers."

Just who the New Lights were is problematical. Some have identified them as simply Methodists; others as "Calvinistic" Methodists. Watson, in his Annals, implies that they were simply converts of Whitefield. Still others connect them directly with Gilbert and William Tennant, Presbyterians, who, to an extent, were followers of Whitefield.

"In New England," said Dr. Coggesshell (*Methodist Review*, 1855), "whenever the clergy (and this was the case with a party among them) did not co-operate with Whitefield and his friends in their labors nor favor the work of which he was the chief promoter and representative, God raised us pious and illiterate preachers by whom separate congregations were formed in several places and who were called Separatists. When the Methodist preachers came into New England nearly a quarter of a century after the death of Whitefield they found some of these Separatist Churches in existence by whom they were well received. A gentleman who was once a member of the Irish Conference under Wesley was induced to become the pastor of one of these churches. It is now (1855), one of the largest and most wealthy Congregational Churches * in New England and out of it members have gone to assist in building up the Methodist Churches in the city in which it is located."

In the course of his ministry in America Whitefield made thousands of converts. These converts he apparently left to follow the course of their own judgment. Many of them, doubtless, found their way, some temporarily, into established churches, such as the Anglican, Presbyterian, Congregational, and Moravian.

Of George Whitefield, Joseph Pilmoor wrote, October 9, 1770, "Of all the pious and useful ministers that have ever

---
* Benevolent Congregational Church, Providence, R. I.

visited America, he was by far the most useful. There are many thousands of souls in this country that have been deeply affected and savingly wrought upon under his ministry and will undoubtedly be a crown of rejoicing to him in the day of the Lord."

"Mr. Whitefield's labors," said Jesse Lee, "as an itinerant preacher had been greatly blessed to the people of America; *and thereby the way was opened* for our preachers to travel and preach the gospel in different parts of the country. And in most places where the people were lively in religion, they were fond of having itinerant preachers visit them."

"Whitefield," says Flanigen, "was really *the advance courier* of Methodism in the open field, the pioneer who went before all the rest, and felled the trees in the forests, and cut away the matter accumulations, the growth of many years of ignorance, neglect, and debauchery."

Referring to the extended period of Whitefield's activity in America from 1739 to 1770 and especially to the 1740 to 1750 decade, Bacon in his *History of American Christianity* says, "It was destined to impress upon the American Church in its various orders for a hundred years to come the character of Methodism." Dr. Charles A. Briggs, a Presbyterian historian, calls the revival under Whitefield "a part of the great Methodist Movement which had a profound effect on all denominations."

A belated recognition of Whitefield's outstanding part in the founding of Methodism is found in the inscription on his monument in the "quad" of the University of Pennsylvania.

"In veneration of his memory this Monument has been erected by the Alumni of this University who are ministers and laymen of the Methodist Church of which he was a founder."

In Great Britain Wesley built the superstructure on the foundations both he and Whitefield had laid. In America Whitefield laid the foundations of Methodism and in most instances Wesley's itinerants reared the superstructure.

Had Whitefield been the organizer or builder Wesley was, Methodism in America would perhaps have taken some definite form years before it did.

CHAPTER V

American Societies—How Recruited. First Societies and Meeting Houses

In 1741 Whitefield expressed the hope that God would "raise up fellow-laborers" in America. In the course of time worthy successors of both his and of Wesley were raised up and owned of God. Some of these were from across the sea, others were native to this soil.

However, most of the successors of Whitefield in the Methodist Movement in America, bear the stamp of Wesley. This applies even to some well-known converts of Whitefield— Thomas Rankin, for instance. The stamp of Wesleyan Methodist was naturally affixed to the Methodist itinerants who came to America after Whitefield, because they were members of the unique organization Wesley had built up, and because, with but a few exceptions, they were appointed by him.

The foundations of Methodism having been laid, it remained for the followers of Whitefield and Wesley to extend them and to rear the superstructure; in other words, to add to theirs new converts and to organize them into Societies.

The people to whom Methodism appealed and with whom were organized the early Societies were not only the unsaved or the unchurched, of whom there were approximately sixty thousand in America, but many who were members of established Churches—Moravians, Lutherans, Presbyterians, Baptists, Dutch Reformed, Swedish, Church of England, and Friends.

Philadelphia with a population at the time of thirty thousand had representatives of all the above denominations. Those who joined the Methodists here, it is said, came largely from the Church of England and from the Moravians. To both of these Churches Wesley had close relations. To the latter he owed his conversion. Their doctrines and manner of worship, also, were akin to those of the Methodists. To some extent the Lutherans contributed toward Methodism.

It may be added here that many of the recruits, to organized as well as unorganized Methodism throughout the colonies, from established churches as well as from the unchurched, were without doubt converts of the revival begun in 1739 and fostered up to as late as 1770 by George Whitefield, himself.

"The Methodism of that day," says Watson in his "Annals," was not so exclusive as now—it collected people of any faith who professed to believe in the sensible perceptions of divine regeneration, etc., and required no other rule of association than a desire to flee the wrath to come and having the form of godliness were seeking after the power thereof."

Methodists denied claim to being, and to any intention of establishing, a church. In his "Statement of Faith and Purpose" made at St. George's, Philadelphia, Sunday, December 3, 1769, Article 1, Pilmoor said: "The Methodist Society has never designed to make separation from the Church of England or be looked upon as a Church." This, of course, was Wesley's position. Therefore, in many instances Christians held dual membership—in the Methodist Society and in an established Church—usually the Church of England.

Several of the clergy were particularly friendly toward the Methodists and aided them in their work. Rev. Devereux Jarratt in Virginia, Dr. McGaw in Delaware, later of Philadelphia, and Rev. Stringer in Philadelphia attended and sometimes assisted in the meetings of the Methodists. It is said that Jarratt actively and extensively co-operated with the Methodists in their evangelistic labors. "The Conference acknowledge their obligations to the Rev. Mr. Jarratt for his kind and friendly services to the preachers and people, from our first entrance into Virginia and more particularly for attending our conference in Sussex, in public and private, and advise the preachers in the South to consult him and to take his advice in the absence of brother Asbury." (Minutes of 1782.)

Dr. Von Wrangel of old Swede's, Philadelphia, to whom we have referred, not only advised his members to hear but urged certain persons (John Hood and Lambert Wilmer) to join the Methodists.

Some of the clergy, apparently, accepted Wesley's statements; or at least did not regard the Methodist Societies as Churches.

The Societies, themselves, were considered as belonging to

the Church of England and in most instances the Methodists received the ordinances from the clergy of that denomination.

At the Conference of 1780, held in Baltimore, the following questions were asked and answered: "Shall we continue in close connection with the Church and press our people to a closer communion with her?" Answer, "Yes." "Will this Conference grant the privilege to all friendly clergy of the Church of England, at the request or desire of the people, to preach or administer the ordinances in our preaching houses and chapels." Answer, "Yes."

Under date of Sunday, September 1, 1784, Asbury wrote in his Journal: "We had a solemn meeting season at the love-feast (St. George's) in the morning, most of the Society present; we afterward went to St. Paul's (Church of England), heard a sermon by Mr. McGaw and received the sacraments."

It may be added here that Wesley did not consider even the services of the Methodist Societies in the same class or as substitutes for the public worship of the Established Church. "Our own service is public worship," said he, "Yes, in a sense; but not such as supersedes the Church service. We never designed it should. We have an hundred times professed the contrary. It presupposes public prayer like a sermon at the University. If it were designed to be instead of Church service it would be essentially defective. For it seldom has the four grand parts of public praise: deprecation, petition, intercession, and thanksgiving. . . . . If the people put ours in the room of the Church Service we hurt them that stay with us and ruin those that leave us. For then they will go nowhere but lounge the Sabbath away, without any public worship at all. I advise, therefore, all the Methodists in England and Ireland, who have been brought up in the Church, constantly to attend the Services of the Church, at least, every Lord's day."

Even Wesley's itinerants were not to be dignified by the title of "minister." They were to be considered and to consider themselves simply "preachers."

In the work of extension and organization in the beginning in America a number of itinerants (or "local preachers") and several Societies played important parts.

Philip Embury—In 1747 Wesley crossed the Irish Sea for the first of many visits to Ireland. His fame had gone before and multitudes flocked to hear him. It is said that on one occasion a priest came along ringing a bell and calling upon his flock to "return to their own fold and not listen to this wolf."

On one of his trips to Northern Ireland, at Ballingrane, Wesley came upon a community of German refugees, and their descendants, from the Rhine Palatinates. He described them "as about the lowest type of an irreligious, swearing, drunken community that I have ever met." He began to preach to them and later on he speaks of them as "the model of quiet, deep, and earnest religious hope." Among Wesley's converts at Ballingrane in 1752 was Philip Embury and perhaps others of his family.

Embury was born at Ballingrane, December 25, 1728. He was a carpenter by trade. It is said he was licensed to preach at the Irish Conference held in Limerick, Wednesday, June 21, 1758. In 1760, in company with a number of other Methodists, among whom were his three brothers and their families, a sister and her family and Paul and Barbara (Ruckle) Heck his cousins, he sailed for America, landing at New York on August 1.

Robert Strawbridge—About the same time that Embury came to America, another Irish Methodist, in the person of Robert Strawbridge, landed on these shores. Strawbridge was born at Drumsnaugh, Ulster County, Ireland. The exact date of his birth and conversion do not appear to be known. While he evidently preached in his native land it is not definitely known either where or if ever he was regularly licensed.

Thomas Webb—born 1724, a non-commissioned officer in the British Army, who saw service at Louisburg and Quebec. In the latter engagement he lost his right eye, over the socket of which he wore a green shade.

Returning to England in 1764, he was spiritually awakened under the preaching of Wesley but was not actually converted until the following year. Subsequently being licensed by Wesley to preach, Webb began his public ministry at Bath.

To Philip Embury is accorded the honor of having or-

Barbara Heck, the "inspiration" of Embury

Philip Embury, who founded the John St. Society and built Wesley Chapel, N. Y.

Captain Thomas Webb, who founded St. George's, Philadelphia

Robert Strawbridge, who founded a Society and built the Log Meeting House on Pipe Creek, Md.

ganized the "John Street" Society, New York; to Robert Strawbridge that of organizing the "Pipe Creek" Society in Maryland and to Captain Webb that of organizing a group of Philadelphia Methodists into the St. George's Society.

No one of these three societies, however, can properly be called *"The* Mother Society" or *"The* Mother Church" of American Methodism. While Captain Webb labored in Philadelphia as well as in New York, he did not represent in any sense the New York Society. The three Societies had separate and distinct origins and in their activities bore no relation or responsibility to one another. In a sense, there were three "Mother Societies" from whom directly or indirectly many but not all other Societies sprang.

If the expression, "The Mother Church," is used in the narrow sense of age, the claim of the New York Society to being the first Society formed, is made also by the Maryland Society. If the Pipe Creek Society in any real sense still "carries on," she is entitled to the distinction of being the oldest of the three original Societies.

From the very beginning there have been two rival claims to the distinction of being the first Society organized by the Methodists in America. As is generally known, our brethren in New York claim that the John Street Society founded by Philip Embury in 1766, was the first Society. On the other hand our brethren in Maryland claim that Robert Strawbridge organized the first Society as early as 1763 or 1764 in Frederick County. Without desiring to pass upon the relative merits of the claims, we present them together with the grounds upon which the rival claimants contend for the distinction of being the "first Society."

The New York Society's claim is supported by a paragraph in the "Historical Statement" printed in the *Discipline,* which now (*Discipline,* 1939) reads as follows: "In the year 1766 Philip Embury, a Local Preacher from Ireland, began to preach in New York City and formed a Society, now John Street Church. Another local preacher, Thomas Webb, Captain in the British Army, soon joined him and began preaching. About the same time Robert Strawbridge, from Ireland settled in Frederick County, Maryland, preaching there and forming some Societies."

The above paragraph differs in a number of particulars from the one found in the original statement at the beginning of the Bishop's "Historical Statement" in 1790, as follows:

"And during the space of thirty years past certain persons, members of the society emigrated from England and Ireland and settled in various parts of this country. About twenty years ago Philip Embury, a local preacher from Ireland, began to preach in the City of New York, and formed a society of his own countrymen and the citizens. *About the same time* (the italics ours) Robert Strawbridge, a local preacher from Ireland, settled in Frederick County in the State of Maryland, and preaching there, formed some Societies. In 1769 Richard Boardman and Joseph Pilmoor came to New York (as a matter of fact they landed and began their work at Philadelphia), who were the first regular Methodist preachers on the continent. In the latter end of the year 1771 Francis Asbury and Richard Wright, of the same Order came over."

In 1791 the following changes were made—second sentence, (1790) for "About twenty years ago" to "In the latter end of the year 1766." The following was inserted as the next sentence:—"In the same year Thomas Webb preached in a hired room near the barracks; and in the year 1767 the rigging-house was occupied." The following was also inserted:—"The first Methodist church in New York was built in 1768 or 1769." In 1792 the clause relating to "the rigging-house" is omitted. In 1796 the sentence, "And during the space of thirty years past," etc. is omitted. The next sentence begins "In the year 1766 Philip Embury, etc." instead of "About twenty years ago."

From the foregoing it would appear that too much stress should not be laid upon the statement in the "Historical Statement." The variations from the original are too apparent. As a matter of fact even the authors of the original were not sure of their ground although at the time they implied their belief that the John Street Society had been organized first. The tendency of successive statements was to make definite what at first was only implied.

The claim of the Maryland Society to priority rests first upon the date of its organization, then upon a certain statement made by Asbury in his Journal.

The date of the organization of the John St. Society 1766, is definite. The date of the organization of the Maryland Society is not quite so definite. It is claimed, however, that the Pipe Creek Society was organized "in 1763 or 1764." If either of these dates can be substantiated, the priority of Strawbridge's Society is established. While admitting some uncertainty as to the exact year, the Maryland folks claim sufficient evidence to prove it was the one year or the other. In addition Asbury's statement in his Journal, May 5, 1801, is cited.—"The settlement at Pipe Creek is the richest in the state; here Mr. Strawbridge formed the first Society in Maryland—and America."

Lednum says, "The evidence adduced warrants the assertion that the first Methodist Society raised up in America .... belongs to Maryland."

The natural question then arises, as Lednum puts it, "Why did Coke and Asbury in their early accounts etc., as found in the *Discipline* (1790) make it appear that organized Methodism began in New York and others the same?" "Because," answers he, "they so understood it, not making it their business to inquire particularly into the history of Strawbridge's movements. Others never took the pains to investigate the matter. Others still have copied the errors without questioning them."

That Coke and Asbury were not positive is evident from the fact that while they say "Captain Webb preached *the same year*, they say "about the same time Robert Strawbridge .... formed some societies." When, in the course of time, Asbury had the facts he seems to correct himself.

After the question of priority of organization is settled, there arises the question of permanence. Was the Strawbridge Society permanent, did it last, and does it actually exist and "carry on" today? We know that the John St. Society in New York and Old St. George's in Philadelphia are still alive and performing all the functions of a regular Society or church. Is this true of the Society founded by Strawbridge? If not then the John St. Society is Methodist's oldest and St. George's her next oldest Society.

The Pipe Creek Society and "Log Meeting House," Maryland

The bare facts concerning the organization of the Maryland Society seem to be as follows:

Immediately on arriving in America Strawbridge proceeded to Frederick County, Maryland. He had no sooner provided and arranged his dwelling, a log house about two miles south of New Windsor, than he opened it for religious services and in it preached to his neighbors regularly.

In time the first class meeting, consisting of six members, was held; the meetings alternating between the home of Strawbridge and one John England. Shortly after starting his first class Strawbridge began another at the home of Andrew Poulson. In 1763 or 1764 the two classes were merged and with several additions, organized into a Society.

Beside Frederick County, Strawbridge preached in Hartford County and elsewhere in Maryland. Under date of Saturday, November 4, 1769, Joseph Pilmoor wrote in his Journal, "The work that God began by him (Capt. Webb) *and Mr. Strawbridge*, a local preacher from Ireland, soon spread throughout the greater part of Baltimore County."

On Monday, May 26, 1772, after he had crossed the Susquehanna, on his way south, Pilmoor proceeded to Bushtown and Gunpowder Neck. Here he writes, "God has undoubtedly begun a good work in these parts by the ministry of John King, Robert Williams, and Robert Strawbridge." On Monday, December 30, of the same year, Asbury "rode in company with Mrs. Rachel Hulys, Mrs. R. and the widow W. to Nathan Perrigs and preached to a large number of people." Again on September 21, 1773, he says, "I rode to Patapsco Neck and after preaching reduced the class to some order." It is claimed that this class was the outcome of the labors of Strawbridge. However the testimony of both Pilmoor and Asbury points to effective activities of Strawbridge in and about the region.

The first Methodist house of worship to be erected in America (if we except Whitefield's "Academy," Philadelphia, and allow Maryland's claims) was a Log Meeting House erected in 1763 or 1764 on Pipe Creek, a mile south of New Windsor, Maryland, by Strawbridge. The Meeting House, measuring 24x24 feet stood, we are told, from 1764 to 1844 "when it was built into a barn adjoining." Beneath its pulpit Strawbridge buried two of his children. In 1914, a marker bearing the following inscription, was erected. "On This Spot Stood The Log Meeting House Erected About 1764."

Strawbridge was more or less of an independent—claiming not only the right to baptize and administer the Lord's Supper but declining to recognize the authority of, or be restricted by Wesley's assistants and even wringing from them certain concessions. In 1776 he moved to a farm near Baltimore, where, in 1781, he died.

The "John Street" Society and "Wesley Chapel," New York

While Strawbridge had evidently begun and was pursuing his labors down in Maryland, Embury, his fellow-countryman, was bideing his time in New York. "We have no record," says Simpson, "of Embury conducting any religious service until 1766."

Six years after his arrival in New York from Limerick, Ireland, at the earnest solicitation of his cousin, Barbara Heck, Embury began to preach. Unusual circumstances apparently brought about the exercise of his long neglected gifts and graces. Finding some of her kinsmen playing cards, Barbara gathered up the cards, threw them into the fire, and then went forth to stir up her neglectful cousin.

"Brother Embury," said Barbara, "you must preach to us or we shall all go to hell and God will require our blood at your hands." To this Embury replied, "How can I preach for I have neither house nor congregation." "Preach in your own home and to our own company first," was the rejoinder. According, Embury at once began to preach in his own home at No. 10 Augustus Street. Here a Class and later the Society, called John Street, from its final location, was formed with the following members: Embury, Mrs. Embury, Paul and Barbara Heck, John Lawrence, and "Betty," a colored servant.

Soon Embury's house became too small and a room was

rented in the worst section of the town, near the barracks. Here, Captain Webb, who had "sold out" of the British Army and been stationed at the Barracks in Albany, coming to New York in February, 1767, found the Methodists worshiping. Webb, who was a convert of Wesley and a local preacher, soon won the confidence of the members and took a keen interest in the affairs of their Society. He assisted Embury in the meetings and frequently preached, usually with his sword laid across the Bible.

The Society having increased in numbers soon moved from the room near the barracks to a rigging loft, at what is now No. 120 Williams Street.

On March 29, 1768, lots on John Street were conveyed by deed by "Mary Barclay, executrix and Andrew Barclay, Leonard Lispenard, and David Clarkston, executors of the last will and testament of Henry Barclay, late of the city of New York, clergyman, deceased, on the one part and Philip Embury, William Lupton, Charles White, Richard Sause, Henry Newton, Paul Heck, and Thomas Taylor, all of the city of New York, and Thomas Webb, of Queens County, of the other part."

The following appeal was then made for funds. "A number of persons desirous to worship God in spirit and truth, commonly called Methodists (under the direction of the Rev. Mr. John Wesley) whom it is evident God has been pleased to bless in their meetings in New York, thinking it would be more to the glory of God and the good of souls had they a more convenient place to meet in, where the Gospel of Jesus Christ might be preached without distinction of sects or parties; and, as Mr. Philip Embury is a member and helper in the Gospel, they humbly beg the assistance of Christian friends, in order to enable them to build a small house for the purpose, not doubting but the God of all consolation will abundantly bless all such as are willing to contribute to the same."

Although the Philadelphia Society (St. George's) does not appear on the list of subscribers to the building fund there is documentary evidence that at least £30 were contributed by it.

IN ENGLAND AND IN AMERICA

In a letter to his brother written from Charleston, South Carolina, May 13, 1769, a Thomas Bell, writes concerning the John St. Society, and its building enterprise: "There is another of our preachers who was a captain in the army; he was convinced of the truth before he left England; his name is Mr. Webb. God has been pleased to open his mouth. So the Lord carries on a very great work by these two men (Embury and Webb). They were, however, sore put to it in building their house; they made several collections about the town for it; and they went to Philadelphia, and they got part of the money there. I wrought upon it six days."

Captain Webb is credited with contributing the £30 but, inasmuch as Philadelphia does not appear on the list, and Webb did collecting there, there is some warrant for concluding that the money credited to Webb was actually money collected by him.

Embury, a carpenter by trade, labored on the building and built also the first pulpit. David Morris, another carpenter, received more than £100 and Samuel Edmonds more than £500 for their work.

The chapel then erected, called "Wesley Chapel" has been described as "a substantial one of stone, faced with blue plaster, 60x42 feet . . . . and was provided with a chimney and fire place." It had, also, a gallery, access to which was gained by a ladder. The cost of the enterprise has been estimated at between £600 and £800. On October 30, 1768, Embury dedicated the Chapel—preaching at the time on Hosea 10: 12.

Arriving in New York Tuesday, March 27, 1770, Pilmoor writes in his Journal:

"Wednesday, 28. As there has been a great uneasiness among the people of this City about the settlement of the Chapel that was built for the Methodists, we called the Trustees together and examined the writings—by comparing them with the plan on which the Chapels in Europe are settled, we found them to be *essentially wrong*. The Trustees were invested with absolute power over both Preacher and People and could do just as they wanted without being accountable to any one. This we judged to be not only contrary to the whole economy of the Methodists, but likely to prove hurtful to the work of God, and therefore endeavored to persuade them to have it altered. The reasons we gave had such weight that the Trustees freely resigned their trust, and agreed to destroy the writings, which was immediately done by the consent of the whole. Afterwards a proper settlement was made according to the general plan and the Chapel was regularly settled. After spending a few days together . . . . we parted with full determination to live or die for the Lord Jesus."

The claim that Maryland makes to the distinction of having built within its confines the first Methodist house of worship, is also made by, and, for New York. Wesley Chapel, it is contended, was the first structure as it is claimed John St. was the first Society.

In 1818, during the pastorate of Samuel Howe, unfortunately, the original Chapel gave way to a second structure. This building was dedicated by Dr. Nathan Bangs.

"Twenty-three years after the erection of the second church," writes Dr. Upham in "The Story of John Street," "it became necessary, on account of the widening of the street, either to reconstruct the building or to supplant it by a new one. A counter proposal was urged, viz: to sell the property and devote the proceeds to missionary purposes. Happily a decision was reached to rebuild and the trustees issued an appeal that contained, in part, the following words: The trustees solicit aid from their brethren at home and abroad to enable them to promote their enterprise, believing as they do that, by perpetuating to other and distant generations the privilege of worshipping their father's God where they first erected the standard of the cross and proclaimed a free and present and full salvation, they do what the voice of the whole Methodist Episcopal Church would demand at their hand."

The present church, called the "John Street Church," built in 1841 was dedicated by Bishop Hedding. Material from the first and most of that from the second church was used.

The ministerial life of Philip Embury was brief. Four years after the founding of the John Street Society he left

New York and settled near Salem, Washington County, N. Y., where he preached until his death in August, 1773.

Barbara Heck, whose name is so closely associated with, and equal-revered as that of her cousin, died in 1804. Her body lies buried in the Blue Church yard on the St. Lawrence, near Prescott, Ontario, but "her spirit goes marching on" and her memory will always be kept green. Only God knows whether there would be a "John Street" Society were it not for Barbara Heck.

Captain Webb, the third important figure in the history of the New York Society, did not confine himself either to that city or Society. Sometime in 1767 he moved to the vicinity of Jamaica, Long Island, where his wife's people resided. Webb preached in various places on the island. Late in 1767 he made the first of many visits to Philadelphia and associated himself closely with the Methodists there. Beside New York and Philadelphia he labored in New Jersey, Delaware, and to an extent in Maryland. He returned to England finally in 1778 and resided near Bristol. He died suddenly December 20, 1796, and was buried on Christmas Eve in a vault in the Crypt of Portland Chapel, which he was instrumental in building.

St. George's, Philadelphia

Philadelphia in the early days was the metropolis of the new world, the "London of America," as Asbury later called it. It was a busy seaport where ships called constantly, especially from Britain, and discharged their cargo and their passengers.

It does not seem strange, therefore, as both history and tradition has it, that Whitefield's labors here should be augmented not only by his own converts but by those of Wesley, both itinerant and lay, from Great Britain. Here, in fact, all of Wesley's first and early missionaries and itinerants landed and began their labors in America.

One of the most active and effective of Whitefield's converts in Philadelphia and vicinity, of whom we have definite knowledge, was Edward Evans. Evans, converted sometime in 1739 or 1740, became one of the original trustees of Whitefield's "Academy." (Watson's "Annals.") He first joined the Moravians ("Old Philadelphia Churches") but withdrew to engage, up until 1769, in independent evangelistic work. When Pilmoor and Boardman arrived Evans definitely cast in his lot with the Methodists who, at the time were worshiping in Loxley Court, but had "obtained a permanent footing in the province two years before."

While a member and trustee of the Philadelphia Society, Evans continued to do evangelistic work in association with Pilmoor in New Jersey, and in the city and its environs.

Writing October 13, 1771, Pilmoor bears the following testimony to the character and labors of this early Methodist itinerant: "Mr. Evans was savingly converted to God about thirty years ago under that precious man of God, Mr. Whitefield, and has maintained an unspotted character from the beginning. When Providence brought Mr. Boardman and me to America he united with us most heartily, and was made a most useful instrument amongst us, as he frequently went into the Jerseys to preach. The people were exceedingly fond of him, built a pretty chapel (at Grinage, or Greenwich, near Gloucester, N. J.), and insisted on having him for their minister. After he had been with them a few months he took fall-fever, which soon brought him to his grave. As he lived so he died—full of faith and full of obedient love."

Lednum in the Introduction to his "Rise of Methodism," tells on good and direct authority of a ship carpenter who preached in a shed or stable on Dock Creek "long before Captain Webb began to visit this port." Lednum says he "*supposed* that, with the exception of Whitefield, Webb was the first Methodist who preached in Philadelphia" until he was informed otherwise. Lednum seems to have been unaware of the existence of Evans, also.

The presence of other Methodists in Philadelphia before the coming of Wesley's itinerants and perhaps before the arrival of Webb is indicated by the fact that Pilmoor and Boardman were accosted on the street by one who had been in society in Ireland and had met Boardman there.

The evidence seems convincing that Methodism had not

only been introduced in Philadelphia by Whitefield but by others who followed him and preceded Webb.

The nucleus of the Philadelphia Society was a "class" or group of Methodists who met under the leadership of a James Emerson, in a sail loft, belonging to, or rented by a Samuel Croft, on Dock Creek (now Dock Street.)

How long this class existed prior to 1767, if it did exist before that date, or who actually began it, we have not been able to determine.

It is significant, however, that the preaching site of the unknown ship carpenter was close by the site of St. George's first meeting place and, perhaps, suggests the circumstances under which the class originated.

However, there is no doubt that in the year 1767, coming to Philadelphia, Captain Webb found and formed into a Society the following Methodists: James Emerson and wife, Miles Pennington and wife, Robert Fitzgerald and wife, and John Hood. If not at the time very shortly after the following were added—Lambert Wilmer and wife, Duncan Steward and wife, Burton Wallace and wife, Mrs. Hood and Samuel Croft. Croft is said to have been the first convert of the Society.

By October, 1769, St. George's had one hundred members. In a letter to Wesley, quoted in full elsewhere, dated—Philadelphia, October 31, 1769, Pilmoor wrote:

"Reverend Sir,

"By the blessing of God we are safe arrived here after a tedious passage of nine weeks. We were not a little surprised to find Captain Webb in town, and a Society of about a hundred members who desire to be in close connection with you. This is the Lord's doing and it is marvelous in our eyes."

Beginning with from seven to fourteen in 1767 indicates an increase of almost fifty members a year—an unusually rapid growth for the time and circumstances.

When on October 24, 1769, Pilmoor and Boardman arrived in Philadelphia from England they were welcomed by Captain Webb. Webb took the same active interest in the Philadelphia Society that he took in the New York. His name appears on the Deed to the Fourth Street property.

From the Dock Street sail loft the Society moved to a room at No. 8 Loxley Court (now Leather Place) in a building formerly used as a "pot" or public house. Here, we shall see, they were worshiping when Williams, Pilmoor, and Boardman arrived.

"The room in Loxley Court," says Pilmoor, "soon became too small for the constantly increasing congregation and more ample accommodations were looked for.

Thursday, November 23, 1769. We met to consult about getting a more convenient place to preach in. What we had would not contain half of the people who wished to hear the word, and the winter was approaching, so that they could not stand without. Several places were mentioned, and application was made, but to no purpose. Though the ministers in general were pretty quiet, they did not approve of our preaching in their pulpits. In this I could not blame them, especially as we form a Society of our own, distinct from them and their congregations. What we should do I could not determine; ground to build upon might have been easily purchased, but we had no money, and besides we wanted the place *immediately*. At length we came to an agreement to purchase a very large shell of a church that was built by the Dutch Presbyterians, and left unfinished for want of money.

"As the poor people had ruined themselves and families by building it they were obliged to sell it to pay their creditors. It was put up at public auction and sold for seven hundred pounds, though it cost more than two thousand."

The building, 55x85 feet in size, far exceeded in cost the calculations of the builders, and those responsible for the amount expended were finally thrown into the debtor's prison and the property was advertised for public sale.

On Thursday, November 23, 1769, the building was purchased for 650 pounds by Miles Pennington, a member of and representing the Methodist Society.

On the very day of purchase the Methodists, under the leadership of Pilmoor, and numbering about 100 members, took up their abode in the new edifice, which had remained unfinished and unoccupied until then.

On Friday, November 24, 1769, the day after its purchase,

the building was dedicated by Pilmoor. "Friday, November 24, 1769, I preached," writes he in his Journal, "in our new church to a numerous congregation with great freedom of mind. God gave me liberty of spirit to open that noble passage of Scripture, 'Who art thou O great mountain? Before Zerubbabel thou shalt become a plain, and he shall bring forth the headstone thereof with shoutings, crying, grace, grace unto it.' Peradventure that God who enabled him to finish the temple at Jerusalem will in His providence and blessing make way for us to finish the church we have bought and set apart for His praise."

Listen to the prayer of Pilmoor. "May Thy Divine presence always abide in it, and the dew of heaven continually descend upon those who assemble there to worship Jehovah, the Lord of Hosts."

The first Sabbath, November 26, 1769, in the new place of worship, "was a great day to the rejoicing congregation." Captain Webb preached in the morning. In the evening Pilmoor preached, he says, to 2,000 hearers. A collection was taken at the evening services for the payment of the church and amounted to over sixteen pounds.

On September 14, 1770, the property, first conveyed to Miles Pennington June 14, 1770, by William B. Hockley, was conveyed by deed by Pennington to Richard Boardman, Joseph Pilmoor, Thomas Webb, Edward Evans, Daniel Montgomery, John Dowers, Edmund Beach, Robert Fitzgerald, and James Emerson for £650.

The following is the "special trust clause" contained in the Deed which conforms to Wesley's "Model Deed" of 1750.

"Nevertheless upon special trust and confidence and to the intent that they and the survivors of them and the trustees for the time being do and shall permit John Wesley, late of Lincoln College, Oxford, clerk, and such other persons as he from time to time and at all times during his natural life shall appoint, and no other persons to have and enjoy the free use and benefit of the said premises so that the said John Wesley and such persons as he appoints may therein preach and expound God's Holy Word, and after his decease upon further trust and confidence and to the intent that the said trustees and the survivors of them, and the trustees for the time being do and shall permit Charles Wesley, late of Christ Church College, Oxford, clerk and such other persons as he from time to time and at all times, during his life shall appoint, and no others, to have and enjoy the free use and benefit of the said premises for the purposes aforesaid, and after the decease of the survivors of them the said John Wesley and Charles Wesley thereupon further trust and confidence and to the intent that the said Richard Boardman, Joseph Pilmoor, Thomas Webb, Edward Evans, Daniel Montgomery, John Dowers, Edmund Beach, Robert Fitzgerald and James Emerson and the survivors of them and the trustees for the time being shall and do from time to time and at all times hereafter forever permit such persons as shall be appointed at the Yearly Conference of the people called Methodists in London, Bristol, and Leeds, and no others, to have and enjoy the free use and benefit of the said premises for the purposes aforesaid. Provided always that the said persons preach no other doctrine than is contained in the said John Wesley's notes upon the New Testament and four Volumes of Sermons. Provided also that they preach in the said house in the mornings and evenings of Sundays and of such other days of the week as by custom the Methodists may from time to time be set apart for that purpose, and upon this further trust and confidence that as often as any of them the said trustees or of the trustees for the time being shall die or cease to be a member of the Society commonly called Methodists, the rest of the said trustees or the trustees for the time being shall as conveniently may be choose another trustee or trustees in order to keep up the number of nine trustees forever. In witness the said parties to these presents have interchangeably set their hands and seals hereunto dated the day and year first above written.

 Sealed and Delivered
 in the presence of
  Charles Shnyder   Miles Pennington
  L. Weiss

 In his Journal, Tuesday, September 11, 1770, Pilmoor states,

"The Methodist Church in Philadelphia is secure for our preachers as the Chapels in London and York."

St. George's is the first Methodist house of worship to be called a church. Pilmoor so speaks of it. The original edifice on John Street was referred to, as were all other Methodist edifices in this country and England, as chapels. Asbury in the course of time, doubtless because of its size—it has a seating capacity of over a thousand people—gave it added dignity by calling it "the Cathedral of Methodism."

The purchase price did not include the ground, which had been taken up on an annual ground rent of 70 pounds sterling, redeemable within ten years by the payment of 400 pounds.

On Monday, September 23, 1782, "I began," says Asbury, "begging for the Society (St. George's) that we might, if possible, relieve our preaching house from the encumbrance of ground rent. I soon got £270."

On June 25, 1802, the "ground rent was extinguished."

The lot was apparently shaped like a right angle, and included the ground upon which the church stands and a vacant lot on New (then Story) Street, upon which the building, 326, was later erected.

The Name. The building now known as St. George's Church, designed to be a German Reform Church, and to be called Georg Kirchen (George Church), probably in honor of the reigning King of England.

After their acquisition of the building and for a number of years the Methodists referred to it as "our preaching house," and "our new meeting house." At the suggestion, probably of Pilmoor, the name was modified to St. George's, after the patron Saint of England, who was martyred during the Diocletian persecution, A.D. 303, and was venerated both in the Eastern and Western Churches. Numerous orders and societies were founded in his honor.

It is suggestive that Pilmoor was very closely associated with an organization called "The Sons of St. George" (organized April 23, 1772) to which he bequeathed one-half the residue of his estate amounting to $8,162.52.

The building, which appears to have been "a mere shell" when purchased, stood originally about two feet above the street level, with stone piers as its support and requiring several steps to enter. The front entrance was in the center and opened directly into the main and only room. The interior was destitute of paint, plaster, and furnishings.

In keeping with the Wesleyan Conference ruling of 1765, old-fashioned slat-backed benches resting on the dirt floor accommodated the first congregations. Indeed, not until after the Revolutionary War was any pretense made at "flooring" and then a "rough floor" was laid in the east end, the other half being left in the original condition. Several important events, then, among them the first three Conferences of American Methodism, were held on the dirt floor of an unpainted, unplastered church building.

In 1784 the walls were plastered and in 1790 the church was floored from end to end and more attractive and comfortable seats installed.

In 1762 Old St. Paul's Episcopal Church, 3rd below Pine Street, was built "with a design to be more in accord with Wesley's church conceptions than was tolerated in other Anglican Churches." Here Pilmoor, Boardman, Asbury, and others attended service. Here, also, our Society at Philadelphia received the Sacraments prior to 1785.

The pulpit of St. Paul's, resembling a "watch box" with the top off, stood about twenty feet from the east wall of the church and just to the south of the north gallery.

The altar was elevated several steps from the floor against the east wall and in front of the altar was an altar rail.

When, therefore, the Methodists completed the interior of their edifice they very naturally copied both their pulpit and chancel after those in St. Paul's. On the north side of the auditorium just to the south of the north gallery and twenty feet from the east wall, at a spot identical with that of St. Paul's, the Methodists built, in place of "the wide square box which served temporarily as a pulpit," the "watch box" type of pulpit.

It held but one person at a time, and was reached by "frame steps" around which was a banister. Over the pulpit hung a "sounding board."

"About 20 feet from the east end, inside," says Watson's

1. Wesley Chapel (John St., N. Y.)
   1768-1818

2. St. George's (Phila.)
   1769 to present

4. Log Meeting House (Md.)
   1764-1844

3. Barratt's Chapel (Frederica, Del.)
   1780 to present

5. Lovely Lane (Md.)
   1775-1786

"Annals," there stood a square thing not unlike a watch box, with the top sawed off, which in that day served as their "pulpit of wood," from whence the Rev. Mr. Willis (1791) used to read prayers previous to the sermon, from Mr. Wesley's Liturgy, and John Hood (lately living) raised the hymn standing on the floor."

In 1815 the high pulpit (called by Wesley a "tub pulpit") was moved and in 1845 was removed entirely. The reproduced pulpit of today is a faithful reproduction on the original site of the original pulpit.

When, in December, 1784, the Methodist Episcopal Church was organized and Methodist preachers were ordained and authorized to administer the Sacraments, arrangements, including an altar rail, for Communion in St. George's became necessary. A pewter Communion set, one cup of which has been preserved, was imported from England.

In 1792 galleries were constructed, at a cost of £362, on the north, south, and west sides.

"Sunday, October 11, 1795," says Asbury, "I preached in the evening in St. George's where to my surprise the galleries were filled."

The church was at first lighted by candles set in black tin sconces, or candlesticks, oblong in shape, which hung on the walls. Candle chandeliers hung from the ceiling.

The first Cash Book (1769-1775) reveals the cost of the sconces: "I doz. sconces 15 shillings." Candles were bought by the pound, the price varying from 14 to 19 cents, 34 to 100 pounds a month were used. The candles would be burned to the socket and the "butts" or "stumps" sold at 8 and 10 cents a pound.

The building was furnished with stoves, probably wood or charcoal stoves and is described as "a dreary, cold-looking place in winter time, when from the leaky stovepipe, mended with clay, the smoke would frequently issue, and fill all the house."

The character of the stoves and the unfinished condition of the church prior to 1800 made heating to a comfortable degree difficult. The women brought "wooden stoves" or foot-warmers such as were commonly used in the market places.

In 1836 excavation under the building permitted facilities for Sunday school and Class purposes. At the same time a slight lowering of the front door permits access on the level to the "basement."

In the second floor room of an old building built in 1812 adjoining the church, for Sunday School, Class, and Conference purposes, Asbury held, April 20-26, 1815, his last Conference in Philadelphia. Here are preserved many valuable papers and relics. Among the most prized of these are letters and the Bible, razor and spectacles of Asbury.

In 1921 efforts were made to remove the old church to a new site to allow the proposed Delaware River Bridge to have the right of way. Led by Bishop Thomas B. Neely these efforts were successfully resisted. The plans for the Bridge were changed to allow its erection fourteen feet farther south and permit St. George's to remain intact on its original site.

Writing to the author, the late Dr. Edward L. Watson, President at the time of the American Methodist Historical Societies, declared *"No church has the record of Old St. George's."* This statement is true whether the reference is to the edifice or to the Society, and will become increasingly apparent as these chapters are perused.

"Lovely Lane" Chapel, Baltimore, Maryland

Was completed in March, 1775. In December, 1784, the memorable "Christmas Conference," at which the Methodist Episcopal Church was organized, Francis Asbury ordained and Asbury and Thomas Coke "set apart" as General Superintendents, was held in Lovely Lane.

Unfortunately, again, Lovely Lane Chapel, which should have been permitted to exist for the inspiration of Methodists of all generations, ceased to be in 1786. The site on which it stood on German Street near South Street, is now occupied by the Merchant's Club of Baltimore, on whose building a bronze tablet proclaims the momentous events of over a hundred and fifty years ago.

IN ENGLAND AND IN AMERICA

Barratt's Chapel, Frederica, Delaware

Built in 1780 and, fortunately, like Old St. George's, is still standing. This Chapel was the meeting place on November 14, 1784, of Thomas Coke and Francis Asbury. Here the Sacrament of the Lord's Supper (at which a Methodist Itinerant, in the person of Richard Whatcoat assisted, to the surprise of Asbury) was for the first time administered under Methodist auspices. At Barratt's Chapel it was, also, agreed to summon the itinerants to the proposed conference at Baltimore the coming December.

CHAPTER VI

The Arrival and Initial Activities of Williams, Pilmoor, and Boardman

In 1768 the Methodists in New York under Embury, particularly Thomas Taylor, a member of the John Street Society, and some in Maryland who had been awakened under the ministry of Robert Strawbridge, appealed to Wesley to send preachers to America to assist them. The following is an extract from the letter, already quoted, of Taylor:

"There is another point far more material (than the financial) and in which I must importune your assistance, not only in my own name, but also in the name of the whole society. We want an able and experienced preacher, one who has both gifts and grace necessary for the work. God has not, indeed, despised the day of small things. There is a real work of grace begun in many hearts by the preaching of Mr. Webb and Mr. Embury; but although they are both useful, and their hearts in the work, they want many qualifications for such an undertaking; and the progress of the Gospel here depends much upon the qualifications of preachers.

"In regard to a preacher, if possible we must have a man of wisdom, of sound faith, and a good disciplinarian: one whose heart and soul are in the work; and I doubt not but by the goodness of God such a flame will be soon kindled as would never stop until it reached the great South Sea. We may make many shifts to evade temporal inconveniences; but we cannot purchase such a preacher as I have described. Dear sir, I entreat you, for the good of thousands, to use your utmost endeavors to send one over. I would advise him to take shipping at Bristol, Liverpool, or Dublin, in the month of July, or early in August: by embarking at this season he will have fine weather in his passage, and probably arrive here in the month of September. He will see before winter what progress the Gospel has made.

"With respect to money for the payment of the preacher's

passage over, if they could not procure it, we would sell our coats and shirts to procure it for them.

"I most earnestly beg an interest in your prayers, and trust you, and many of our brethren, will not forget the church in this wilderness.

"I remain with sincere esteem, Rev. and dear sir, your very affectionate brother and servant,

THOMAS TAYLOR."

Captain Webb and Dr. Von Wrangel, pastor of Old Swedes, Philadelphia, had likewise urged the needs and claims of that city upon Wesley. On his way back to Sweden, Von Wrangel had formed the acquaintance of and dined with Wesley.

Under date of October 14, 1768, Wesley wrote in his Journal, "I dined (at Bristol) with Dr. Von Wrangel, one of the King of Sweden's chaplains, who has spent several years in Pennsylvania. His heart seemed to be greatly united to the American Christians: and he strongly pleaded for our sending some of our preachers to help them, multitudes of whom are like sheep without a shepherd."

"Tuesday, 18," continues Wesley, "he (Von Wrangel) preached at the new room to a crowded audience and gave general satisfaction by the simplicity and life which accompanied his sound doctrine."

The influence brought to bear upon Wesley had its effect and when the appeal made at the Bristol Conference in 1768 was renewed at Leeds in August, 1769, two preachers, Joseph Pilmoor and Richard Boardman, volunteered and were dispatched to America.

Joseph Pilmoor was born at Tadmouth (or Tadmoor), Yorkshire, England, October 31, 1739. He was converted under Wesley at the age of 16 and placed by him in the Kingswood School, where he studied English Literature, Latin, Hebrew, and Greek. After four years of training he was employed as a "lay-helper." In 1765 he was admitted into Conference and stationed at Cornwalls. In 1767 and 1768 he traveled in South Wales.

Richard Boardman is supposed to have been born at Gillimoor, Ireland, in 1738. Sometime prior to 1765 he began to itinerate. Lockwood says, "He traveled successively the Grimsby, Limerick, and Cork Circuits, closing this period of his labors on the Dales Circuit near the source of the River Tees."

The absence of an authentic Journal of Boardman, such as we have of Pilmoor, is deeply regretable.

Before Pilmoor and Boardman set sail, however, an Irish local preacher, Robert Williams by name, had embarked for America, arriving in all probability in Philadelphia, on or before September 2, 1769. Williams, it is said, had arranged to accompany a Mr. Ashton of Dublin to this country. On hearing that Ashton was about to embark, Williams sold his horse to pay his debts, and with only his saddlebags, a loaf of bread, and a bottle of milk, hastily left Castlebar for the place of embarkation, relying on his friend to pay his passage over.

It is thought by some that Williams was at the Conference at Leeds when Pilmoor and Boardman were appointed. This is hardly likely. The Conference did not begin until Tuesday, August 1; we know it was not over until after the fourth, and that Williams was in America on September 2. This would allow only twenty-eight days for the passage, against sixty-three by Pilmoor, and fifty by Asbury, although the possibility must be admitted since Whitefield made the passage back to England in 1765 in exactly twenty-eight days.

There is some debate as to whether Williams landed in New York or in Philadelphia, and whether he began his labors with the John Street or with St. George's Society. Claim for New York is based, apparently, on an entry in John Street "Cash Book" dated September 20, 1769. An earlier date, *September 2, 1769*, however, in *St. George's "Cash Book,"* together with certain well known and authenticated activities, tend to support the claim that Philadelphia was the port of Williams' arrival, and St. George's the first American Society to which he ministered.

Ignorance of the existence of the entry in St. George's "Cash Book" doubtless explains the acceptance and spread of the error concerning New York. In all probability John Lednum is responsible for the publicity given to John Street's entry.

His ignorance of the entry in the "Cash Book" of St. George's, of which he was pastor in 1827, is easily explained. The fact is Lednum himself did not have access to St. George's oldest record. The reason is as follows: In 1801 a group of St. George's members organized themselves into what came to be known as Union Methodist Episcopal Church. In the group was Samuel Harvey, secretary of the Board of Trustees of St. George's. With him went St. George's Cash Book, dating from August, 1769. On January 1, 1863—62 years later, the Board of Trustees of St. George's appointed a committee "to wait upon the party or parties" having the above book in their possession, with the request that they hand over the same to the proper custodians. April 5, 1888, Rev. Robert Corson, the pastor of St. George's, was requested to wait on the Trustees of Union Church and endeavor to secure the book in their possession. On January 3, 1889, Dr. Corson, having by certain means secured the old Cash Book from Union, presented it to the Board of Trustees of St. George's. Later the Trustees of Union demanded its return, but the request naturally was refused, as it was pointed out "that the entries in the book showed conclusively that it belonged to St. George's Church."

However, on or about September 2, 1769, Williams made his appearance at the Loxley Court quarters of the Philadelphia Society. According to their records, £1. 2s. 6d was paid for traveling expenses, 5s. 7½d for his washing, and significant and suggestive enough, "2s. 2½d for shrub on Boat." Provision was made for Williams from time to time until December, 1771.

Williams brought with him to America some of John Wesley's tracts, sermons, books, and the hymns and songs of Charles. These he immediately began to sell and to reprint with the result that at the first Conference in 1773, his acts were called in question and his activities limited.

On October 7, 1769, a little over a month after Williams' arrival, the treasurer of St. George's paid John Dunlap & Co. for printing 400 hymns. Late in 1769 or early in 1770, Dunlap & Co. printed "Wesley's Hymns and Spiritual Songs, etc." These publications were in all probability printed under Williams' direction and from copies furnished by him. These were doubtless the first hymns published and bound for an American Society.

In a letter to Thomas Rankin, which was transmitted to Wesley, Dr. Jarratt says, "In the counties of Sussex and in Brunswick (Va.), the work from the year 1773 was chiefly carried on by the labors of the people called Methodists. The first of them that appeared in these parts was Mr. Robert Williams, who, you know, was a plain, artless, indefatigable preacher of the Gospel."

To return now to Pilmoor and Boardman: Hearing the appeal from America at Bristol in 1768, Pilmoor writes that during the following year, which he spent chiefly at Pembrokeshire, he was "frequently under great exercise of mind, respecting the dear Americans and found a willingness to sacrifice everything for their sakes. Accordingly, when the proposal for sending missionaries to America was mentioned, I told in the fear of God what was on my mind and offered myself for the service. At the same time Mr. Richard Boardman offered himself to go likewise. Mr. Wesley and the preachers in the Conference heartily approved of the proposal and immediately appointed us as missionaries to that country. As we had been for years in connection, and were well known among the preachers, we judged their concurrence, with what we believed to be a call from God, of the utmost importance, which made us rest fully satisfied with our appointment. As we had then sufficient reason to believe it was of God, and as the brethren in connection with us were also perfectly satisfied with our appointment, they generously made a collection among themselves toward the payment of our passage over. Afterward it was mentioned in London, Bristol, etc., and money enough was soon raised to send us over the Atlantic."

Concerning the Conference at Leeds in 1769 the Leed's *Intelligencer* of August 8 stated: "For the week past the Rev. John Wesley has held a kind of visitation, but what they call a Conference, in this town, with several hundred (?) of his preachers from most parts of Great Britain and Ireland. When he settled several routes for the succeeding year, etc., and

A page from Old St. George's Cash Book. Note reference to Robert Williams—Sept. 2, 1769. Note also "Printing of Hymns"—Oct. 7, 1769

after collecting a large sum of money for the purpose of sending out missionaries for America, he yesterday morning set out for Manchester."

"When Conference was over," continues Pilmoor, "I took leave of Mr. Wesley and the preachers and set off to see my relations. I was somewhat afraid the trial of parting with me would be too great for them, especially my mother, but God had prepared her for it before I came; she seemed to give me freely up to Him and was much resigned to His will. This was a fresh token of the will of God concerning my going, and greatly encouraged my soul, so that I had not the least remaining doubt that it was my duty to go. The way was made plain before me, every obstacle was entirely removed and I was fully satified about it.

"On Sunday, 13th, after preaching at Kovringham and Sheriffhutton in my way, I came to York, where I had appointed to meet Mr. Boardman.

"At ten o'clock we took coach for London, where we arrived in peace at eight o'clock on Tuesday night. The rest of the week we spent in making preparations for our voyage to Philadelphia.

"When we had been a few days in London the Rev. Mr. George Whitefield sent for us. As he had been long in America, he knew what directions to give us, and treated us with all the kindness and tenderness of a father in Christ. Difference in sentiment made no difference in love and affection. He prayed heartily for us and commended us to God and the word of his grace, so we parted in love, hoping soon to meet where parting is no more.

"Sunday, 20th. At five I preached in the foundry to a numerous congregation. Mr. Charles Wesley met the Society, and afterwards sent for Mr. Boardman and me into his room, where he spoke freely and kindly to us about our sea voyage and the important business in which we had engaged. After giving us much good advice he sent us forth with his blessing in the name of the Lord.

"Monday, 21st. After preaching once more in the foundry we took leave of our dear London friends, went to the Carolina Coffee House, where we met Capt'n Sparks, with whom we were to sail. We took the coach for Gravesend, where we embarked in the evening on board the Mary and Elizabeth for Philadelphia."

After a passage of nine weeks from London, on the 24th of October they landed at Gloucester Point, six miles below Philadelphia.

"When we got on shore," writes Pilmoor, "we joined in a doxology and gave praise to God for our deliverance and all the mercies bestowed upon us during the passage.

"When we had rested a little while at a public house, Mr. Boardman and I walked up to the city, where we were kindly received and entertained by Captain Sparks and his wife. He behaved to us with the greatest civility during the five weeks we were on board his ship, and his generosity at the last was truly noble. May our God and Saviour abundantly reward and bless him for all his kindness to us, both in time and eternity. Having no knowledge of any society in Philadelphia, we had resolved to hasten to New York as soon as possible, but God had work for us to do that we knew not of."

While Pilmoor and Boardman apparently for some reason were ignorant of the existence of the Philadelphia Society, Wesley himself not only knew of, but had the Society in mind when he dispatched the two to America. "Tuesday, August 1 (1769) our conference began at Leeds. On Thursday I mentioned the case of our brethren in New York. For some years past several of our brethren from England and Ireland had settled in North America and had in various places formed societies, *particularly in Philadelphia* and New York" (Wesley's Ecclesiastical History, Vol. IV, page 261).

Again, on October 14, 1768, as we have seen, he dined with Von Wrangel, the rector of Old Swedes, Philadelphia, who pleaded for preachers to help the American Christians. One can readily believe that the Philadelphia Society was, in a measure at least, the subject of the conversation.

It is not to be wondered at, however, that two comparatively young itinerants (Pilmoor was 30 and Boardman 31) should be ignorant of much of the Methodist situation in America.

Continuing his account of his and Boardman's arrival in

Philadelphia, Pilmoor says, "As we were walking along one of the streets a man who had been in Society in Ireland and seen Mr. Boardman there, met with us and challenged him. This was very providential, for he informed us they had heard that two preachers were arrived, and he was then out seeking us. He took us home with him, and in a little while Captain Webb, who had been in the city for some days, came to us and gave us a hearty welcome to America. Our souls rejoiced to meet with such a valiant servant of Jesus in this distant land, especially a she was a real Methodist. In the evening we had the happiness to hear a Gospel Minister in St. Paul's Church. He preached a very useful sermon on 'Behold the Lamb of God that taketh away the sin of the world.'"

When Pilmoor and Boardman arrived in Philadelphia they found, as Williams had before them, the Society worshiping in what had been a "pot" or public house at No. 8 Loxley Court, to which they had moved from the sail loft on Dock Street sometime before.

The next day (October 25) after arrival Boardman "preached to a small but serious congregation" in Loxley Court "on the call of Abraham to go forth into the land of promise."

After preaching to the Society in Philadelphia, Boardman set off on the following day for New York via Trenton.

Almost immediately on arrival he entered into the following agreement with the John Street Society:

"Mr. Richard Boardman, assistant to and preacher in the Connexion with Rev. John Wesley, also Philip Embury, local-preacher, and William Lupton, a trustee and steward (in New York), thinking it necessary that some regulations should be made for the preachers in New York, agreed, on the 1st of November, 1769: First, that each preacher, having labored three months in New York, shall receive three guineas, to provide himself with wearing apparel. Secondly, that there shall be preaching on Sunday morning and Sunday evening; also on Tuesday and Thursday evenings; and the preacher to meet the Society every Wednesday evening."

Under date of November 4, 1769, Boardman writes to Wesley.

"Reverend Sir,—After nine weeks' voyage of great difficulties, we safely arrived in Philadelphia. Several said there had not, in the memory of the oldest man on the continent, been such hard gales of wind as for these few months past. Many vessels have been lost, while others got in with loss of masts and much damage to their cargoes. We observed shipwrecks all along the coast of Delaware. I never understood David's words as I now do: 'They that go down to the sea in ships, that do business in great waters; these see the works of the Lord, and his wonders in the deep.' In calm serene weather I found much exercise of mind—strong temptations and great dejection; in rough stormy weather when it appeared morally impossible the vessel should live long, amid conflicting elements, I found myself exceedingly happy, and rested satisfied that death would be gain. I do not remember to have had one doubt of being eternally saved, should the mighty waters swallow us up. This was the Lord's doings. O, may it ever be marvelous in my eyes.

"When I came to Philadelphia I found a little society and preached to a great number of people. I left brother Pilmoor there and set out for New York, coming to a large town (Trenton) on my way and seeing a barrack, I asked a soldier if there were any Methodists belonging to it. 'O yes,' said he, 'we are all Methodists; that is, we should be glad to hear a Methodist preach.' 'Well,' said I, 'tell them in the barrack, that a Methodist preacher just come from England, intends to preach here tonight.' He did so, and the inn was surrounded with soldiers. 'I asked where do you think I can get a place to preach in?' (it being dark). One of them said, 'I will go and see if I can get the Presbyterian meeting house.' He did so; and soon returned to tell me he had prevailed and that the bell was just going to ring to let all the town know. A great company soon got together and seemed much affected.

"The next day I came to New York. Our house contains about seventeen [he probably meant seven] hundred hearers. About a third of those who attend the preaching get in; the rest are glad to hear without. There appears such a willingness in the Americans to hear the word as I never saw before. They have no preaching in some parts of the back settlements.

I doubt not, but an effectual door will be opened among them. O, may He now give His son the heathen for His inheritance.

"The number of blacks that attend the preaching affects me much. One of them came to tell me she could neither eat nor sleep because her master would not suffer her to come to hear the word. She wept exceedingly, saying, 'I told my master I would do more work than I used to do if he would but let me come; nay I would do everything in my power to be a good servant!'

"I find a great want of every gift and grace for the great work before me. I should be glad of your advice. But, my dear sir, what shall I say to almost everybody I see? They ask, 'Does Mr. Wesley think that he shall ever come over to see us?'

"I am, dear sir, your affectionate son and servant,

R. BOARDMAN."

To return now to Pilmoor, whom Boardman left at Philadelphia: "I agreed," says he in his Journal, "To stay some time in Philadelphia, to try what might be done for the honor of God and the salvation of immortal souls.

"In the evening, Thursday, the 26th, we had a fine congregation of attentive hearers, but I was greatly straitened in my own mind, and felt but very little freedom to preach. God was pleased to humble me by leaving me to myself, and make me ashamed of my own unworthiness. Others may, perhaps, preach very fluently, and with great accuracy without any assistance from above, but that is nothing to me. I find it an easy matter to *talk*, but to *preach* the gospel with the Holy Ghost sent down from Heaven is widely different.

"Friday, October 27th. In the evening our congregation was large. My mind was at liberty, and God gave the word free course among the people. When He is present it is a pleasure to preach. Under the Divine influences of His Spirit my soul exults in Hope of success, but without Him I can do nothing."

Writing on the same day, only three days after his arrival, concerning Edward Evans to whom we have referred, Pilmoor continues: "I spent an hour comfortably with Mr. Edward Evans, an old Disciple of Jesus, one who has stood fast in faith for nearly thirty years. He is a man of good understanding and sound experience in the things of God, and his conversation was both entertaining and profitable.

"Sunday, October 29. We had a fine congregation at seven in the morning, to whom I explained and enforced part of the first Psalm; afterwards I attended worship at St. Paul's, where we had a profitable sermon by Mr. Stringer. Having appointed preaching on the common (Franklin Square) adjoining the city, at five o'clock, I went and found a vast multitude gathered together. So I got upon the stage erected for the horse race, and was presently surrounded with several thousands of genteel persons, who all behaved with the utmost attention while I declared Jesus Christ, the prophet, priest, and King of His people. After preaching I met the little Society, *in our own room* (Loxley Court), and exhorted them to walk worthy of their high calling and adorn the gospel of Christ. This was the first Sabbath I spent in America, and it was truly delightful. My soul was abundantly blessed in preaching the word of life to others, and seemed perfectly willing to sacrifice everything for their good.

Monday, October 30. As I wished to fill up every moment of my time for God, I began preaching at five o'clock in the morning and found it a time of love."

Pilmoor then addressed the following letter to Wesley:

Philadelphia, October 31, 1769.

"Reverend Sir,—By the blessing of God we are safely arrived here after a tedious passage of nine weeks. We were not a little surprised to find Captain Webb in town, with a society of about a hundred members who desire to be in close connexion with you. This is the Lord's doing, and it is marvellous in our eyes.

"I have preached several times and the people flock to hear in multitudes. Sunday night I went out upon the common (now Franklin Square). I had the stage appointed for the horse-race for my pulpit, and I think, between four and five thousand hearers, who heard with attention still as night. Blessed be God for field preaching! When I began to talk of preaching at five o'clock in the morning the people thought it would not answer in America. However I resolved to try and had a very good congregation. There seems to be a very great and effectual door opening in this country, and I hope many souls will be gathered in. The people in general like to hear the word, and seem to have some ideas of salvation by grace. They seem to set light to opinions. That which is the most prevalent, is 'universal salvation.' And if this be true, then, perhaps (as Count Zinzendorf observed), 'we may see the devil falling before the Saviour and kissing his feet.' I have been to visit Mr. Stringer, who is well. He bears a noble testimony for our blessed Lord Jesus; and I hope God does bless him.

When I parted with you at Leeds, I found it very hard work. I have reason to bless God that I ever saw your face. And though I am well now four thousand miles from you, I have an inward fellowship with your spirit. Even while I am writing my heart flows with love to you and to all our dear friends at home. In a little while we shall meet in our Father's Kingdom,

> 'Where all the storms of life are o'er,
> And pain and parting are no more.'

"This, reverend and dear sir, is and shall be the earnest prayer of your unworthy son in the Gospel,

J. PILMOOR."

"November 1—Mr. Robert Williams called on me on his way from New York to *Maryland*. He came over to America about business, and being a Local Preacher in England Mr. Wesley gave him a license to preach occasionally under the direction of the regular preachers. During his stay in the city he preached several times, and seems to have a real desire to do good.

"His gifts are but small, yet he may be useful to the country people who are in general as sheep without a Shepherd.

"Saturday, 4.—Captain Webb came up from Wilmington, where he had been for a few days on a visit, and brought us tidings "that Jesus, the great Shepherd, had blessed his labors in the gospel and made them successful in turning men from darkness unto light, and from the power of Satan unto God.

"The work that God *began* by him and *Mr. Strawbridge, a local preacher from Ireland,* soon spread through the greater part of Baltimore County, and several hundreds of people were brought to repentance and turned unto the Lord.

"Sunday, 5.—At seven in the morning Captain Webb gave us an excellent discourse on 'Poverty of Spirit,' and I trust many of the hearers are beginning to experience it. We had a blessed time at St. Paul's at the sacraments. My soul did truly eat *Christ's flesh* and drink *His blood* and found meat indeed.

"In the afternoon at two o'clock I preached to some thousands of people in the New Market (Front and Market Streets), who all behaved as if they felt the awful presence and power of God."

Rules Read to Multitude.—"At six in the evening I read and explained the rules of the Society to a vast multitude of serious people. The first time, I suppose, the rules were ever read in America to such a multitude of people. God has opened a great and effectual door in this place for the preaching of the Gospel, of all that I have seen in such a manner that I am filled with wonder and with praise.

"Many persons who are engaged in religious matters take pains to be as *secret* as they can, but I wish to be as *public as possible*, because I think everything that is of God will bear the light, and whatever is contrary thereto ought to be *discovered* that it may be *amended.*

"November 6.—After preaching at five in the morning, Mr. Williams set off for Maryland. As he is very sincere and zealous, I trust God will make him a burning and shining light in that *dark part of the country*, where the poor people have been so *long neglected that they are* quite ignorant of the Gospel way of *Salvation.*

"In the evening we had a large congregation of attentive hearers to whom I preached, after which met a small company of people and spoke to them about the state of their souls.

"The Lord was remarkably present at our public meetings during the whole of this week. I generally preached twice a day besides meeting classes and conversing with the people about the state of their souls. Nine persons were admitted to the Society, and one found peace with God. The Lord is making bare His arm in the sight of the heathen, and many of the poor Africans are obedient to the faith."

Pilmoor evidently roomed at No. 8 Loxley Court, above the Society meeting place which, apparently, was on the street floor.

He continues:

"On Saturday night the people crowded into the room as long as they could, and many were obliged to stand without in the street while I explained and applied these words of the Baptist—'Whose fan is in His hand, etc.' After which several young persons met together for prayer, one of whom was deeply affected and groaning for redemption through the blood of the Lamb.

"Mr. Webb met with them and was greatly drawn out in prayer to God for him. *As I sat in my room* my mind was impressed with a strong desire *to go down and join with them; I did so,* and it was a time of great life and power as the poor creatures cried out in the bitterness of their souls for an interest in the blood of atonement and would not *rest* without a blessing from God. I stand and wonder at the amazing goodness of God that He should condescend to work by such an unworthy instrument. But He has chosen the weak and foolish of the world to confound the wise and mighty."

CHAPTER VII

An Important Statement of Faith. Inauguration of the Prayer Meeting, Watch Night, Love Feast

In the evening of Sunday, December 3, 1769, a "crowded audience" at St. George's greeted the pastor, Joseph Pilmoor. Referring to this service Stevens in his History of Methodism, says, "Many other notable gatherings have been held within its walls, but none more significant than this. The memories that cluster around Old St. George's," he continues, "give it a peculiar interest. From its pulpit on the first Sunday in December, 1769, Pilmoor made an important statement of the faith and body of principles of Methodism, proclaiming it to be an organization having no schismatic aim, but seeking earnestly the revival of *spiritual religion.*"

This statement, made by Pilmoor, was doubtless the first public utterance in America, if not anywhere, of Methodism's purpose and principles.

The following is of Pilmoor's own account:

"Sunday, December 3. In the evening I preached to a crowded audience, on a *judgment* to come, and the behaviour of the people was such as became the solemnity of the subject. Indeed the people in general behaved to us with utmost respect and civility, not only in the church while we worshipped Jehovah, but in all other places.

"As I would not wish to do anything in *secret* that will not bear the light, nor even *mislead* or *impose* upon people, I resolved to lay before the congregation the only design we had in coming to America, and the reason of our buying the church, that they might be able to judge for themselves whether they ought to encourage us or no. Accordingly I read in public the following particulars:

"1. That the Methodist Society has never designed to make a separation from the Church of England or be looked upon as a church.

"2. That it was first and is still intended for the benefit of

Interior of Old St. George's

all those of every denomination who being truly convinced of sin and the danger they are exposed to, earnestly desire to flee from the wrath to come.

"3. That any person who is so convinced and desires admittance into the Society will be readily received as a *probationer*.

"4. That those who walk according to the oracles of God, and thereby give proof of their sincerity, will readily be admitted into full connection with the Methodists.

"5. That if any person or persons in the Society walk *disorderly* and transgress the holy laws of God we will admonish him of his error; we will strive to restore him in the spirit of meekness; we will bear with him for a time; but if he remains incorrigible and impenitent, we must then of necessity inform him he is no longer a member of the Society.

"6. That the church now purchased is for the use of this Society for public worship of Almighty God.

"7. That a subscription will immediately be set on foot to defray the debt on said church, and an exact account kept of all the benefactions given for that purpose.

"8. That the deeds of settlement shall be made as soon as convenient and exactly according to the plan of the settlement of all the Methodist Chapels in England, Scotland, and Ireland. I then told the people we left our native land, not with a design to make divisions among or promote a schism, but to gather together in one the people of God that are scattered abroad, and revive *spiritual religion*. This is our one point, Christ that died for us, to live *in us* and reign over us in all things."

The "Intercession" or Prayer Meeting—On Friday, December 8, 1769, Pilmoor inaugurated at St. George's the "Intercession." This service he refers to in his Journal under the above date. "We had," says he, "our first Intercession, and it was a time of love." Again, Friday, March 23, 1770, "We had a time of refreshing at the intercession." It is significant that after the intercession a love feast (the first by the Methodists in America) was held. This was in keeping with the custom of the English Methodists of holding a "Watch night" or "Love Feast" after the fast day and prayer service.

On "August 31, 1770," Pilmoor writes, "The Intercession on Friday was a time of love." At this time and thereafter a capital "I" is always used in Pilmoor's Journal in the spelling of "The Intercession."

Pilmoor speaks frequently in his Journal of "The Intercession," of the weather conditions that prevailed, and of visiting afterward the sick and the "poor prisoners in goal." "Friday, November 23, 1771, I had," says he, "the presence and blessing of the Lord, especially at the Intercession. I have regularly kept up *this meeting* both here (New York) and in Philadelphia since my arrival in America, and have abundant reason to bless God for the immeasurable benefit He has from time to time bestowed on us." While Pilmoor speaks frequently of the Intercession, he never mentions a "Prayer Meeting." The "Intercession" in America, like that of the "fast day" and "Intercession" in Great Britain, was invariably held on Friday and usually in the daytime, although evening service also was frequently held.

This service we have traced elsewhere to the National day of fasting and prayer kept regularly by the Methodists in Great Britain. Its characteristics and subsequent purpose "to intensify zeal in the work and to prepare for the duties of the Sabbath" convinces us that it was the immediate forerunner both here and in Great Britain of what is known today as the Prayer Meeting.

In 1791 the preachers were instructed to "appoint prayer-meetings" wherever they could in "Large Societies." The General Conference of 1792 ordered that "The preacher who has Charge of a Circuit, shall appoint prayer-meetings wherever he can on his Circuit."

It is significant that the Prayer Meeting in Philadelphia was originally held, not on Wednesday, as is the general custom today, but on Friday. All the old Philadelphia Churches followed, for some time, the early custom of holding Prayer Meeting, Fridays. Just when the "Intercession" in America became the "prayer meeting" or when day services during the week were abandoned we have been unable to determine.

"Sunday, December 17. After preaching at seven to a few serious hearers," . . . . writes Pilmoor, "I went to the Quaker Meeting to *wait* upon the Lord. Sunday, January 14. Mr. Robert Strawbridge, a local preacher from Maryland, gave us a useful discourse at seven in the morning." Tuesday, January 16. Pilmoor preached "eight miles from the City"; on Sunday, 21, after "preaching in our own Church" he preached to the Swedes at Kingcess. On Sunday, March the 4th, on his way to the City, he preached in the English Episcopal Church, at White Marsh, of which later he became rector.

The First Love Feast in America—"Friday, March 23, 1770," writes Pilmoor, "in the evening we had our first American Love Feast in Philadelphia, and it was indeed a time of love. The people behaved with much propriety and decorum, as if they had been for many years acquainted with the economy of the Methodists. Perhaps this favorable beginning will encourage the people to wish for such a season again, and may help to prepare them to eat bread together in the Kingdom of God."

Monday, March 26, 1770, writes Pilmoor, "I set off in the morning for New York—Mr. Francis Harris, a gentleman of Philadelphia, took me with him in his Chaise, and as I was to preach at Pennypack, a vast number of my friends accompanied me so far to hear my last sermon for the present.

"Tuesday, 27. We set off early in the morning and arrived in New York about eight o'clock on Wednesday evening—knowing it was a preaching night we hastened to the Chapel, and found the congregation assembled and Mr. Boardman preaching the word of God with life and power.

Wednesday, 28. Pilmoor examines the Deeds of Wesley Chapel, finds them "essentially wrong" and persuades the trustees to destroy them and have others drawn in conformity with the plan on which the Chapels in England are settled. (See Chapter V.)

Mr. Boardman sets off with Mr. Harris in his Chaise for Philadelphia. Pilmoor stayed in New York.

"On Thursday, the 19th of April, I crossed over," says he, "to Long Island, and rode on with a friend to Jamaica to visit Capt. Webb."

On May 6, 1770, George Whitefield arrived from the

South, in Philadelphia, where at the time, Boardman labored. On the 24th Whitefield is still in Philadelphia.

"Sunday, May 13, 1770," writes Pilmoor, "In the evening I was greatly enlarged at the preaching but more at the lovefeast. It is the first that has been kept by the Methodists in New York and the Lord was remarkably present.

"Saturday, June 25, 1770, I had the honor to wait on the Rev. George Whitefield and congratulate him on his safe arrival in New York. He was remarkably loving and affectionate and desired me to be quite free and frequently call on him.

"Sunday, 26. As Mr. Whitefield was to preach, I began at six o'clock that the people might be at liberty to attend him. In the evening I did not think it proper to interfere with him and therefore did not preach in our Chapel."

On July 25 Pilmoor met Boardman at Princeton. Boardman goes on to New York. Pilmoor returns to Philadelphia.

On August 18, 1770, John King arrives at Philadelphia from England. (See next chapter.)

Tuesday, October 9, Pilmoor receives "the melancholy news of the death of that excellent saint of God, Mr. George Whitefield."

On the thirteenth he goes with Edward Evans "to Metchen, a place about twenty miles from the city (near Centre Square, Montgomery County, Pa.) to open up a new chapel (Bethel) which had been built by a few persons who love the Redeemer." About three o'clock he preached, Evans exhorted and in the evening they held a love feast.

While in America Pilmoor was not without temptation to leave the itineracy nor without tempting offers to be ordained and unite with the Anglican Church. One such offer he refers to in his Journal, October 20, 1770. "I had the pleasure," says he, "of dining at the Mr. D. Roberdaws, where I met Mr. Turnbull, a gentleman from Turtola in the West Indies. He offered me a living of £400 a year and would have taken me over to England, got me ordained and put me in possession of the Church. I told him I had no objection to ordination, but I could not consent to settle in one congregation for life as I believed I might do more good in the Itinerant way."

IN ENGLAND AND IN AMERICA

Watch Night Service—While the Watch Night closely corresponded to the Vigiliae of the early church, the custom of the Methodists in America is traceable directly to that of the Kingswood miners, already referred to, in 1742.

According to the Old Cash Book a Watch Night Service was held in St. George's, Thursday, November 1, 1770, the first of which, as far as we can find any record, held in America.

On Monday, November 5, Pilmoor leaves again for New York while Boardman returns to Philadelphia.

On Monday, December 31, 1770, Watch Night Services were held both at St. George's (Cash Book) and in Wesley Chapel, New York.

Concerning the Watch Night in New York, Pilmoor writes, "We had our Watch Night. The mob had threatened great things but the terror of the Lord made them afraid and we continued till midnight, that we might end the old and begin the New Year in the service of God."

CHAPTER VIII

The Arrival of King, Asbury, and Wright

For two years Pilmoor and Boardman labored chiefly in Philadelphia and New York, exchanging places every three to five months, preaching meanwhile in adjacent towns, villages, and the countryside.

Late in March, 1770, and again late in July, 1770, these two itinerants exchanged places, resulting in Boardman going to New York and Pilmoor to Philadelphia.

August 18, 1770, Pilmoor notes in his journal the arrival at Philadelphia of "a new herald of peace," John King.

King was born in Leicestershire, England, of "well-to-do, Church of England parents. He studied at Oxford and at a London medical college." In 1776 he was converted under Wesley and in 1770 sailed for America where he labored in New Jersey, Virginia, and North Carolina until 1777 when he located. He died at a very advanced age near Raleigh, N. C.

King was the recipient of the following interesting letters from Wesley.

May 17, 1775.

"My dear Brother: Always take advice or reproof as a favor; it is the surest mark of love. I advised you once, and you took it as an affront. Nevertheless, I will do it once more.

"Scream no more, at the peril of your soul. God warns you by me, whom he has set over you, speak as earnestly as you can, but do not scream. Speak with all your heart, but with a moderate voice. It was said of our Lord, 'He shall not cry'; the word properly means, He shall not scream.

"Herein be a follower of me, as I am of Christ. I often speak loud, often vehemently, but I never scream; I never strain myself; I dare not; I know it would be a sin against God and my own soul. Perhaps one reason why that good man Thomas Welsh, yea, John Manners, too, were in such grievous darkness before they died was because they shortened their own lives.

"O, John, pray for an advisable and teachable temper? By

Francis Asbury—First American Bishop who preached in St. George's, October 28, 1771, the first of 16,590 times in America, beginning an itinerary that covered 270,000 miles

nature you are very far from it; you are stubborn and headstrong. Your last letter was written in a very wrong spirit. If you cannot take advice from others, surely you might take it from Your affectionate brother."

July 28, 1775.
"Taking opium is full as bad as taking drams. It equally hurts the understanding, and is, if possible, more pernicious to the health than even rum or brandy. None should touch it, if they have the least regard either for their souls or bodies."

"I met," writes Pilmoor concerning King, "with a particular trial, a young man waited on me, who said he was just arrived from England, and had been a preacher among the Methodists. But upon examination I found he had no letter of recommendation from Mr. Wesley, nor any of the Senior Preachers in England or Ireland, hence I could not receive him as a Minister in connection with us, nor suffer him to preach among our societies in America. However, as he appeared to be a good young man, I resolved to deal tenderly with him and treat him with all the kindness in my power, as a stranger in a distant land, and told him I would do everything in my power for him, only I could not employ him as a preacher; as this did not satisfy him he departed from me, and was determined to preach whether I approved of it or not, so I left him for the present to pursue his own business, and was fully determined to be on my guard against all impostors."

King, however, was not to be discouraged and, therefore, persisted in preaching in the outdoor places of the city. Sunday, August 26, 1770, Pilmoor writes: "In the evening at six I wondered to find so few people in the Church (St. George's), but soon found out the cause of it. Mr. John King (the young man who was with me a few days ago wanting to be employed as a preacher) had publicized himself and was preaching in Potter's Field to a great multitude of people. When he had done they hastened away to the Church, which was soon filled."

"Having conversed much with him," writes Pilmoor later, 'since he arrived in the city, and found him to be a zealous and good man, I thought it would be well to try him, so I appointed him to preach before me and the leaders of the Church." On Friday, August 31, 1770, King accordingly preached his probationary sermon in St. George's, and was licensed by Pilmoor. Subsequently, as we shall see, King introduced Methodism into Baltimore.

On Thursday, February 8, 1771, Boardman arrived in New York and Pilmoor left on Sunday for Philadelphia, via Elizabeth Town, Trenton, and Burlington.

"This," writes Pilmoor, "has been the most dangerous, fatiguing and disagreeable journey I ever undertook—and there was no necessity for it at present; only my friend Boardman would come to New York and I could not think of leaving Philadelphia without a preacher.

"Tuesday, March 5, 1771. Received a letter from London informing me that Mr. Wesley preached a funeral on the death of that great man of God, Mr. Whitefield. What a pity, Mr. Wesley and he were ever divided, however, difference of opinion did not separate them in affection for they loved as brethren and undoubtedly will rejoice together in the Kingdom of God.

"Monday, April 15, having had a pressing invitation, I set off in the morning for Wilmington. In the evening, I found a fine congregation ready to receive the word of the Lord, and He enabled me to preach with freedom and power.

"Thursday, April 18, I met with Mr. John King, the person I sent into these parts several months ago and have the happiness to find, God has made him an instrument of abundance of good among the country people."

Pilmoor then went to Newark (Del.), Christeen (?) Bridge, and New Castle, returning on the 20th to Philadelphia.

On Sunday, the 21st, King preached in the morning. "How wonderfully improved since he arrived in America!" comments Pilmoor. Continuing he writes, "As I had Mr. Williams and Mr. King both in the city, I was glad to accept their assistance."

Friday, May 10, after meeting Pilmoor was, "agreeably surprised to meet Mr. Jarvis from New York." On return home he finds Boardman. On Monday, the 13th, he took stage with Jarvis for New York, reaching there on Tuesday.

With New York as his center, Pilmoor labors in New

Rochelle, a French settlement, East Chester, West Chester, Rye, on Long Island, and Jamaica.

August 11, Williams preaches in New York and on the 13th Pilmoor goes by stage to Philadelphia, arriving on the 14th. On the 15th Boardman departs for New York.

With Philadelphia as his center, Pilmoor labors in the neighboring towns of Gloucester, Chestnut Hill, and Germantown (Philadelphia).

Tuesday, October 1, Pilmoor goes to Burlington, arriving about seven in the evening. On Wednesday, October 2, he writes, "I preached at the Court House—Having a desire to try Bristol . . . . we all went over in a boat and I preached in the Court House, but here my labor was almost in vain; for the Bristol Gallios care but little for any of these things."

The year 1771 marks the arrival in America of two more appointed missionaries of Wesley, Francis Asbury, and Richard Wright, the former of whom was to become the outstanding figure of all time in the history of American Methodism.

At the Conference in Bristol (England), 1771, Wesley sounded the second call for preachers to go to America. "Our brethren in America," said he, "call aloud for help. Who are willing to go over and help them?" Five volunteered. The two appointed were Francis Asbury and Richard Wright.

Francis Asbury was born August 20, 1745, near the foot of Hamstead Street Bridge, Parish of Harnworth, four miles from Birmingham, Staffordshire, England.

"At 12 years of age," writes he, "the Spirit of God strove frequently and powerfully with me, but being deprived of proper means and being exposed to bad company, no effectual impression was left on my mind. When between 13 and 14 the Lord graciously visited my soul again. I then found myself more inclined to obey, and carefully attended preaching in W. Brunswick, so that I heard Stillingfleet, Rylaud and others, who preached the truth. I then began to watch over my inward and outward conduct. The next year Mr. M's came in to those parts. I was then 15, and young as I was, the word of God soon made a deep impression upon my heart, and brought me to Jesus Christ, who graciously justified my guilty soul through faith in His precious blood. About 16 I experienced a marvelous display of the grace of God. At 17 I began to hold some public meetings, and between 17 and 18 began to exhort and preach. About 21 I went through Staffordshire and Gloucestershire, in the place of a traveling preacher, and the next year through Bedfordshire, Sussex, etc. In 1769 I was appointed assistant in Northamptonshire, and the next year traveled in Wiltshire.

"On August 7, 1771, the Conference began in Bristol, England. Before this I had felt for half a year strong inclinations in my mind that I should visit America, which I laid before the Lord, being unwilling to do my own will, or run before I was sent. During this time my trials were very great, which, I believe, the Lord permitted me to prove and try me in order to prepare me for future usefulness.

"At the Conference it was proposed that some preachers should go over to the American Continent. I spoke my mind and made an offer of myself. It was accepted by Mr. Wesley and others, who judged I had a call."

Although on December 10, 1772, Asbury received a letter from Wesley appointing him "Assistant" and another on December 24, 1783, directing him to act as "General Assistant" and to receive no preachers from Europe that were not recommended by Wesley, nor any in America that would not submit to him, it seems, from Asbury's own words and actions and from the Minutes of the American Conferences, that his original appointment was that of General Assistant. He evidently supplanted Boardman and Pilmoor and in turn was supplanted by Rankin. In the Conference at Kent County, Delaware, in 1779, as we shall see, the itinerants decided that Asbury "ought to act as General Assistant in America . . . . 2d because originally appointed by Mr. Wesley." The Conference of 1782 "unanimously chose" brother Asbury to act according to Mr. Wesley's original appointment, and preside over the American conferences and the whole work."

"From Bristol I went home," continues Asbury, "to acquaint my parents with my great undertaking, which I opened in as gentle manner as possible. Though it was grievous to flesh and blood, they consented to let me go. My mother is one of the tenderest parents in the world; but I believe she was blessed in the present instance with Divine assistant to part with me. I visited most of my friends in Staffordshire, Warwickshire and Gloucestershire, and felt much power and life among them. Many of my friends were struck with wonder when they heard of my going; but none opened their mouths against it, hoping it was of God. Some wished their situation would allow them to go with me.

"I returned to Bristol in the latter end of August, where Richard Wright was waiting for me, to sail in a few days for Philadelphia. When I came to Bristol I had not one penny of money; but the Lord soon opened the hearts of friends, who supplied me with clothes and ten pounds; thus I found, by experience, that the Lord will provide for those who trust in him.

"On Wednesday, September 4, we set sail from a port near Bristol; and having a good wind, soon passed the channel. For three days I was very ill with sea sickness, and no sickness I ever knew was equal to it. The captain behaved well to us. On the Lord's Day, September 8, Brother Wright preached a sermon on deck, and all the crew gave attention.

"Thursday, September 12," on board ship, Asbury wrote in his journal, "I will set down a few things that lie on my mind. Whither am I going? To the new world. What to do? To gain honor? No. If I know my own heart. To get money? No, I am going to live to God and to bring others so to do. In America there has been a work of God; some moving first among the Friends, but in time it declined; likewise by the Presbyterians, but among them also it declined. The people God owns in England are the Methodists. The doctrines they preach and the discipline they enforce, are, I believe, the purest of any people now in the world. The Lord has greatly blessed these doctrines and this discipline in the three kingdoms; they must, therefore, be pleasing to him. If God does not acknowledge me in America, I will soon return to England. I know my views are upright now; may they never be otherwise."

After a stormy voyage of fifty days, Asbury and Wright reached Philadelphia, Sunday, October 27, 1771.

Pilmoor happened at the time of Asbury's arrival to be in charge of the Philadelphia work. Boardman was in charge at New York.

Arriving in Philadelphia, Asbury and Wright were directed to the house of a Mr. Francis Harris, "by whom," writes Asbury, "we were brought in the evening to a large church (St. George's), where we met a considerable congregation. Mr. Pilmoor preached. The people looked on us with pleasure, hardly knowing how to show their love sufficiently, bidding us welcome with fervent affection, and *receiving* us as the angels of God. Oh that we may always walk worthy of the vocation wherewith we are called! When I came near the American shore my heart melted within me, to think whence I came, where I was going, and what I was going about. But I felt my mind open to the people and my tongue loosed to speak. I feel that God is here, and find plenty of all we need."

Sunday, October 27, Pilmoor notes in his Journal the arrival at Philadelphia from Europe of Asbury and Wright. "We have long expected them," says he, "and now I trust the Lord will be with them and make His face to shine on all their labors." Monday Pilmoor spent in introducing the new arrivals "to his particular friends in the city."

On Monday, October 28, 1771, Asbury preached in St. George's the first of 16,500 times in America, beginning an itineracy that covered 270,000 miles. The text of his first sermon he failed to record.

On Tuesday he accompanied Pilmoor to Grenage Chapel. On Sunday, November 3, Wright preaches and on the 4th a Watch Night is held with all three itinerants present—Asbury preaching.

On Wednesday, October 30, according to the records of Old St. George's, Richard Wright preached his first sermon in America. On November the 4th a Watch Night Service was held, all three itinerants—Asbury, Wright, and Pilmoor—being present, Pilmoor preaching.

On "Tuesday, November 6, I preached," says Asbury, "at Philadelphia, my last sermon before I set out for New York, on Romans VIII 30-32: 'He that spared not his own son but delivered him up for us all, how shall he not with him freely give us all things.' This also was a night of power to my own and many other souls."

On November 7 Asbury set out for New York, via Burlington, New Jersey. On Monday, the 12th, he continued on to New York, where he found Richard Boardman "in peace but weak in body." On Tuesday, November 13, 1771, Asbury preached in Wesley Chapel, John Street, "to a large congregation on I Cor. II-2."

On the 11th Williams and Wright set off for Wilmington, leaving Pilmoor alone in Philadelphia.

Tuesday, November 20, 1771—"I remain," writes Asbury, "in York, though unsatisfied with our being both in town together. I have not yet the thing I seek—a circulation of preachers, to avoid partiality and popularity. However, I am fixed to the Methodist plan, and do what I do faithfully to God. I expect trouble is at hand.

"Thursday, 22nd—At present I am dissatisfied. I judge we are to be shut up in the cities this winter. My brethren seem unwilling to leave the cities, but I think I shall show them the way."

On December 9 Pilmoor receives a letter from Boardman and on the 10th Mr. Harris leaves in his chaise "to fetch Mr. Boardman from New York."

On December 21 Boardman arrives in Philadelphia and Pilmoor departs for New York, reaching there on Thursday, December 26, 1771.

Thursday, December 26, 1771. "As some disaffected persons had insinuated I should meet with a cold reception in New York," writes Pilmoor, "my friends made a point of showing themselves, so that I never met with so kind reception before.

"Tuesday, December 31. In the afternoon, had Mr. Sauce, Mr. C. White, and Mr. M. Molloy to speak with me about certain Letters they had written to London and Dublin about Mr. Boardman and me, but they all denied writing the words which Mr. Wesley transmitted to us so we concluded to drop the matter and bury all past grievances."

On April 2, 1772, Asbury is again in Philadelphia. "I came," writes he, "to Philadelphia and finding Brother Boardman and Brother Wright there was much comforted. Brother B's plan was that he should go to Baltimore, Bro. P. to Virginia, and Bro. W. to New York, and that I should stay three months in Philadelphia. With this I was well pleased."

CHAPTER IX

*Appointment and Arrival of Rankin and Shadford.
Extended Labors of Boardman and Pilmoor*

In 1773 St. George's was called upon again to welcome to America three more of Wesley's itinerants, this time in the persons of Thomas Rankin, George Shadford, and Joseph Yearbry.

At the British Conference at Leeds in 1772, Captain Webb once more urged Wesley to send preachers to America. His urging, perhaps, together with another reason, as we shall shortly see, doubtless led to the decision to send Rankin and Shadford.

Thomas Rankin was born in Dunbar, East Lothian, Scotland, and converted at Edinburgh under the preaching of George Whitefield. After a trip to America, where at Charleston, S. C., he spent some time, he returned to England to come again under the spell of Whitefield's preaching with the result that he began to preach. After more than ten years of service we find him at the Leed's Conference.

It is said Rankin and Shadford "volunteered for service in 1772." The Minutes of 1772, however, show Rankin and Shadford designated as "Assistants," the former appointed to York, the latter to N. Wiltshire. Before the next Conference it had apparently been decided that both should come to America. The Minutes of the London Conference in August, 1773, show them appointed here but they are already on the ground.

The main reason, probably, for the appointment of Rankin, particularly, and Shadford was the loose manner in which the Societies here were, in some instances at least, conducted. This condition had been communicated to Wesley and had called forth his censure. On December 31, 1771, Pilmoor refers in his Journal to "certain letters .... written to London and Dublin about Mr. Boardman" and him, the words of which Wesley had transmitted to them. "Mr. Boardman and I," writes Pilmoor, "had been shamefully misrepresented to Mr.

Thomas Rankin, who presided at the first Conference of American Methodism, at Old St. George's, July 14, 15, 1773

Wesley and Mr. Rankin was sent over to take the whole management upon himself."

That in some instances there was poor judgment exercised in the selection of leaders, laxity in the enforcement of the Rules, partiality toward city pastorates and admission to society meetings without either ticket or membership is clear.

Asbury in his Journal refers frequently to these causes for complaint. In his Journal, Tuesday, April 28, 1772, he writes: "I intended to go out of town (Philadelphia) but could not get a horse. So I stayed with Bro. W and heard that many were offended at my shutting them out of society-meeting, *as they had been greatly* indulged before. But this does not trouble me. While I stay, the rules must be attended to; and I cannot suffer myself to be guided by half-hearted Methodists. An elderly Friend told me very gravely, that the opinion of the people was changed, within a few days, about Methodism; and that the Quakers and other dissenters had *laxed* their discipline; that none but the Roman Catholics kept it up with strictness! But these things do not move me."

On August 4, 1772, Wright held a "general love-feast" in New York which Asbury said, "is undoing all he has done."

On October 10, 1772, Asbury writes in his Journal, "I received from Mr. Wesley a letter in which he required strict attention to the *Discipline*, etc."

In striking contrast to Asbury's attitude is that of Pilmoor, revealed in the following entry in his Journal, May 17, 1772, "After preaching I hastened back to the city (Philadelphia) to preach in the evening. But O what a change—when I was here before the great church would hardly hold the congregation, now it is not near so full. *Such is the fatal consequence of contending about opinions and the ministering of the discipline.* It grieves me to the heart to see people scattered that we have taken such pains to gather, but I cannot help it without opposing the measures of Mr. Wesley's delegate and that would breed much confusion so I am obliged to go weeping away."

In the course of time the new appointees to America, Rankin and Shadford, accompanied by Joseph Yearbry, an English local preacher, Mrs. Webb, a bride of four months, and

Captain Webb, who paid the passage, embarked. When about to sail Wesley wrote to Shadford, "Dear George, the time has arrived for you to embark for America; you must go down to Bristol, where you will meet with Thomas Rankin, Captain Webb and his wife. I let you loose, George, on the great continent of America; publish your message in the open face of the sun and do all the good you can."

Leaving Rankin and his companions on the high seas, let us turn again to the itinerants already in America.

Writing to Wesley, May 5, 1770, Pilmoor said: "Brother Boardman and I are chiefly confined to the cities, and therefore, at present cannot go much into the country, as we have much more work on our hands than we are able to perform. There is work enough for two preachers in each place; and if two of our brethren would come over, I believe it would be attended with a blessing, for then we could visit the places adjacent to the cities which we cannot pretend to do, till we can take care of them."

On the arrival of Asbury and Wright in 1771 and, therefore, feeling relieved of the responsibilities of Philadelphia and New York, Pilmoor and Boardman felt free to extend their labors to other sections—Boardman to the North and Pilmoor to the South.

Concerning Boardman's itinerary we can find very little. About to return, however, to Philadelphia he writes from New Castle, Delaware, to Mary Thorne: "May 25, 1773, I have been through my circuit; the rides are long, the roads bad, the living poor, but what more than compensates for these difficulties is a prospect of advancing the Redeemer's Kingdom in bringing sinners to the knowledge of the truth as it is in Jesus. In the greatest part of this round the people are wicked and ignorant to a most lamentable degree, destitute of the fear and regardless of the worship of God. But such a reformation is wrought among them as shows the amazing love and almighty power of God. It would do you good to hear them (when the business of the day is done in the fields) wrestling in prayer with God and singing His praise with joyful lips.

Very dear friend, I trust you find your own soul alive to God—growing in grace, advancing in knowledge (viz.) of

Christ's love, the devil's malice, your great nothingness. Expect much, you cannot be disappointed. Do what little you can to bring much glory to God. Forsake yourself and sometimes your beloved retirement to stir up yourself to go forward. Charge your heart neither to murmur or repine, but to trust without wavering, to believe without doubting, to be active without fainting. Very soon, you shall praise and adore without ceasing. My kind love to Mr. and Mrs. Dowers, to Mr. Robinson, to any that ask after. Your affectionate friend, R. Boardman."

Concerning Pilmoor's itinerary to and through the south his Journal furnishes the following information:

"Thursday, April 30, 1772, at New York. Mr. Williams met the people in the morning and I began to prepare for my journey southward. As we have now got preachers to take care of the people that God has graciously raised up by us in New York and Philadelphia and all adjacent places, Mr. Boardman and I have agreed to go forth in the name of the Lord, and preach the gospel in the waste places of the wilderness and seek after those who have no shepherd. Friday Mr. Boardman arrived from Philadelphia in his journey toward the North and we were much comforted together."

Friday, May 8, Pilmoor left New York for Philadelphia, via Staten Island, Elizabeth Town Point, Penny Town, Somerset, Princetown (Princeton), and Trenton. At Princetown he met Mrs. Thorne and Mrs. Shippen from Philadelphia. On Thursday, May 14, he arrived at that city.

On Monday, May 26, at nine o'clock in the morning Pilmoor set off for the South, "determined to follow my Lord whereever he should be pleased to lead me." From Philadelphia he proceeded to Dublin, Reading, Lebanon, and Lancaster. Crossing the Susquehanna he went forward five miles where, at a Mrs. Dallums he found "honest Robert Williams preaching." Accompanied by Williams, Pilmoor goes on to Bushtown and Gunpowder Neck, where he "met a few in private as a Society." "Here," he writes, "God has undoubtedly begun a good work in these parts by the ministry of Messrs. John King, Robert Williams, and Robert Strawbridge."

Leaving King, whom he apparently picked up somewhere

on his way, at the Forks of Gunpowder, he proceeds with Williams to Baltimore. Thursday, June 11, he arrives in Baltimore, where he preaches in the Dutch Church and to almost a thousand people on the "green." On the 22d he meets a few serious people in the Dutch Church and "proposes to form a Society." Later he preached at the "Point" where he formed a Society of twenty-five persons.

With Batlimore as his center he preached at Bushtown, Deer Creek, the Forks of the Gunpowder and the surrounding country.

Writing July 9 at Baltimore, Pilmoor says, "There is now an open door in this town and nothing is wanting but a good, lively, zealous preacher for the people are many of them well affected to the cause of God and wish us prosperity in the name of the Lord. My heart is much united with them and would like well to continue longer in these parts but the tutelary cloud moves southward and I am called to go forward." On Friday, the 10th, he leaves Baltimore for Annapolis, thence to Norfolk and Portsmouth.

Using Norfolk and Portsmouth, where he organizes Societies, as centers to which he returns frequently, Pilmoor visits Great Bidge, Cranny Island, Williamsburgh, and Yorktown. Monday, September 26, he sets forth for North Carolina, returning again, however, to Portsmouth and Norfolk.

Writing November 23, he says, "Had I left Norfolk where some persons would have had me, I should have no Society either there or at Portsmouth and now we have a goodly company in each place."

In his Journal Pilmoor refers frequently to the presence and preaching of both Williams and Watters in the neighborhood.

Sometimes Williams preached in his presence. On one occasion Williams would not preach and Pilmoor was compelled to preach for him.

On December 13, he takes leave of his friends at Norfolk and Portsmouth and begins his journey toward South Carolina. In time we find him at Newburn. Of the people of Newburn he writes, Wednesday, December 30, 1772, "In all my travels through the world I have met with none like the people of Newburn! Instead of going to Balls and Assemblies as people of fashion generally do, especially at this season of the year, they came driving in their coaches to hear the word of the Lord and wait on God in His ordinances!"

On Monday, January 18, 1773, late in the evening Pilmoor reaches Charles Town, South Carolina, which appeared to him to be "an indifferent place." On Friday, January 22, at six in the evening he preached there his first sermon. On Monday, February 1, he begins to prepare for his journey to Georgia. "As I proposed," says he, "to return to Philadelphia by land, I judged it best to leave my horse at Charles Town to rest until I come back from Savannah."

On Friday, February 5, he arrives at Savannah, a town, at the time of "3,000 inhabitants white and black, the houses part of brick, the rest of timber, and very large but exceedingly neat: . . . three churches, one for the English Episcopalians, one for the Lutherans, one for the Independents." On Wednesday he visits the Orphans's House (Whitfield's), twelve miles from Savannah. While in Savannah Pilmoor had opportunity to preach on but three occasions, twice in private families. "Therefore, having no longer any Divine call in this place, on Monday morning (February 15) "I took," says he, "my leave of Savannah in company with Mr. Zubley for South Carolina."

Working his way north on Tuesday, April 6, he arrives at Norfolk and, on the 10th, at Portsmouth. On Tuesday, April 27, assisted by Williams, "at eight in the evening our first Watch Night," says he, "in Virginia began." Monday, May 3, he left Norfolk, thence to Nancemond, Suffock, and Smithfield, where he met Watters.

Crossing the James River to Williamsburgh he proceeds to New Kent Court House, and New Castle where having "a strong desire to preach to the inhabitants," he "hired a boy to go around the town to inform them." From New Castle his way lay through Hanover Court House, Caroline Court House, Fredericksburg, Dumfrers, Colchester, and Alexandria Court House.

At Alexandria he was robbed of £40 which he was taking from a gentleman in Norfolk to one in Burlington. Fortunately all but £8 was recovered. From Alexandria Pilmoor continues to Georgetown, Maryland, thence to Blandensburg and Baltimore.

On Saturday, May 29, he meets Boardman at Josiah Dallum's outside of Baltimore, "Just before we went to rest," writes he, "Mr. Boardman came. As I had not seen him for more than a year my heart rejoiced exceedingly at our meeting and we found our spirits most closely united in the fellowship of the Gospel and the Communion of Saints."

From Mrs. Dallum's at Deer Creek, where he first preached in Maryland, he proceeds to Mr. Stedam's in New Castle. By Mr. Stedam he was taken by boat to Wilmington. From Wilmington he travels to Chester, to Kingsess and thence Philadelphia, arriving at 6 P.M. on June 1. At Philadelphia Pilmoor says, "I was received by my honorable friend, Mr. John Wallace, as if I had been an angel of God."

On June 3 Rankin and his companions arrive in Philadelphia from England.

Writing in his Journal on June 3 Pilmoor says, "It is now above a year since I left the city. I set out with a consciousness of *duty* and was determined to obey what to me was a *call* from above. I was totally unacquainted with the people, the road, and everything else; only I knew there were multitudes of souls scattered throughout the vast extent of country and I was willing to encounter any difficulty and undergo the greatest hardships, so that I might win them to Christ, resolved to follow the leadings of Providence, and go wherever the 'Tutelary Cloud' should direct. With this view I turned my face toward the South; I went forward above a thousand miles through the Provinces and visited most of the towns between Philadelphia and Savannah, in Georgia, where I have preached the Gospel of Christ. . . . . Capt. Webb and his lady with two preachers, Rankin and Shadford, arrived from England."

Asbury who, also, was in the city at this time writes in his Journal: "June 3, to my great comfort arrived Mr. Rankin, Mr. Shadford, and Capt. Webb. Mr. R. preached (June 4, St. George's Records) a good sermon on these words: 'I have set before thee an open door, etc.' He will not be admitted as a preacher. But as a disciplinarian he will fill his place. "

St. George's Old Cash Book records the following payments:

June 9, 1773. Paid for 3 quarts of wine for Mr. Shadford, 5s.

June 10. Paid for 3 quarts of wine to Mr. Rankin and Shadford, 5s. 6d.

June 18. Paid for washing for Messers Rankin and Shadford to Nancy Loyd, £1. 5s. 9d.

June 18. Paid for porterage of Mr. Rankin's (goods from ship), 2s. 6d.

June 18. Paid for washing for Mr. Rankin, to Wm. Byrnes, 8s. 6d.

"Friday, June 4, was a day of sharp tribulation, indeed," writes Pilmoor. "Since I came to America I have had innumerable trials and many of them from persons I least of all expected. For more than two years Mr. Wesley, who should have been as a compassionate father to us, has treated us in a manner not to be mentioned. During that time we have not had so much as a single letter that we could read to the people; nothing but jealous reflections, unkind suspicions, and sharp reproofs came from under his hand, which greatly discouraged us in the work, and would certainly have driven us away if we had not regarded the work of the Lord above everything this world can possibly give. . . . .

"June 5, in the evening, Mr. Shadford gave an exhortation which he called, 'True Old Methodism,' and seemed to intimate that people wanted it till now."

On the 5th and sixth of June, 1773, Asbury is in Burlington, N. J. On the 10th he is in Trenton.

About the 11th of June Rankin leaves Philadelphia for Newark, via Trenton, and Shadford for Chester.

St. George's Cash Book:

"Traveling expenses to Mr. Rankin–N. York, £1. 10s.

"Horse hire for Mr. Shadford to Chester, etc., 7s. 6d.

On the 11th of June Asbury and Rankin meet in Trenton. "Friday, 11th," says Asbury, "Mr. R. came to Trenton. After dinner and prayer we set off together for Princeton. On Saturday we reached New York, and our friends there having previous notice of our coming, kindly met us on the dock where we landed. The sight of Mr. W., with some concurring circumstances, affected Mr. R. so that he appeared to be rather cast down in mind."

On Wednesday, June 23, Asbury writes, "On my return to New York I found Mr. R. had been well employed in settling matters pertaining to the Society."

Asbury again leaves New York, but returns early in July. Either before or after his return, Rankin departs for Philadelphia to preside at the first Conference of American Methodism and to definitely assume the supervision of the societies and preachers in America, with the authority of Wesley and the title of "General Assistant." This supervision, which practically supplanted Pilmoor, Boardman, and Asbury, extended over a period of five years.

"Saturday, July 11 (1773)," writes Asbury, "I preached twice with great plainness to a large number of people, and then set off, in company with Mr. J., toward Philadelphia."

Chapter X

First Conferences of American Methodism

Up until 1773 no regular Conference of preachers had been convened, but matters in which they, or the Societies were interested were cared for at quarterly meetings.

The first three Conferences of American Methodism were held in St. George's Church, Philadelphia, in 1773, 1774, and 1775. The first Conference was held on July 14, 15, 1773, with Thomas Rankin presiding.

Philadelphia was chosen for this first, and the following two important Conferences, doubtless because it was the most suitable place for such gatherings. Conveniently located for the middle and southern colonies, it was also the largest city of the colonies, having a population of 30,000, compared to 15,000 in New York, and 5,000 in Baltimore.

"Conference," says Pilmoor, "appointed to meet Tuesday, July 13. Several met in the church at 6 A.M., but as two of the preachers" (Asbury was one) "hadn't arrived, we agreed to meet the following day."

Concerning this Conference Pilmoor writes: "Wednesday morning we met, and entered upon our business in the fear of the Most High God. As Mr. Boardman and I had been shamefully misrepresented to Mr. Wesley, and Mr. Rankin sent over to take the whole management upon himself, it was expected we should have pretty close work. Had we given place to *nature*, and followed our own temporal *interests*, it would have been so; but we considered, and preferred the interests of religion and the honor of God above all the riches and honors the whole world can bestow, and were determined to submit to anything consistent with a good conscience rather than injure the work of the Lord. In this spirit we were kept during the Conference; we consulted together under the tender visitations of the Almighty, and were favored with the presence and blessing of God. So the enemy of souls was disappointed, and all our matters were settled in peace. It was now near four years since Mr. Boardman and I arrived in

America; we have constantly labored in the great work of the Lord, and have preached the gospel through the Continent for more than a thousand miles, and formed many Societies, and have above a thousand members, most of whom are well grounded in the doctrines of the gospel and savingly converted unto God. This hath God wrought, and we will exalt and glorify His adorable Name."

On Thursday, July 15, the second day of the Conference, Asbury arrived. "I did not find," writes he, "such perfect harmony as I could wish for. There were some debates amongst the preachers in this Conference relative to the conduct of some who had manifested a desire to abide in the cities and live like gentlemen. Three years out of four have been already spent in cities. It was also found that money had been wasted, improper leaders appointed, and many of our rules broken."

That Asbury was a moving spirit in this debate one may conclude from the opinion he expressed very shortly after his arrival in America. Writing at New York, January 1, 1771, he said, "I find that the preachers have their friends in the cities and care not to leave them. There is a strong party-spirit. For my part I desire to be faithful to God and man."

The purpose of this Conference was twofold: "To unify the somewhat scattered work and to suppress irregularities that had crept in relative, especially, to proceedings of Robert Strawbridge and Robt. Williams, who were employing methods out of accord with the practice of English Methodists."

None of the English or Irish preachers who had come to America to assist in the work of establishing Methodism was ordained, and consequently did not have authority to administer the ordinances.

Robert Strawbridge, however, who labored in Maryland, began to baptize and administer the Communion soon after his arrival in America, and at a quarterly meeting in Maryland defended his actions. The matter was brought up in the First Conference, when it was decided that—

"Every preacher who acts in connection with Mr. Wesley and the brethren who labor in America, is strictly to avoid administering the ordinances of baptism and the Lord's Supper." Asbury says an exception was made in the case of Strawbridge, who was permitted to administer the ordinances "under the particular direction of the assistant."

Further, "All people among whom we labor," declared they, "were to be earnestly exhorted to attend church and to receive the ordinances there, but in particular manner to press the people of Maryland and Virginia to the observance of this minute."

The Methodist Societies were originally governed by the General Rules, drawn up by the Wesleys in 1743, and by regulations adopted in the Conferences in England which were held yearly from 1744. These regulations were first published in the Minutes from year to year. They were afterward collected and printed, with slight alterations, in a tract called "The Large Minutes."

The same rules and regulations, so far as applicable, governed the Methodist Societies in America.

At the First Conference the preachers put themselves definitely under the authority of Wesley.

"1. Ought not the authority of Mr. Wesley and that Conference to extend to the preachers and people in America, as well as in Great Britain and Ireland?"

"Ans. Yes."

Second, the preachers formally recognized the doctrine and discipline of the Methodists as contained in the English Minutes to be the sole rule of their conduct.

"2. Ought not the doctrine and discipline of the Methodists, as contained in the Minutes, to be the sole rule of our conduct, who labor in connection with Mr. Wesley in America?"

"Ans. Yes."

3. At this Conference it was decided that "no person or persons be admitted into our love feasts oftener than twice or thrice unless they become members; and none to be admitted to the Society meetings more than thrice."

4. One of the first English itinerants, Robert Williams, who reached Philadelphia from England nearly eight weeks before Pilmoor and Boardman, brought with him Wesley's books, tracts, sermons and hymns. These, as we have seen, he sold or had reprinted and found ready sale for them.

On October 10, 1772, Asbury says, "I received a letter from Mr. Wesley in which . . . . He also enjoined that Mr. W. might not print any more books without his consent." On Wednesday, March 24, 1773, Asbury states, "I was somewhat troubled to hear of Mr. W., who had printed some of Mr. Wesley's books for the sake of gain. This will not do. It does by no means look well."

In keeping with Wesley's injunction and probably at Asbury's suggestion, at the first Conference, Williams was permitted to sell the books he already had, but to print no more without the authority of Wesley (when it could be gotten) and the consent of his brethren.

5. Every "assistant" was to send an account of the work of God in his circuit to the General Assistant.

The list of appointments made at the First Conference follows:

New York—Thomas Rankin (to change in four months).

Philadelphia—George Shadford (to change in four months).

New Jersey—John King, William Watters.

Baltimore—Francis Asbury, Robert Strawbridge, Abraham Whitworth, Joseph Yearbry.

Petersburg—Robert Williams.

Neither King nor Watters traveled at this time in New Jersey. After the Conference Rankin called on Philip Gatch to fill the appointment of Watters, which he did, accompanied by King.

The number of Methodists reported at the First Conference was: New York, 180; Philadelphia, 180; New Jersey, 200; Maryland, 500; Virginia, 100. Total, 1,160. Preachers, 10.

Concerning this First Conference of American Methodism, Ezra Tipple, in "Francis Asbury, a Prophet of the Long Road," has the following to say: "While there was at this time apparently no thought of a separate American organization, nevertheless some things were accomplished besides making of rules. I think it not too much to say that *at this First Conference in* 1773, rather than at the Christmas Conference in 1784, *the* Methodist Church had its birth."

All the preachers present at that First Methodist Conference in America were Europeans, namely; Rankin, Boardman, Pilmoor, Asbury, Wright, Shadford, Webb, King, Whitworth, and Yearbry—ten in number.

Whitworth's name does not appear after the second American Conference in 1774. He was, as we have seen, instrumental in the conversion of Benjamin Abbott, but was later expelled.

It is claimed by some that William Watters was present at the First Conference. The claim arises from a hasty reading or a misunderstanding of Watter's autobiography. In October, 1772, Watters, in company with Robert Williams, left his home and traveled to Norfolk, Portsmouth, Alexandria, and Charleston. After a serious illness and an absence of eleven months, he returned home via Baltimore—never, apparently, being near Philadelphia.

"In November, 1773," writes Watters, "I again left home for the second time, being appointed for Kent Circuit, on the Eastern Shore of Maryland."

There is no doubt that Asbury was present at the First Conference, but Watters writes in October, 1773 (page 34), "Here I met with Mr. As——y at my good friend's G. P——ys, which was the *first time* I ever saw him."

There is, also, no doubt that Rankin was at the First Conference and that he presided—Watters says (page 35), "During my stay at home I first met with Mr. Rankin at one of my brothers'."

Wright's stay in America was brief. While here he labored chiefly in Philadelphia and New York. At the First Conference he received no appointment. Sometime between that and the Leeds Conference, August, 1774, he returned to England. Asbury says (May 25, 1774), "we agreed (at the Second Conference) to send Mr. Wright to England." At the Leeds Conference a few months later, Wright was appointed to West Cornwall.

Apparently Wright was not acceptable to Thomas Rankin. It is significant, as we have seen, that when Rankin went to New York in 1773, in company with Asbury, and found Wright there he was very much exercised. The "sight of Mr. W.," according to Asbury, seemed to have a very depressing effect on Mr. Rankin, although the next day "Mr. R. found his spirits raised and was much comforted."

Two other entries in Asbury's Journal, however, may not only indicate the reason for Wright's return but also explain Rankin's reaction to their meeting at New York.

Monday, August 4, 1772, "I set off," writes Asbury on Manday, "in a boat for New York; and arriving about five o'clock found Mr. W. (Wright) who that night had preached his farewell sermon, and told the people he did not expect to see them any more. I have always dealt honestly with him, but he has been spoiled by gifts. He has been pretty strict in the society but ended all with a general love-feast: which I think is undoing all he had done."

Lord's day (May) 29, 1774, "I visited Mr. W. who is going to England; but found he had no taste for spiritual subjects. Lord, keep me from all superfluity of dress and from preaching empty stuff to please the ear, instead of changing the heart! Thus has he fulfilled as hireling his day."

The appointment of Rankin as General Assistant, while it did not change much the matters that called for correction, did have the effect of stirring up the feelings of those who had been laboring in America. Pilmoor, in particular, was affected. Neither he nor Boardman took an appointment at the first Conference and at the close of the year both felt constrained to leave the country, the latter never returning.

On his return to England Pilmoor "desisted" for a time from traveling. From 1776 till 1784 he served under Wesley in England, Ireland, and Scotland. When in 1784, Wesley selected the "Legal Hundred" that were to constitute the Conference, he omitted Pilmoor. Deeply aggrieved Pilmoor applied for ordination to and was ordained by Bishop Seabury in November, 1784. Having returned to America, Pilmoor eventually became rector of St. Paul's Episcopal Church, Philadelphia. After a pastorate of twenty-one years he died, July 24, 1825, and was buried under the chancel of the very church in which he and Boardman worshiped on the first night of their arrival in America and which he served for so many years.

The Second, and almost equally important, *Conference of*

American Methodist was held in St. George's, May 25, 1774, and lasted three days.

This Conference reported 2,073 members. 17 preachers were present, and appointments were made as follows:

New York—Francis Asbury (to change in three months).
Philadelphia—Thomas Rankin (to change in three months).
Trenton—William Watters.
Greenwich—Philip Ebert.
Chester—Daniel Ruff, Joseph Yearbry (to change with William Watters and P. Ebert).
Kent—Abraham Whitworth.
Baltimore—George Shadford, Edward Drumgole, Richard Webster, Robert Lindsay.
Frederick—Philip Gatch, William Duke.
Norfolk—John King.
Brunswick—John Wade, Isaac Rollins, Samuel Spragg.

"All the preachers to change at the end of 6 months. At this Conference another feature of the itinerary was adopted, namely; that of admitting young preachers on trial, the time at first being one year, a little later, two. In addition, "Every preacher who is received into full connection is to have the use and property of his horse, which any of the circuits may furnish him with."

"Every preacher to be allowed 6 pounds, Pennsylvania currency, per quarter, and his traveling charges besides."

This Conference began the custom, also, of examining the preachers. "Ques. 4. Are there any objections to any of the preachers? Ans. They were examined one by one."

Writing in his Journal, Wednesday, May 25, 1774, concerning this Conference, Asbury says: "Our conference began. The overbearing spirit of a certain person excited my fears. My judgment was stubbornly opposed for a while, and at last submitted to. But it is my duty to bear all things with a meek and patient spirit. Our conference was attended with great power; all things considered, with great harmony. We agreed to send Mr. W. (Wright) to England; and all acquiesced in the future stations of the preachers. My lot was to go to York (New York). My body and mind have been much fatigued during the time of this conference. If I were not conscious of the truth and goodness of the cause in which I am engaged I should by no means stay here. Lord, what a world is this! Yea, what a religious world! O keep my heart pure, and my garments unspotted from the world! Our conference ended on Friday with a comfortable intercession."

At this time were "admitted" *the first two native American Methodist itinerants*—Philip Gatch and William Watters, both born in 1751. This was their first Conference. Watters for the first time preached in St. George's before a Conference of preachers.

The Third Conference of American Methodism was held in St. George's, May 17, 1775. 18 out of 19 preachers were present. King was absent. They reported 3,148 members, and were appointed:

New York—James Dempster.
Philadelphia—Samuel Spragg.
Greenwich—William Duke.
Chester—Richard Webster.
Kent—Philip Gatch, John Cooper.
Norfolk—Francis Asbury.
Trenton—John King, Daniel Ruff.
Baltimore—Martin Rhodda, Richard Owens, John Wade.
Frederick—William Watters, Robert Strawbridge.
Brunswick—George Shadford, Robert Lindsay, Edward Drumgole, Robert Williams, William Glendenning.

This Conference proclaimed "a general fast for the prosperity of the work and for the peace of America, on Tuesday, the 18th of July." At this time it was decided that "the 'preachers' expense, from the Conference to their circuits, be paid out of the yearly collection."

Concerning the Conference of 1775 Asbury writes, "From Wednesday till Friday we spent in conference, with great harmony and sweetness of temper."

Although his name appears in the appointments of 1775 for Brunswick, Williams married, located, and died a short time after Conference. Tuesday, September 26, Asbury wrote in his Journal, "Brother Williams died. The Lord doeth all things well; perhaps brother W. was in danger of being entangled in worldly business and might thereby injure the cause

Bishop Asbury, in the Old St. George's Pulpit

of God. So he was taken away from evil to come. Thursday, 28, I ventured to preach a funeral sermon at the burial of Brother Williams. He has been a very useful, laborious man, and the Lord gave him many souls to his ministry; perhaps no man in America has ministered to the awakening so many souls as God has awakened by him."

The Wesleyan Conference Minutes of August, 1774, list James Dempster and Martin Rodda as appointed to America. The Minutes of August, 1775, list, in addition, William Duke, John Wade, Daniel Ruff, Edward Drumgole, Isaac Hollings, and Richard Webster, who were admitted that year into Conference. The American Minutes, May, 1774, list Duke, Ruff, Drumgole, and Hollings as "admitted on trial" and all five appointed to stations. The names of Dempster and Rodda do not appear until the American Minutes of 1775.

No appointments were made by Wesley after 1775 except in 1784 when Coke, Whatcoat, and Vasey were appointed.

Richard Owens, appointed to Baltimore in 1775, was "one of the first local preachers on the continent, traveling for weeks and months in the back settlements, in the infancy of the work. He gave himself up to the work for the two last years of his life." He died at Leesburg, September, 1786. (Minutes, 1787.)

From 1773 to the organization of the Methodist Episcopal Church, December, 1784, but one Conference annually, except in 1779, was held. 1773-1774 and 1775, in St. George's; 1776, Baltimore; 1777, Deer Creek, Md.; 1778, Leesburg, Va.; 1779, Fluvanna and Kent County, Del.; 1780, Baltimore, 1781, Choptank, Del.; 1782, 1783, and 1784, at Ellis Preaching House, each adjourning to Baltimore. These Conferences were styled, "Some conversations between the Preachers in Connexion with Rev. Mr. Wesley."

During the early years the Methodists had their largest gain in the South, particularly in Maryland, Virginia, North Carolina, and Delaware, rather than in Pennsylvania, New Jersey, or New York. The more rapid gain in the South in the opinion of Lednum, "was not due to the preachers, the doctrines they taught, nor in the difference of temperament of the people, but in the different religious trainings they had received."

The fact that Methodism was growing more rapidly in the South, especially below the Potomac, made the South therefore, the more logical place for the Conferences, and from 1776 to 1787 the Conferences were held exclusively in that section.

However, there was another reason that doubtless had some weight in the decision to hold the Conferences in the South. This reason is clearly revealed by Ezekiel Cooper in his "Funeral Discourse on death of Asbury," in St. George's, April 23, 1816.

"During the seven years of the Revolutionary War, between 1775 and 1783, they (The Methodists) had, more especially, almost unsupportable difficulties, violent oppositions, bitter persecutions, and grievous sufferings to endure. So many of the preachers being Englishmen, and Mr. Wesley, who was considered founder and chief ruler of the Methodist Societies, and his directions, opinions and advices having great influence upon their rules of conduct in America; and he being in England and known to be a loyal man to his King, and of course unfriendly to the American measure and revolution; these things occasioned jealousies and suspicions to arise among many, that the Methodists were, politically a dangerous people. Also, the moral views, the religious principles, and the conscientious scruples of the people called Methodists, not being favorable on general principles, to the spirit of war; on this ground also, the temper and spirit of the times, combining with other prejudices and passions of the day, excited jealousies and suspicions, which occasioned an evil report, of alarm, to be raised and propagated that the Methodists, preachers and people, were unfriendly and opposed to the American revolution.

"However untrue or incorrect those inferences were against the Methodists, yet nevertheless, perhaps some of them were to blame. I feel no disposition to conceal it, that a few of the preachers were imprudent, and reprehensible, in some things; and gave too much cause for such suspicions. Rodda, in particular, acted improperly and quit the country in 1777 under circumstances unfavorable to his reputation as a preacher of the gospel and hurtful to the cause of religion. Capt.

IN ENGLAND AND IN AMERICA

Webb, also, did not act so well as he ought to have done as a Christian preacher, nay, even as a British officer, his conduct was exceptionable. Rankin, likewise, had spoken so freely and imprudently on public affairs that it excited jealous fears that his opinions and influence would be of dangerous consequences to the American cause. However, he left the country in 1777."

"Some of the British preachers who were at that conference" (Deer Creek, May 20, 1777), says Lee, "intended to return to England: but they agreed to stay and continue preaching among the Americans, until their way should be quite open and for them to return to their native country. About the middle of September, Mr. Rankin and Mr. Rodda left the continent, and sailed for Europe. But sometime before they embarked, Mr. Rodda had taken some imprudent steps in favor of the Tories: a company of them having collected in Delaware state, below Philadelphia. Mr. Rodda's conduct brought many sufferings and much trouble, on the Methodist preachers and people."

Wesley's "Calm address to our American Colonies" only tended to increase the suspicion and hostility dwelt upon by Cooper.

"The spirit of the times," continues he, "the passions and prejudices of the people, the jealousies and suspicions subsisting against Asbury as an Englishman, and as a principal Methodist preacher, were such that he could not with safety travel openly and at large. In 1778, when the storm was at its highest and persecution raged furiously, he being in serious danger prudently and advisedly confined himself for personal safety to the little state of Delaware, where the laws were rather more favorable and the rulers and influential men were somewhat more friendly." There he found an asylum in the home of Thomas White, one of the Judges of the Court in Kent County.

"The reason" for Asbury's retirement, to use his own words, "was as follows. From March 10, 1778, on conscientious principles I was a non-juror, and could not preach in the State of Maryland; and therefore withdrew to the Delaware State, where the clergy were not required to take the State-oath;

though with a clear conscience, I could have taken the oath of the Delaware State had it been required; and would have done it, had I not been prevented by a tender fear of hurting the scrupulous conscience of others . . . . on Tuesday . . . . G. S. left me . . . . Friday, 13 . . . . three thousand miles from home—my friends have left me—I am considered by some as an enemy of the country . . . . Lord stand by me."

Partly, therefore, because of the antagonism toward them and the suspicion in which they were generally held, it became matters of wisdom for the English itinerants to hold the conferences in which they were leading spirits, not only as far away as possible from centers of anti-British sentiment but to retire shortly from the country.

Had Wesley had his way, probably because of the relations between Asbury and Rankin as well as the attitude of America toward English preachers, as early as 1775 Asbury, also, would have returned to England. Writing to Rankin March 1, that year Wesley said, "I advise brother Asbury to return to England the first opportunity"; April 21, "But I do not advise him (Asbury) to go to Antigua. Let him come home without delay." But, on August 13, same year, also to Rankin, Wesley said, "I am not sorry that Brother Asbury stays with you another year. By that time it will be seen what God will do with North America and you will easily judge whether our preachers are called to remain any longer therein."

Long before the Conference of 1779 met in Kent County, Delaware, with the exception of Asbury and Robert Williams and John King, who died in America, the English itinerants had all departed. This Conference, therefore, expressed its judgment that Asbury should act as General Assistant in America, because of his age, because he was originally appointed by Wesley and because of his "being originally joined with Rankin and Shadford by express orders from.Wesley." "Ques. 13, How far shall his powers extend? Ans. On hearing every preacher for and against what is in debate, the right of determination shall rest with him according to the Minutes."

CHAPTER XI

Organization of the Methodist Episcopal Church General Conferences to 1824

Sacramental services it seems were held among the early Methodists of England and in their own Chapels. The Sacrament of the Lord's Supper formed part of every morning service at the Bristol Chapel. As the converts in the Revival increased, we are told the number of communicants multiplied. "In 1771," writes Wesley in his Journal, "we had 650 Communicants at Bristol." In other places in his Journal he mentions the length of these Communion services. They continued the morning service until late afternoon.

On the other hand, for nearly a score of years the Methodist Societies in America were not only without an ordained ministry, without the Sacraments in their own places of worship, but without the Sacraments at all except as they were fortunate enough to receive them from the clergy of and in an established church—usually the Church of England.

The Revolution forced the majority of these clergy to return home to England, leaving the Methodists practically without the Sacraments. This condition led Asbury to request of Wesley some mode of church organization for the Methodist Societies (now numbering 60, with a membership of 18,000 and with 104 itinerant preachers, Minutes, 1785), whereby they could have the Sacraments in a legitimate way. Wesley tells us that he opposed a proposition that the English bishops "ordain a part of our preachers for America" and that he "desired the bishop of London to ordain one only but could not prevail."

In February, 1784, Wesley conferred with Thomas Coke at City Road Chapel, London, and told him of Asbury's request, stating that he had decided to provide a mode of church organization according to a plan modeled after that of the ancient church of Alexandria, where the presbyters, on the death of a bishop, exercised the right of ordaining another from their own number.

Wesley then asked Coke to accept ordination at his hands as a presbyter, after the custom of the early apostolical church. After considering the matter for about two months, Coke said he was ready to co-operate in any way possible.

Thereupon "Wesley took a momentous step," we quote Dr. Platt, "when he took upon himself to ordain Methodist preachers, so that the Methodist people in America, and later in Scotland and England, might receive the Sacrament of the Lord's Supper at the hands of their own preachers, by whose ministry they had been brought into the joy and assurance of personal salvation.

"It was in a house, No. 6 Dighton Street, a little up the hill from Charles Wesley's house in Charles Street, that this historic event took place at five o'clock one September morning.

"This act and deed of John Wesley in the house of his physician and friend in Bristol, Dr. Castelman, was also the decisive and irrecoverable action that slowly but inevitably led to the ultimate separation of the people called Methodists."

On September 2, 1784, John Wesley, assisted by Dr. Coke and Rev. James Creighton (an ordained presbyter of the Church of England) ordained Thomas Vasey and Richard Whatcoat deacons, and a day later, elders.

Coke was consecrated superintendent of the Methodist Societies in America.

The certificate of ordination reads as follows: "To all to whom these presents shall come, I, John Wesley, late fellow of Lincoln College in Oxford, presbyter of the Church of England, sendeth greeting. Whereas many of the people in the Southern Provinces of North America, who desire to continue under my care, and still adhere to the dictrine and discipline of the Church of England, and greatly distressed for the lack of ministers to administer the sacraments of baptism and the Lord's Supper, according to the usage of said church, and whereas, there does not appear to be any other way of supplying them with ministers; Know all men, that I, John Wesley, think myself to be providentially called at this time to set apart some persons for the work of the ministry in America. And, therefore, under the protection of Almighty God, and with a single eye to his glory, I have this day set apart as Superintendent, by the imposition of my hands and prayer (being assisted by other ordained ministers), Thomas Coke, doctor of civil law, a presbyter of the Church of England, and a man whom I judge to be well acquainted for that work. And I do hereby recommend him to all whom it may concern, as a fit person to preside over the flock of Christ. In testimony whereof, I have here unto set my hand and seal, this the second day of September in the year of our Lord, one thousand seven hundred and eighty-four. John Wesley."

Coke, Whatcoat, and Vasey then set sail for America, bearing two letters from Wesley, one setting forth that the urgent condition in America had led him to set apart Coke as superintendent; the other addressed to "Dr. Coke and Mr. Asbury, and our Brethren in North America."

November 3, 1784, Coke, with his companions, landed in New York. The same evening he preached his first sermon in this country in Wesley Chapel. He preached again the next morning, and in the afternoon started for Philadelphia, where he was entertained by Jacob Baker, merchant on Market Street and a trustee of St. George's.

On Sunday, November 7, Coke preached in St. George's. On Sunday, the 14, Coke, Whatcoat, and Vasey met Francis Asbury at Barratt's Chapel, Frederica, Delaware.

"Sunday, November 14," writes Asbury, "I came to Barratt's Chapel; here, to my great joy, I met these dear men of God, Dr. Coke and Richard Whatcoat; we were greatly comforted together. . . . . Having had no opportunity of conversing with them before public worship, I was greatly surprised to see Brother Whatcoat assist by taking the cup in administration of the sacrament. I was shocked when first informed of the intention of these my brethren in coming to this country; it may be of God. My answer then was, if the preachers unanimously choose me, I shall not act in the capacity I have hitherto done by Mr. Wesley's appointment. The design of organizing the Methodists into an Independent Methodist Episcopal Church was opened to the preachers present, and it was agreed to call a general conference to meet at Baltimore the ensuing Christmas; as also that Brother Garrettson go off to Virginia to give notice to our brethren in the South.

"Friday, December 24, "we rode to Baltimore, where we met a few preachers. It was agreed to form ourselves into an Episcopal Church and to have superintendents, elders and deacons."

On December 27 the Conference, now known as the Christmas Conference, at which Dr. Coke and Francis Asbury presided, was begun at Lovely Lane Chapel. Sixty out of eighty-three (Minutes, 1784) preachers were present. Coke, who opened the Conference, read the following letter:

Bristol, September 10, 1784.

"To Dr. Coke, Mr. Asbury, and our brethren in North America:

1. "By a very uncommon train of providences, many of the provinces of North America are totally disjoined from the British empire, and erected into independent states. The English government has no authority over them, either civil or ecclesiastical, any more than over the states of Holland. A civil authority is exercised over them, partly by Congress, partly by the state assemblies. But no one either exircises or claims any ecclesiastical authority at all. In this peculiar situation some thousands of the inhabitants of these states desire my advice; and in compliance with their desire I have drawn up a little sketch.

2. "Lord King's account of the primitive church convinced me, many years ago, that bishops and presbyters are the same order, and consequently have the same right to ordain. For many years I have been importuned, from time to time, to exercise this right, by ordaining part of our traveling preachers; but I have still refused, not only for peace sake, but because I was determined as little as possible to violate the established order of the national church to which I belonged.

3. "But the case is widely different between England and North America. Here are bishops who have a legal jurisdiction. In America there are none, and but a few parish ministers; so that for some hundred miles together there is none either to baptize or administer the Lord's Supper. Here,

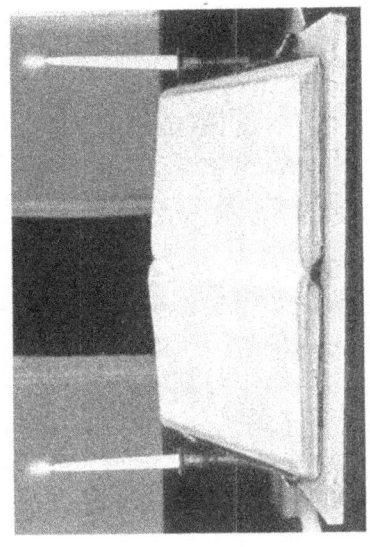

Asbury's Bible, at Old St. George's

Francis Asbury, first American Bishop

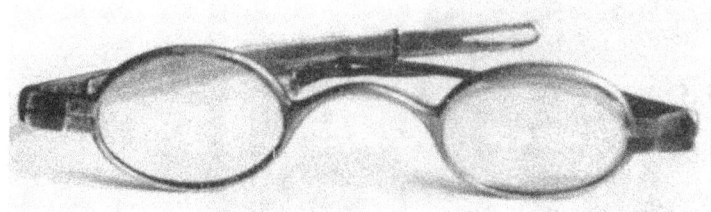

Spectacles of Bishop Francis Asbury Elected December, 1784

Spectacles of Bishop William McKendree Elected in 1808.

Possession of Old St. George's.

therefore, my scruples are at an end; and I conceive myself at full liberty, as I violate no order, and invade no man's right, by appointing and sending laborers into the harvest.

4. "I have, according, appointed Dr. Coke and Mr. Francis Asbury to be joint *superintendents* over our brethren in North America; as also Richard Whatcoat and Thomas Vasey to act as elders among them, by baptizing and administering the Lord's Supper.

5. "If any one will point out a more rational and scriptural way of feeding and guiding those poor sheep in the wilderness, I will gladly embrace it. At present I cannot see any better method than that I have taken.

6. "It has indeed been proposed to desire the English bishops to ordain part of our preachers for America. But to this I object (1), I desired the bishop of London to ordain one only, but could not prevail. (2) If they consented, we know the slowness of their proceedings, but the matter admits of no delay. (3) If they would ordain them *now*, they would likewise expect to govern them. And how grievously would this entangle us! (4) As our American brethren are now totally disentangled both from the state and from the English hierarchy, we dare not entangle them again, either with the one or the other. They are now at full liberty to follow the Scriptures and the primitive church. And we judge it best that they should stand fast in that liberty wherewith God has so strangely made them free.   John Wesley."

Acting on Wesley's suggestion it was unanimously agreed that circumstances made it expedient for the Methodist Societies in America to become a separate body from the Church of England, of which until then they had been considered members.

It was also decided, without disent, to be known as the Methodist Episcopal Church—a title proposed by John Dickins.

Knowing the sentiments and the determination of Asbury not to accept the appointment by Wesley as superintendent unless unanimously chosen by the preachers themselves, doubtless influenced the Conference to make the Episcopal office elective and the bishops or superintendents "amenable to the body of ministers and preachers."

"When," says Asbury, "the Conference was seated, Dr. Coke and myself were unanimously elected to the superintendency of the church and my ordination followed (December 27) after being previously (December 25) ordained deacon and (December 26) elder." Rev. Philip Otterbein, a German minister, assisted in the consecration of Asbury as Superintendent.

Wesley offered a liturgy he had prepared and advised that it be used by the itinerants in Sunday services, read the liturgy Wednesday and Friday, and pray extemporaneously on other days.

Whatcoat says that Wesley's "liturgy was accepted, and the sacraments were to be administered and persons were to be ordained, after election by Conference, the form of ordination to that prescribed by Wesley in his prayerbook."

The Conference adopted rules of Discipline as arranged by Coke and Asbury and added to the 24 Articles of Religion one on the Rulers of the United States of America.

Twelve elders were elected and ordained, two of whom were to serve in Nova-Scotia (Freeborn Garrettson and James O. Cromwell), and one (Jeremiah Lambert) in the West Indies.

Three deacons (John Dickins, Caleb Boyer, and Ignatius Pigman) were elected and ordained.

Various rules or regulations were adopted after "debating" and "determining all things," as Asbury says, "by a majority of votes." Such questions as the following were taken up and answered: How often to permit strangers to be present at the meeting of the Society; at Love Feasts; how to prevent improper persons getting in, and when to admit new members. Rules were adopted concerning dues, marriage, "spiritous liquors," and the conduct, expulsion, death of a Superintendent. Twelve rules were formed for the government of all the preachers.

The annual salary of the elders, deacons, and helpers were fixed at "$64 and no more"; for each preacher's wife, $64; for each preacher's child under six years, $16, from six to eleven, $21.33.

Rules concerning slaves, directions concerning the Lord's

Supper, baptism and marriage, visiting and dealing with the negligent, were laid down.

At this Conference a plan was adopted for raising money to support or help preachers and their families. The money was to be collected from the traveling preachers ($2.67 on admission to the Conference and $2.00 annually) and applied to the support of the preachers. It was called "The Preachers' Fund." Out of this Fund "every worn out preacher shall receive, if he wants it, $64.00 a year," a widow, "if she wants it, $53.33," but none shall be entitled to anything from this fund until he has paid $6.67," etc.

Asbury says of this Conference—"We were in great haste, and did much business in a little time." It is said, also, that the Conference was composed of the youngest group of men that ever framed a constitution or organized a Church or State. Asbury himself was only 39.

From 1784 to 1792 the business of the Church was done in what were called and were, strictly speaking, "district conferences."

"It was very inconvenient," says Bangs (His. Methodist Episcopal Church, page 302), "for all the members of the conference to assemble together in one place to transact their business. Hence the bishops had appointed several separate conferences for the despatch of their ordinary affairs.

"But anything which was done in these separate conferences was not binding, except simply the ordinations and stationing the preachers, unless sanctioned by them all. And as this could rarely be expected, constituted as human nature is, it was plainly seen that there was danger of their falling to pieces, or having divers administrations."

However, the point we are to bear in mind here is; that all questions of general interest were passed upon by all the conferences and nothing of that character would be binding unless sanctioned by all.

The Christmas Conference of 1784, at which the Church was organized, was a General Conference in the sense only that all preachers who could be secured were present.

Jesse Lee says that it was later thought that "general conferences" would be impracticable "on this extensive continent," that they "would be attended with a variety of difficulties and many inconveniences to the work of God." It was therefore judged, by *the conferences* of 1789, expedient to form a Council of chosen men out of the several districts as representatives of the whole connexion, who would meet at stated times with authority to "mature everything they should judge expedient; 1. To preserve the general union; 2. render and preserve the external form of worship; 3. preserve the essentials of Methodist doctrine and discipline; 4. correct abuses and disorders and to mature everything they thought necessary for the good of the Church for promoting and improving our colleges and places of education." Unanimous assent of the Council alone was to be binding. Bishops and Presiding Elders were to be members providing the members should never be fewer than nine. Bishops had the power to call the Council.

But the plan was very quickly seen to be dangerous. It placed too much power in the hands of the Bishops who, together with the Presiding Elders, who were their appointees and could be changed by them at will, composed the Council. Again, nothing unanimously assented to by the Council would be binding in any district until agreed upon by a majority of the conference held for that district. "If then," as Lee says, "one district should agree to any important point and another district should reject it; the union between the two districts would be broken and in the process of time our United Societies would be thrown into disorder and confusion. The plan produced such difficulties and brought such opposition that could not be reconciled that nothing would or could give satisfaction to the preachers but the calling together of all the travelling preachers in a general conference to which after some time the bishop (Asbury) consented."

Therefore, after but two meetings of the Council were held —one in December, 1789, and the other in the later part of 1790, the first General Conference, after that of 1784, met in November, 1792, at Baltimore.

1792

No copy of the Journal of the first General Conference

has ever been found. At the General Conference of the Methodist Episcopal Church in 1892 Dr. (later Bishop) Thomas B. Neely compiled a fairly complete account of the proceedings of the Conference of 1792. It may be said, however, after comparison with Lee's "History of the Methodists in the United States of America," that much of Neely's information may have been gained from that source.

The General Conference of 1792 was composed of all the travelling preachers who were in full connection at the time.

On the second day of the Conference James O'Kelly of Virginia offered the following amendment to the law that made it the duty of the Bishop to fix the appointments of the preachers: "After the Bishop appoints the preachers at Conference to their several circuits, if any one think himself injured by the appointment, he shall have the liberty of appeal to the Conference and state his objections; and if the Conference approve his objections, the Bishop shall appoint him to another circuit."

After considerable debate John Dickins moved that the matter under discussion be divided into two questions, "First— Shall the Bishop appoint the preachers to the circuits? Second —Shall a preacher be allowed an appeal?" The first question was answered unanimously in the affirmative, the second in the negative by a large majority.

As O'Kelly's amendment related more to Asbury's administration than to Coke's, who, as Neely points out, was frequently absent from the country, Asbury not only refused to preside at but absented himself from the session while the matter was under discussion. He sent, however, the following letter:

"My Dear Brethren,—Let my absence give you no pain— Dr. Coke presides. I am happily excused from assisting to make laws by which myself am to be governed; I have only to obey and execute. I am happy in the consideration that I never stationed a preacher through enmity or as a punishment. I have acted for the glory of God, the good of the people and to promote the usefulness of the preachers. Are you sure that if you please yourselves the people will be fully satisfied? They often say, 'Let us have such a preacher'; and sometimes, 'We will not have such a preacher—we will sooner pay him to stay at home.' Perhaps I must say, 'His appeal forced him upon you.' I am one—you are many. I am as willing to serve you as ever. I want not to sit in any man's way. I scorn to solicit votes; I am a very trembling, poor creature to hear praise or dispraise. Speak your minds freely; but remember you are only making laws for the present time; it may be that as in some other things, so in this, a future day may give you further light. I am yours, etc.

Francis Asbury."

By 1792 the plan of the Council, adopted in 1789, had met with great apposition on the part of both preachers and people. Soon after the General Conference of 1792 opened Lee says, "The Bishop and preachers in general showed a disposition to drop the Council and all things belonging thereto." Asbury finally requested that the name of the Council might not be mentioned in the conference again.

In 1791 the preachers were instructed to "appoint prayer-meetings wherever they could in Large Societies." In 1792 it was ordered that "The Preacher, who has charge of a Circuit, shall appoint prayer-meetings wherever he can on his Circuit." Fasts, also, were ordered to be held "in every Society on the Circuit, on the Friday preceding every Quarterly Meeting; and that a memorandum of it be written on all the Class Papers."

A Superannuate was defined as one "so worn out in the interant service as to be rendered incapable of preaching constantly but at the same time is willing to do any work in the ministry which the conference may direct and his strength will enable him to perform."

Rules were made allowing preachers to receive money if offered to them (but not to charge) for performing the marriage ceremony.

A rule was adopted intended to keep all preachers as nearly as possible on an equal footing in money matters.

The General Conference of 1792 made it necessary that a Bishop be elected by the General Conference rather than by a majority of the members of the conferences as heretofore. The consecration of a Bishop was to be, hereafter, not by the laying on of hands by one Bishop but by three, or one Bishop and two Elders, or, when no Bishop is present, by three Elders.

The preachers and stations had heretofore been in charge of "assistants" and they in turn were under a "General Assistant"—terms borrowed from the Wesleyan custom and referring to their relation to Wesley. In 1792 the office of Presiding Elder was defined and the titles later appears for the preacher in charge of a District. The "District Conference" was decided upon for the title of the annual conferences which were held in different sections of the country. The General Conference determined the boundaries, the membership and the business of the District Conference.

It was determined that the district should be formed according to the judgment of the Bishop yet not as to include more than twelve nor less than three circuits on a district.

This General Conference legislated concerning the admission of Preachers into the Conference, the salaries of preachers, the instruction of children, the trial of preachers, members, non-members, marriage, stewards, dress, ritual, worship, etc.

At the suggestion of the Book Committee, of which Thomas Haskins, Treasurer of St. George's was chairman, an allowance annually of $200 was allowed Dickins "for a dwelling-house and for a book-room," $80 for a boy, 53 dollars 1-3, for fire wood; and, 333 dollars to clothe and feed himself, his wife, and his children. In all, 666 dollars 1-3." (See chapter on "The Book Concern.")

At this General Conference the Quadrennial Conference was created and named the General Conference.

1796

The General Conference of 1796 met in Baltimore, Thursday, October 20. One hundred and twenty preachers out of two hundred and twenty-nine entitled to membership, were present.

At this Conference the feeling was strong that the number of bishops be increased. Most of the labor and responsibility rested upon Asbury, Coke having given little time to the work of oversight and having frequently absented himself from the conferences. Besides he was not a citizen. At his request, however, the matter of electing another Bishop was "laid on the table" for a half day. Later he "offered himself to the American Connexion, if the brethren saw fit to take him as a permanent Bishop." Owing to conditions, however, that prevailed in the British Conference, and the pressure brought to bear on him to return to England, Coke was unable to abide by his offer.

Up to 1796 the bishops had the right of appointing as many conferences as they judged fit. As a result, as many as fourteen conferences were held in one year and some of them not far apart, "to the general dislike of the preachers."

To quote the General Conference Journal, October 20, 1796:

"For several years the annual conferences were very small, consisting only of the preachers of a single district, or of two or three small ones. This was attended with many inconveniences. 1, There were but a few of the senior preachers, whose years and experiences had matured their judgment, who could be present at any one conference; 2, The conference wanted the dignity which every religious synod should possess and which always accompanies a large assembly of gospel ministers; 3, The itinerant plan was exceedingly cramped from the difficulty of removing preachers from one district to another. All of these inconveniences, it was thought, would be removed on the plan adopted, and at the same time the conferences were so arranged that all the members respectively may attend with little difficulty."

At the General Conference of 1796 in answer to Question 1. "Are there any directions to be given concerning the Yearly Conferences?

"Answer. There shall be six conferences in the year as follows, viz.: 1, The New England Conference; 2, The Philadelphia Conference; 3, The Baltimore Conference; 4, The Virginia Conference; 5, The South Carolina Conference; 6, The Western Conference." The foregoing were, therefore, the six original Conferences.

The boundaries of the six original Conferences were fixed as follows:

1. The New England Conference, under the direction of which shall be the affairs of our Church in New England, and

in that part of the State of New York which lies on the east side of the Hudson's River: Privided, that if the bishops see it necessary, a Conference may be held in the province of Maine.

2. The Philadelphia Conference, for the direction of our concerns in the remainder of the State of New York, in New Jersey, and in all that part of Pennsylvania which lies on the east side of the Susquehanna River, the State of Delaware and all the rest of the Peninsula.

3. The Baltimore Conference for the remainder of Pennsylvania, the remainder of Maryland and the Northern Neck of Virginia.

4. The Virginia Conference for all that part of Virginia which lies on the south side of the Rappahannock River, and for all that part of North Carolina which lies on the north side of the Cape Fear River, including also the circuits which are situated on the branches of the Yadkin.

5. The South Carolina Conference for South Carolina, Georgia, and the remainder of North Carolina.

6. The Western Conference for the States of Kentucky and Tennessee: Provided, that the bishops shall have authority to appoint other Yearly Conferences in the interval of the General Conference, if a sufficiency of new circuits be anywhere formed for that purpose.

In the course of time other Conferences were formed, some of them having their nucleus in one or more existing Conferences. For instance, out of the territory originally included in the Philadelphia Conference were organized New Jersey, Newark, Central Pennsylvania, Wilmington, and portions of the Wyoming and Genessee Conferences.

Strictly speaking then, neither the Philadelphia nor any other definitely styled Conference, as such, existed prior to 1796.

The mere fact that a Conference was held in a certain place does not warrant using the name of that place as the title of the Conference, otherwise the Conference would have one title one year, another the next. The same Conference—or group—met at different times in different places. The identical Conference that met, for instance, in Baltimore in 1777 met at at Deer Creek in 1778; and the same group that met in Philadelphia in 1788 met part in Chestertown, Maryland, and part in Philadelphia in 1789. Today the Conference is a corporate body, and its name is fixed and unaffected by changes in the place of its sessions.

At the General Conference of 1796 the attendance at the yearly conferences was limited to "Those who are in full connexion, and who are to be received into full connexion."

Plans of "deeds of settlement" for preaching houses were drawn up and authorized.

"The propagation of religious knowledge was declared next in importance to the gospel" and the printing of the Methodist Magazine was ordered.

The plans of the "Chartered Fund," drafted by Thomas Haskins, treasurer of St. George's Church, Philadelphia, and signed by him and the other trustees of the said church, were presented and adopted. Later this "Fund" was incorporated and sponsored by St. George's. (See chapter on "Chartered Fund.")

General Rules for Seminaries of Learning were adopted.

Rules regarding slavery were adopted and in addition yearly conferences were authorized to make whatever regulations they judged proper respecting the admission of persons to official positions.

Members who marry unawakened persons who haven't "the form and do not seek the power of godliness" were ordered expelled or put back on trial.

Salaries of preachers' wives were fixed at $64 annually—the same for traveling preachers.

1800

The General Conference of 1800 met in Baltimore on Tuesday, May 6. It was to have met on the 20th of October, but due to the fact that yellow fever prevailed for several seasons in Baltimore in that month, it was decided by the annual conferences of 1799 to meet in May. This action was approved by the General Conference.

A motion was made, but defeated, at this Conference to make the General Conference a delegated body.

The difficulties under which Asbury had to labor and the

conditions in the British Conference that made it impossible for Coke to fulfil his engagement to his American brethren are revealed in the correspondence between the Leed's Conference and Asbury.

In 1797 the Conference at Leeds addressed a letter "to Mr. Francis Asbury and all the Conferences of the people called Methodists in America." This letter and its reply are interesting and illuminating. The letter expressed the difficulties confronting British Methodism and the desire that Dr. Coke might be permitted to "return to Europe to assist in healing the breach which designing men had been making amongst them." Some, it seems had arisen "who under the pretense of liberty and from the desire of being heads of a party" endeavored to overturn the itinerancy and discipline and to destroy them root and branch. Dr. Coke, declared the British Conference, had often been a peacemaker among them, and they had "frequently experienced salutary effects of his advice and exertions in behalf of that part of the Connexion. It is on this ground that we must request the return of our friend and brother, Dr. Coke..... He has informed us of the engagements he has made to you. But you must share him to us for a time, at least, while these convulsions continue in our Societies; and the sooner you permit him to return the greater will be the favour."

Replying to this letter November 29, 1797, Asbury and the Virginia Conference wrote that there was "but one grand responsive body which is our General Conference and (that) it was in and to this body the Doctor entered his obligations to serve his brethren in America and no Yearly Conference, no official character dare assume to answer for that Grand Federal Body. By the advice of the Yearly Conference now sitting in Virginia I write to inform you that in our own persons and order we consent to his return and partial continuance with you and earnestly pray that you may have peace, union and happiness together."

Again Asbury continues, "With respect to the Doctor's returning to us, I leave your enlarged understanding and good sense to judge. You will see the number of souls upon our American Minutes; and as men of reading you may judge over what vast continent these Societies are scattered. By a probable guess we have perhaps from one to two thousand Travelling and Local Preachers. Local Preachers are daily arising and coming forward to receive ordination; and the regulations and ordinations of the six Yearly Conferences form a mighty concern. From the Conference held in Charleston, South Carolina, to the Conference in the province of Maine, there is a space of 1,300 miles, and only one worn out Superintendent, who was this day advised by the Yearly Conference wholly to desist from preaching till next spring, on account of his debilitated state of body; and the situation of our affairs requires that he should travel about 5,000 miles a year through many parts unsettled, and other thinly settled countries. I have now with me an Assistant, who does everything for me he constitutionally can, but the ordaining and stationing of the Preachers can only be performed by myself in the Doctor's absence.

"We have to lament that our Superintendency is so weak that it cannot constitutionally be strengthened till the ensuing General Conference. How I have felt and must feel under such critical and important circumstances, I leave to you to judge."

After the opening of the Conference of 1800 Coke read an address from the British Conference which expressed the desire for his return to England. Coke explained that the address was not his own and that he had not been consulted concerning it. The Conference granted the request with the understanding that Coke return to America by the next General Conference.

The Bishops obtained leave under certain conditions to ordain local deacons of colored people. The first to be so ordained was Richard Allen.

The salaries of the traveling preacher was fixed at $80. The children were to receive, until the age of seven, $16 annually and from seven to fourteen, $24.

Preachers were directed to advise the brethren of each circuit to purchase ground, erect thereon a parsonage and furnish it with at least heavy furniture. Where circuits could not buy or build, parsonages were to be rented.

For some years after the organization of the Church, the

Bishop was more than a mere presiding officer. He both voted and made motions. Exercising his privilege Asbury at this time "moved" that the annual conferences be directed to keep a record of their proceedings and to send a copy to the General Conference.

Richard Whatcoat was at this time elected Bishop. The vote cast was 59 for Whatcoat, 55 for Jesse Lee.

The boundaries of the New York Conference were defined as to include all the state of Connecticut and all that part of the states of Massachusetts, Vermont, and New Hampshire which is now included in the districts of New York and New London, together with all that part of the state of New York east of the Hudson River.

1804

The General Conference of 1804 met in Baltimore, May 7. One hundred and seven preachers, representing seven annual conferences, were present. Coke, Asbury, and Whatcoat presided. Of the one hundred and seven preachers Philadelphia and Baltimore were represented by sixty-seven. All preachers who had traveled four years from the time they were received on trial were entitled to a seat. No change, however, in the constitution of the Conference to a delegated body was made.

Bishops were required at this Conference to allow each annual conference to remain in session at least a week.

On motion of Bishop Coke, it was ordered that the *Discipline* be devided into two parts—one containing all that related to temporal and the other, all that related to spiritual interests.

Ezekiel Cooper, Alexander McCaine, and Thomas Lyell were appointed to draft a letter to the Irish and English Conferences in reply to theirs.

A committee of seven was appointed to report on the subject of Slavery. The report was adopted and Section nine was incorporated in the *Discipline* of that year. The members of the church in North Carolina, South Carolina, and Georgia were exempted from the rule of the section.

The general book steward and his assistant were authorized to preserve, alter, or change the phraseology and measure of our pocket hymnbook as they judged best.

The Book Business, by a vote of 36 to 26, was ordered moved from Philadelphia. Conference then voted—38 to move to New York, 36 to move to Baltimore. Ezekiel Cooper was continued as its head with the title of General Book Steward. The duty of appointing the Book Committee was transferred to the New York Conference.

The time of a preacher's probation was henceforth to be reckoned from the time of his reception by the conference.

1808

The General Conference of 1808 met in Baltimore, Friday, May 8. One hundred and twenty-nine preachers representing seven Conferences were present. Bishop Asbury presided. Coke was absent in Europe. Whatcoat had died in Dover, Delaware, on July 5, 1806.

Of the total of one hundred and twenty-nine preachers present, eighty-two were from Baltimore, New York, and Philadelphia. The need of a delegated General Conference was apparent.

On the fourth day a Memorial was presented by the New York Conference, concurred in by the Eastern (New England) Western, and South Carolina Conferences, setting forth the necessity of a delegated body. On the 18th of May the proposition was defeated by a majority of seven votes. On the 23rd the matter was reconsidered and a motion by Enoch George was passed by a large majority that "The General Conference shall be composed of one member for every five of each annual conference" and that "it shall meet on the first day of May, in the year of our Lord 1812 in the city of New York and thence forward on the first day of May, once in four years perpetually."

Having gone back to England after the General Conference of 1804, Coke addressed two letters to the Conference of 1808 —one dated November 26, 1807, and the other January 29, 1808. These letters, together with a printed address from the British Conference, were read by Ezekiel Cooper. The letters expressed the earnest desire of the British preachers that Coke be permitted to reside in England. The letters were referred to a committee who reported the following resolution: "Resolved, that Dr. Coke's name be retained on our Minutes, after the name of our bishops. N. B.—'Dr. Coke, at the request of the British Conference, and by the consent of the General Conference resides in Europe; he is not to exercise the office of superintendent or bishop among us in the United States until he is recalled by the General Conference, or by all the annual Conferences respectively.' "

On Thursday, May 12, William McKendree was elected Bishop, receiving ninety-two of one hundred and twenty-eight votes.

A Committee on the Review of the manuscript, "History of the Methodists in the United States of America"—thought to have been Lee's—deemed "it rather a simple and crude narrative of the proceedings of the Methodists than a history and thought it would be improper to publish it." Later Lee's History was printed at the author's own risk after he had secured several hundred subscribers, in various states.

At this General Conference Ezekiel Cooper resigned as Book Agent. Cooper reported that when he engaged in the Concern in 1799 the whole amount of clear capital stock was not worth more than $4,000 and that he had "not a single dollar in hand belonging to the connexion to carry on the work, or to procure materials or to pay a single demand against the Concern, which at that time was near three thousand dollars in debt."

At the time of the General Conference in 1804, the Concern could show a capital of about $27,000. At this General Conference (1808) the capital amounted to $45,000.

Cooper was voted an extra compensation for his services of $1,000. John Wilson was employed as editor and general book steward at $750 a year. Daniel Hitt was elected assistant.

It was moved "from the chair" that one thousand forms of *Discipline* be prepared for the use of the South Carolina Conference, in which the section and rule on salvery be left out." It is thought that this special edition of the *Discipline* was never printed.

On motion of Jesse Lee the following resolution was passed: "The next General Conference shall not change or alter any part or rule of our government so as to do away episcopacy or to destroy the plan of our itinerant general superintendency; that the General Conference shall have full powers to make rules and regulations for our church under certain (5) restrictions."

1812

In 1812 the first delegated General Conference met in New York, May 1. Ninety delegates, representing eight conferences, were present.

The question of admitting reserve delegates in place of the principals was settled in the affirmative.

A resolution to appoint a secretary who was not a member of the body was passed.

At this General Conference McKendree, who had been elected Bishop in 1808, introduced the custom of reading an address in which the separate matters treated were referred to appropriate committees to consider and report on.

Asbury, as it has been well said, was a "personal ruler" as Wesley had been. He arranged the work and appointed the preachers without consulting any one. McKendree, however, desired to take the Conference or his brethren into his counsels. However, after McKendree had finished reading Asbury arose and addressing him, in substance, said, "You have done today what I never did and I want to know why." McKendree answered, "You are my father and do not need these rules. I am a son and do." (Authorities quote both Asbury and McKendree differently.)

Neely points out that the Church had always retained Wesley's original admonition concerning things to be avoided; Drunkenness, buying and selling spirituous liquors, or drinking them, unless in cases of extreme necessity but the clause "buying and selling spirituous liquors" had in some way dropped out and buying and selling such liquors, if not drinking them, had become "all too common" and even distillers were not absent from among church members.

At the Conference of 1812 James Axley introduced a resolution "That no stationed preacher shall retail spiritual liquors without forfeiting his ministerial character among us." After being postponed for several days the motion to adopt was lost.

In 1816 Axley again presented his resolution and after it had been divided into two parts—"No preacher shall distill" and "No preacher shall retail spirituous liquors without forfeiting his license" it was adopted.

A resolution was adopted at the request of Benjamin Tanner, a Philadelphia artist, son of Bishop Tanner of the A. M. E. Church, requesting Asbury to "sit for his likeness" for an engraved portrait and the Book Agents were directed to "negotiate for a supply of the portraits for the Conference."

The Western Conference was divided at this time into the Ohio and the Tennessee Conferences and the ordination of local deacons to the office of elder was authorized.

In his address to the Conference of 1812 Asbury speaks of his desire to visit Europe. The matter was referred to a committee who reported it "their sincere request and desire that Bishop Asbury relinquish his thoughts of visiting Europe and that he confine his labors to the American continent."

1816

The General Conference of 1816 met at Baltimore, Wednesday, May 1. On May 2, 1814, Coke died while on the Indian Ocean and on March 31, 1816, Asbury had passed away at Fredericksburg, Va., leaving but one bishop of the Church, McKendree.

An address prepared by Asbury was read by McKendree and that of McKendree was read by Thomas L. Douglass of Tennessee.

Enoch George and Robert R. Roberts were elected Bishops.

Eleven Conferences were designated and their boundaries defined.

The chapter in the *Discipline* on slavery was made to read "No slaveholder shall be eligible to any official station in our Church, hereafter, when the laws of the state in which he lives will admit of emancipation and permit the liberated slave to enjoy freedom."

The ratio of representation was increased from five to seven.

The Bishops, or a committee appointed by them, were instructed to prescribe a course of study for condidates for the ministry.

Request from male members of the church in Baltimore to remove the remains of Asbury to that city, granted.

Thursday, May 9, Roszel announced that the remains of Asbury had arrived at the house of William Hawkins, "whereupon the conference resolved to adjourn until 3 o'clock P.M." the next day in order to attend the funeral in the forenoon.

1820

At the General Conference of 1820 a resolution was adopted to make the presiding eldership elective and the presiding elders of a conference an advisory council of the Bishop in stationing preachers. Joshua Soule, who had been previously elected a Bishop, strongly opposed the new rule considering it a curtailment of episcopal prerogative and power, and he therefore refused to be consecrated. Soule finally resigned and his resignation was accepted. The rule however was suspended until the next General Conference. By action of a majority of the annual conferences the rule was judged unconstitutional and the General Conference of 1824 declared it to be "without authority and not to be carried into effect."

1824

At the General Conference of 1824 Soule was again elected Bishop together with Elijah Hedding.

At this conference the Bishops were requested jointly to address a pastoral letter to the Church and the Book Agents were directed to print and distribute to the presiding elders eighty-five thousand copies.

CHAPTER XII

Bishop Asbury's Labors

Coke's Attempt to Unite the Methodist Episcopal Church and the Episcopal Church

"On becoming Bishop of the church," writes Stevens, "Asbury seemed to become ubiquitous throughout the republic. The history of Christianity since the apostolic age affords not a more perfect example of ministerial and episcopal devotion.

"His labors in the new world were, if possible, greater than those of Wesley in the old. It has been estimated that in the 45 years of his American ministry he preached 16,500 times, traveled 270,000 miles, held no less than 224 Conferences and ordained more than 400 preachers." "His diocese extended," writes Ezekiel Cooper, "from Canada and other British possessions to the North and East, into the Spanish possessions, the Floridas, and Mexico to the South and West, 1,500 or 2,000 miles in length; and from the Atlantic to the Mississippi and Louisiana, East and West, the best part of 1,000 miles in breath. Including all the United States and the extensive territories thereof. And he generally went through this whole district once every year. And contented himself with the small allowance of $80 a year and the amount of his travelling expenses.

"That Asbury was fond of power and too tenacious of maintaining his authority and supporting his power I have no difficulty in admitting, honestly and candidly that the objections, when considered on general principles, are too well founded. But is there not an apology sufficient to extenuate the supposed fault contained in the objections? Perhaps no other man could be equally justifiable in wishing, or claiming, or exercising the same degree of authority in the church. Bishop Asbury stood as father and as a patriarch in the Connexion. When and where was the man possessing so much influence and invested with so much authority that ever used it to better purposes, for the good of others and so little to selfish advantages; so little toward his own bodily ease, earthly honor and worldly profit?"

Even in his so-called retirement Asbury was not unemployed. Insinuations to the contrary, as in the case of Jesse Lee, he strongly resented. Writing in his Journal, Sunday, June 24, 1810, he says: "I have seen Jesse Lee's History for the first time; it is better than I expected. He has not always presented me under the most favorable aspective; we are all liable to mistakes and I am unmoved by his. I correct him in one fact. My compelled seclusion, in the beginning of the war, in the State of Delaware was in no wise a season of inactivity; on the contrary, except about two months retirement, from direst necessity, it was the most active, the most useful, and most afflictive part of my life. If I spent a few dumb Sabbaths—if I did not for a short time steal after dark, or through the gloom of the woods, as was my wont, from house to house to enforce that truth I (an only child) had left father and mother, and crossed the ocean to proclaim—I shall not be blamed, I hope when it is known that my patron, good and respectable Thomas White, who promised me security and secrecy was himself taken into custody by the light horse patrol; if such things happened to him, what might I expect, a fugitive and an Englishman? In these very years we added 1,800 members to Society and laid a broad and deep foundation for the wonderful success Methodism had met with in that quarter. The children and children's children of those who witnessed my labors and my sufferings in that day of peril and affliction now rise up by hundreds to bless me. Where are the witnesses themselves? Alas! there remain not five, perhaps, whom I could summon to attest the truth of this statement."

The following extract from a letter from Asbury written at "Hanging Rock, 20 miles Northwest of Camden (N. C.), October 17, 1807," to Rev. Thomas Haskins, Philadelphia, reveals not only the magnitude of Asbury's labors but his consciousness of his responsibilities and of the greatness and danger of his power:

"My dear Son, I hope you are more than ever devoted to God in preaching; and living; time is short. I am greatly

amended in health, than when I wrote last. I have only to say I sit on a joyless height, a pinnacle of power too high to sit secure and unenvied, too high to sit secure without divine aid. My bodily and mental powers fail, I have a charge too great for many men with minds like mine. I hope not to jump down, fall down, or be thrown down by haughty ambition, but I mean to step down as soon and safely and completely as I can; and not to stand alone, but break the fire by having more objects than one. I am happy, the ship is safe in harbor with an increase of 10,000 annually, but how many more if the dead, and removed and expelled were numbered. Understand me right, I mean to live for life, but not alone, the executive is far too weak. 4 years my local labors were little inferior to many traveling preachers. In the year 66 I began my present line of labour, between 40 and 50 times I have x the allegheny mountains, swamps, and rivers of the South going and returning. When a man is in his 62 year it is not safe to trust a great work in his trembling hands. A president of a State of the states ought to know when to retire for fear of damages, and if heaven would insure my life bodily and mental powers would heartily advise my brethren to provide immediately for such a charge! and not to rest it with me, or any one man upon earth. Only to think seven Conferences, 500 travelling, possible two or three thousand local and official men, possible near ten millions in ? or congregations charge, 100,000 in membership. Lord be merciful to me. Amen, pray for   Your father,
                                                            Francis Asbury."

The spirit and zeal of Asbury is revealed by himself in the following letter, also, the original of which is in the possession of Old St. George's, to the Methodist Episcopal Society in Norfolk, Virginia:

"February 8, 1815.

Dearly beloved in the Lord, grace and peace and health and life spiritual and temporal and eternal attend us in our Great Redeemer. You are happily united. You use all the means of grace. You love as brethren and sisters in Jesus. You are frequent and fervent in prayer, you visit the sick and comfort the mourners and sooth the sorrows of the afflicted and dying. Surely we will not fear the terror by night, the arrows that flyeth by day, nor the pestilence that walketh in darkness, nor the destruction that wasteth at noon-day.

Let a thousand fall at our sides and ten thousand at our right hand, the Almighty can preserve us, if we set our love and confidence on, and in Him.

Quick (?) John Early wrote you your friend, Francis, was coming to see you. Sampson like he at other times would go out, as his body cannot keep pace with his mind, a failure in his health, the providence of God, and things generally preventeth his visits once a year, it is not enough we have rode since the month of June 3,000 miles, I would have rode 1,200 from the South Carolina to the Virginia Conference, but the man, the horses fail, roads in bad order, of the affliction in head not heart, we are in immortal till our work is done. So after traveling 700 miles last month. So after coasting from Millidgville to Charleston, and New Bern and Tarborough, we are taking a straight course to Lynchburgh. You ask, watchman, what of the night! We believe the morning cometh and also the night! in the Church of God and this continent. But God's ministers are greatly humbled and united; so also the people of God. Your friend feeleth for you—he still moveth as he hath done from 15 to the 6 month of 70th year of his age—for 49 years he hath visited seaports in Europe and America; he delighteth to do it, still the popularity of these places, the communication, the privileges, the opportunity of preaching to such multitudes of the inhabitants of the sea, upon land. The brethren help those sisters that are doing good. The pious of all denominations in Europe are awake. Sending the printed word into all lands and languages, sending missionaries to Africa, Asia and isles of the seas—educating children in Sabbath schools, the bringing home Abraham's children, and if two parts of the earth should be cut off and die the third shall come through the fire, and yet a little while and Lebanon subject to high cultivation shall be counted for a forest, yet judgment shall dwell in the wilderness and righteousness remain in the fruitful field, the increase of about 30,000 in two years in the Methodist Society

in Europe still declareth God is with His church, His ministers and the latter day glory sweetly drawing near.
We must commend you to God and the word of His grace.
Yours in Jesus,
F. Asbury.

Roanoke, Brunswick County, Virginia.
We desire the stationed preacher or some person may read this epistle to the Society in Norfolk."

"Asbury's manner of life," according to Cooper, "was irreproachable. His prudence and caution as a man and a citizen; his pious and correct department as a Christian and a minister was such as to put at defiance the suspicious mind and the tongue of persecuting slander."

Although for a number of years after the title of Bishop was seldom given to the general superintendents and in addressing them "Brother" or "Mr." was used, the *Discipline* of 1787 refers to them as Bishops for the first time. Shortly after that, it appears, Asbury openly assumed the title. Wesley's reaction is revealed in the following letter he wrote to Asbury under date of September 20, 1788.

"There is indeed a wide difference between the relation wherein you stand to the Americans and the relation wherein I stand to all the Methodists: I am, under God, the father of the whole family. Therefore I naturally care for you all in a manner no other person can do. Therefore, I in a measure provide for you all; for the supplies which Dr. Coke provides for you he could not provide were it not for me, were it not that I not only permit him to collect, but also support him in so doing.

"But in one point, my dear brother, I am a little afraid both the doctor and you differ from me. I study to be little; you study to be great. I creep; you strut. I found a school—you a college. Nay and call it after your own names! O beware! Do not seek to be something! Let me be nothing and Christ be all in all. One instance of this greatness has given me great concern. How can you, how dare you suffer yourself to be called a bishop. I shudder, I start at the thought. Men may call me a knave, or a fool, a rascal or a scoundrel, and I am content but they shall never, by my consent call me *bishop!* For my sake, for God's sake, for Christ's sake put a full end to this. Let the Presbyterians do what they please, but let the Methodists know their calling better.

"Thus, my dear Franky, I have told you all that is in my heart. And let this, when I am no more seen, bear witness how sincerely I am   Your affectionate friend and brother."

In 1791 before going to Europe, Coke endeavored to accomplish the union of the Methodist Episcopal and the Episcopal Churches. He apparently felt such a union would "enlarge the field of action" of the Methodist bishops and conciliate many who were, like O'Kelley, unfriendly to or critical of the office.

To this end Coke held several Conferences with Bishop William White of Philadelphia and corresponded with Bishop Seabury of Connecticut, and Bishop Madison of Virginia.

At the Convention of the Episcopal Church held in New York, September, 1792, Bishop Madison submitted a proposal which has been described as "a composite, reduced from these conferences and correspondence between White and Seabury and Madison, together with those of Coke and other Methodist leaders of kindred mind; and that does not include Brother John (Wesley) or Mr. Asbury."

The following letter is both interesting and revealing.

To Rev. Simon Wilmer:

Near Philadelphia, July 30, 18-4.

Revd Sir:

I recd your Letter of ye 27th inst. under Circumstances which prevented my answering by ye Return of ye Post. With it there was delivered a Letter from ye revd *John McKlaskey, whom I find to be ye Person alluded to in yours. Having written to this Gentleman, my Transcribing of ye Information given him will be an Answer to you also.

"I beg it may be understood that I have never, from ye Sug-

---

* John McK(C)laskey was a Methodist itinerant, and at the time, Presiding Elder.

gestion of my own Mind, given Information of ye Matter concerning which you inquire, except to those whom Dr. Coke expected to be informed of it. Several years passed after ye Transaction, before I had Reason to suppose it known to any others. Within these few years, I have been spoken to on ye Subject two or three Times; when I found myself under a Necessity of Stating Facts in order to guard against Misrepresentation.

"In ye Spring of ye Year 1791, I recd a Letter from Dr. Coke on ye Subject of uniting ye Methodist Society with ye Episcopal Church. An Answer was returned. In consequence of which, Dr. Coke on his coming to Town, made me a Visit, having not then recd my Letter, but having heard that I had written. Our Conversation turned chiefly on ye aforesaid Subject. The general Outlines of Dr. Coke's Plan were a Reordination of ye Methodist Ministers & their continuing under ye Superintendence then existing & in the Practice of their peculiar Institutions. There was also suggested by him a Propriety, but not a Condition made, of admitting to the Episcopacy himself & ye Gentleman associated with him in ye Superintendence of ye Methodist Societies. This Intercourse was communicated at ye Time by Dr. Coke to Dr. Magaw. I do not know of any other Person then informed of it, unless I may except ye Gentleman above alluded to, by whom, if I have been rightly informed, my Letter to Dr. Coke was opened in his absence, such a Freedom being understood, as I supposed to arise out of ye Connection between ye two Gentlemen. But for this Part of ye Statement I cannot vouch. It was understood between Dr. Coke & me that ye Proposal should be communicated to ye Bishops of ye Episcopal Church at ye next Convention, which was to be in Sept. 1792, in New York. This was accordingly done, after which I perceived no Use of further Communication on ye Subject & I have not since seen Dr. Coke nor heard from him nor written to him.

"It appears to me that ye above comprehends either explicity or by Implication, all ye Points to which your Letter leads. It would have been more agreeable to me, if no Occasion of this Testimony had incurred & it is now given merely to prevent ye Matters being understood otherwise than it really is."

The above is what I have written to Mr. McKlaskey & I remain, your affte Brother,   Wm. White.

Does the above letter suggest, as it has been inferred, the answer to the question: "What blocked White's purpose in 1791 to welcome Coke's return to the Church in the new land? Was it Asbury's appropriation of that letter? Or was it the laymen's attitude at the New York Convention?"

Whatever Wesley's feelings may have been about the American Episcopal or the Anglican Church and their relation to American Methodism, he evidently did desire some union of a lasting character *between Methodists throughout the world.* The following letter, the last written by Wesley to America, addressed to Ezekiel Cooper, reveals not only his strong desire for such an indissoluble union but his deep affection for his American brethren.

"Near London, February 1, 1791.

"My dear Brother. Those who desire to write, or to say anything to me, have no time to lose; for time has shaken me by the hand and death is not far behind. But I have reason to be thankful for the time that is past. I felt few of the infirmities of age for four score and six years. It was not until a year and a half ago that my strength and sight failed. And still I am enabled to scrawl a little, and to creep, though I cannot run. Probably I should not be able to do so much did not many of you assist me by your prayers. I have given a distinct account of the work of God which has been wrought in Britain and Ireland for more than half a century. We want some of you to give us a connected relation of what our Lord has been doing in America from the time that Richard Boardman accepted the invitation and left his country to serve you. See that you never give place to one thought of separating from your brethren in Europe. Lose no opportunity of declaring to all men that the Methodists are one people in all the world, and that it is their full determination so to continue.

"Though mountains rise, and oceans roll, To sever us in vain.

"To the care of our common Lord I commit you, and am your affectionate friend and brother.   John Wesley."

N.B. Note omission of Pilmoor's name.

CHAPTER XIII

The Book Concern and the Chartered Fund

In 1769, as we have stated in another chapter, Robert Williams brought with him to America some of John Wesley's books, tracts, sermons, and the hymns and songs of Charles Wesley.

These, Williams immediately began to sell and reprint, with the result that at the Conference in 1773 his acts were passed upon and his activities limited. He was permitted to sell the books, etc., he had, but was to print no more without the authority of Wesley when it could be had or the consent of the brethren. This rule was made applicable to all preachers.

At the same time the principle was laid down, to be strictly adhered to, that profits from the sale of all printed matter were to accrue "to the general interest," i.e. of all the preachers. This was the principle followed by the Wesleyan preachers who considered themselves pre-eminently one body and "nothing was to be done by any individual prejudicial to the whole or any part."

What Williams started, in the course of time, other itinerants adopted and continued with increasing activity until eventually their labors were centralized, and their profits pooled and systematically distributed.

Prior to 1785 Methodist literature, excepting reprints for Williams and hymns printed by Dunlap for St. George's, was printed in England. The first edition of the *Discipline* printed that year (1785) at Dr. Coke's expense, in Philadelphia by Cist, was bound up with "the Sunday Service" and "the Collection of Psalms and Hymns" which had been sent over to America in sheets.

Lee in his "History of the Methodists" says that in the course of the year 1787, Asbury printed the General Minutes or "A form of *Discipline* for the ministers and members of the Methodist Episcopal Church in America," which was "considered and approved at a conference held at Baltimore, Monday, December 27, 1784." In the last section of this *Discipline* appears the following: "As it has been frequently recommended by the preachers and people that such books as are wanted be printed in this country, we therefore propose:

1. That the advice of the Conference shall be desired concerning any valuable impression, and their consent be obtained before any steps be taken for the printing thereof.

2. That the profit of the books, after all necessary expenses be defrayed shall be applied, according to the discretion of the Conference, toward the college (Cokesbury), the preachers' fund, the deficiencies of the preachers, the distant missions or the debts on our churches."

While the printing of Methodist literature, with the exception, as we have seen, of that for Williams and Coke, and perhaps for some others, was done in England, after the publication of Asbury's *Discipline* "we began," says Lee, "to print more of our own books in the United States than we had ever done before; the principal part of the printing business was carried on in New York." By this last clause Lee certainly does not mean to infer that a printing establishment had been set up, but simply that most of the printing done for the itinerants was done by secular concerns in New York.

On Wednesday, April 26, 1786, Asbury arrived in Baltimore. In his Journal he says he "was occupied until Saturday in collecting money for the books and inspecting the accounts of the Book Concern." What Asbury apparently meant was that he inspected the accounts of the various itinerants or the returns they had made of the book business they had done individually. At that time there was no established, centralized book concern with a single responsible head doing business in a designated locality. The expression "Book Concern" was either coined by Asbury or borrowed from the English Methodists, as "Book Steward," "Book Committee," and "Book Room" were later. As a matter of fact ours in the beginning was not "The Book Concern" but the "Printing and Book Business."

However, the demand for Methodist literature was growing, and strenuous efforts were doubtless made to meet it. Naturally the printing of this literature was gradually and in the course of time completely transferred to America. Then, finally, an establishment of our own with a responsible head was deemed imperative.

As we have related elsewhere, from 1784 to the first General Conference in 1792 the business of the Church was done in what were strictly speaking only district conferences, so grouped and located as to accommodate the largest possible number of preachers. The business of these conferences was mostly routine, and was recorded in the form of questions and answers. Business, however, of general interest, such as slavery, instruction of children, temperance, care of the colored folks, requirements for membership, formation of the Council, and at this time particularly, that of establishing a Printing Business, had to be passed upon and concurred in by every conference to become the law or the enterprise of the connection as a whole.

"Anything which was done in these separate conferences *was not binding, except simply the ordinations and stationing of the preachers, unless sanctioned by them all.*" (Bangs His. M. E. Ch. 302.)

In 1789 eleven district conferences, stretching from Georgia to New York, were held. There can be no doubt but what every phase of the contemplated establishment of the printing and book business (*the place to found, locate it and the man best fitted for the job, etc.*) was taken up, discussed and passed upon (sanctioned) in every one of the eleven conferences, so that all that was eventually done was the judgment, not of a single limited group, but of the whole connection.

On May 28, 1789, the last of the eleven district conferences was held in New York. Ten circuits were represented and nineteen preachers, out of a total of one hundred and ninety-six in the connection, received appointments. The matter of establishment of a printing business, which had been taken up and doubtless santcioned in all the other conferences, was taken up and sanctioned there.

The decision to establish the Book Business was then not the decision of a comparatively few itinerants made in a few days, but that of the whole connection over a period of time. To use the words of Lee, employed in reference to the no more important matter of the Council: "It was therefore judged, by the *conferences* of 1789, expedient to" establish a Printing and Book Business.

Just ten days before the district conference in New York a similar conference was held in Philadelphia. Asbury and Coke presided at both conferences. At the Philadelphia conference, doubtless, was Thomas Haskins, an itinerant for a time, trained in the law and a close friend of Asbury. It was with Haskins that Asbury consulted about and who drew up the Articles for the Chartered Fund in 1796. It was Haskins who, as a member of the first "Book Committee," drafted the report for that committee to the General Conference of 1792. At this time he was a trustee of St. George's, and very active in its affairs.

In view of the foregoing it seems very likely that both Haskins and other officials in Philadelphia were consulted about the plans being perfected to establish a Book Business there.

John Dickins was born in 1747 in London. He was educated in that city and at Eton. In 1774 he entered the itinerancy and traveled extensively in Virginia and North Carolina. In 1781 he is noted as desisting from traveling. From 1783 until 1789, excepting 1785, when he was appointed to Bartie, Virginia, he was stationed in New York. At the district conference of 1789, held May 28 in New York, Dickins was appointed to St. George's, Philadelphia, with the understanding that he was to establish the "Printing and Book Business" in that city. His position was designated as "Book Steward." Philip Cox, who served at Mecklenburg, N. C., in 1788 was appointed at Leesburg in 1789 "Travelling Book Steward."

While Dickins was in North Carolina in 1783, Asbury met him at C. I. Clayton's, near Halifax. "Saturday, April 5," writes Asbury in his Journal, "I prevailed with Bro. Dickins to go to New York, where I expect him to be far more useful than in his present station." August 25 Asbury writes, "I set out for New York and found Brother Dickins preaching."

Commenting on the above incident Simpson says, "One writer remarks it was for the purpose of supervising our book business" that Dickins was prevailed upon to go to New York. This was pure assumption and reveals an ignorance of the book situation at that time.

Immediately on his arrival in Philadelphia in 1789, Dickins

set about performing the task assigned him. In this he was greatly and ably assisted by Thomas Haskins.

In 1790 Dickins was given the title of Superintendent of the Printing and Book Business. In 1790 it was also provided that the profits "be applied as the bishop and council shall direct." The Council referred to was, as we have seen a body of men chosen from the several districts to represent the whole connection, and had but a brief existence.

In 1792 the question (question 5) was asked: "How much shall be annually allowed out of the book fund for Cokesbury College till the next General Conference?" Ans. "Eight hundred dollars for the ensuing year; and one thousand sixty-six dollars and two-thirds for each of the remaining three years."

"Question 7. What sum of money shall be allowed to distressed preachers out of the book fund till next General Conference?" "Ans. Two hundred and sixty-six dollars and one-third per annum."

In 1795 Cokesbury College was destroyed by fire and at the General Conference of 1796 all that related to funds for the institution was "struck out." Chapter III, section II from the "Notes to the Discipline" by Asbury and Coke, prepared at the request of the General Conference of 1796 closes with this clause: "And the consideration that all profits" from the printing of books, etc., "shall be lodged in our chartered fund for the benefit of the distressed preachers, both travelling and superannuated, will, we trust form a considerable additional inducement to our brethren to purchase our books."

There has been for years some question as to the source of Dickins's capital. It is certain that no provision was made either for the Concern or for him as Book Agent until 1792.

An old unsigned and undated paper in the handwriting of Thomas Haskins, active in the affairs of St. George's, and drafter and witnesser of the "Agreement" between Ezekiel Cooper and the Philadelphia Conference when Cooper became Agent, proves that it was with his own money that Dickins financed the Concern.

This paper, which evidently is the original draft of the report of the Book Committee to the General Conference of 1792, reads as follows:

"The undersigned, to whom was referred the examination of the accounts of Mr. John Dickins, relative to the business of the Book Fund, respectfully report:

"That in their opinion (after the investigation of the accounts) the principal on which the Books were originally opened and the mode in which they have been kept by Mr. Dickins is fair and correct, that they will not only stand the test of the strictest scrutiny, but strongly mark the knowledge, industry, integrity and disinterestedness of his head and heart in the management of the whole business, and your committee is of the opinion that too much praise cannot be given Mr. Dickins when it is known under what disadvantages he has labored from the commencement of the business up to the present.

"Few instances occur where an Agent or Factor has put at stake his own capital and risqued his all for the benefit of his employer and still fewer, where no compensation, or at least a very inadequate one, has been asked for the use and risque of that capital.

"Yet this is a true state of facts as it respects Mr. Dickins. He began the business for the connexion on his own capital and from an accurate examination of the cash account find he has for 7½ years been in advance on an average £111 .. 18s .. 0; that he has never forborne to make a charge of the whole of the legal interest justly due him, in short, our astonishment at his unexampled good conduct and management is not a little excited on a review of the whole of the business and are of opinion that the Conference will not fail to see Mr. Dickins merits all the confidence reposed in him by them and that nothing on their part will be wanting to render his situation less embarrassing, either by supplying a capital or forbearing to authorize any considerable draught from the Book Fund for 12 or 18 months to come, when in our opinion a sufficient active capital may be found for conducting the business to best advantage for the connection. We forbear to make any further remarks on the business, only that we think, in addition, to Mr. Dickins' present allowance, an additional sum of $200, might, with the greatest propriety, be added to his present allowance, with a sum to enable him to procure a room exclusively to de-

Ezekiel Cooper, successor to John Dickins who founded the "Book Concern" at Old St. George's where both Dickins and Cooper are buried

IN ENGLAND AND IN AMERICA

posit and keep the unbound impressions of the several books he has printed and other materials belonging to the business."

Evidently, as a result of the above, at the General Conference in 1792, Dickins was "allowed $200 for a dwelling house and book room, $80 for a boy, $53 1-3 for firewood, and $333 to clothe and feed himself, his wife and children—in all, 666 1-3 dollars."

The following "powers" were "granted" Dickins at the General Conference or 1792. "1. To regulate the publications according to the state of the finances. 2. To determine, with the approbation of the book committee, on the amount of the drafts, which may be drawn from time to time on the book fund. 3. To complain to the District Conferences if any preacher shall neglect to make due payment for books. 4. To publish from time to time such books or treatises as he and the other members of the book committee shall unanimously judge proper."

The following book committee was designated: "John Dickins, Henry Willis, Thomas Haskins, and the preacher who is stationed in Philadelphia from time to time."

The first book printed was "The Christian's Pattern," by A Kempis, August 17, 1789. The first volume of the Arminian Magazine, the Hymn Book, Saint's Rest and Primitive Physic, were published the same year.

The second volume of the Arminian Magazine was printed late in 1789 and put on sale in January, 1790. The Introduction, dated December 8, 1789, is signed by Asbury "in behalf of the Council." That copies of the first volume were limited is indicated by the "Note—Some of the first volume of this work are yet to be had by timely application."

In 1796 the General Conference declared "the propagation of religious knowledge by the means of the press is next in importance to the preaching of the gospel" and therefore recommends the printing of the Methodist Magazine. The first volume of the Methodist Magazine was printed December (17), 1796, for the year 1797. After the printing of the second volume, like its predecessor, the Arminian Magazine, and for the same reason, lack of patronage, it was discontinued. In

1812 the General Conference ordered it resumed by January, 1813.

Printing of Methodist literature for "The Printing and Book Business" was done at first by Pritchard and Hall, later by Joseph Cruickshank and by Henry Tuckniss—all of Philadelphia.

In the beginning St. George's Church was the Depository, and the business was carried on there by Dickins. In his report (printed in full elsewhere) for the Book Committee to the General Conference of 1792, Thomas Haskins says: "We think, in addition to Mr. Dickins' present allowance, an additional sum of $200 might with great propriety be added to his present allowance, with a sum to enable him to procure *a room exclusively* to deposit and keep the unbound impressions of the several books he has printed and other materials belonging to the business."

This is positive proof that up until November, 1792, Dickins had no room *exclusively* for his books or his business. Where then did he keep his supplies and do business?

He tells us on the title page of the first volume of the Arminian Magazine in the following words: "Sold by John Dickins *in Fourth Street (East Side) near the corner of Race Street*," a description that fits exactly the location of St. George's.

The immediate availability of the church and the absence of financial obligation for its use—which, of itself, was a consideration in view of the fact that Dickins had no other funds at his disposal but his own—made the church the logical place to begin business.

The absence of a street number on the title page of the Arminian Magazine would indicate either the church had no number or that the custom of numbering properties had not as yet been adopted.

It is of course evident that Dickins in time sold his merchandise elsewhere. One imprint in 1789 gives "Fourth St. between Race and Arch." In 1790 two locations are given —"Fourth St. near the Corner of Race," which corresponds with the Church and "No. 43 Fourth St.," which we cannot identify with the Church. In 1791 No. 43 is again given.

In 1792 and 1793 imprints give "182 Race St. near Sixth"

and "182 Race St. between Fifth and Sixth," and "43 Fourth St." The Philadelphia City Directory of 1793 identifies for us the Race Street location as that of Dickins' residence. Until that year neither Dickins nor his business is listed in the Directory. In 1793 the following appears: "John Dickins, minister of the methodist church, 182 Sassafras (Race) St."

In 1794, also, imprints give two locations where merchandise was on sale: "No. 44 N. Second St. near Arch St." and "No. 124 N. Second St."

Sometime after the General Conference of 1792, when at the suggestion of the "Book Committee," Dickins was allowed an additiontal sum of "$200 for a dwelling house and a book room and $80 for a boy," he moved his residence and his business to the same address, "No. 44 N. Second St." Here he continued to reside and do business until his death in 1798.

"The Minutes of the Methodist Conferences from 1793 to 1794 inclusive," published in 1795 give on the title page, "No. 44" and in an advertisement in the back, "No. 50 N. Second St." No. 44 and No. 50 are doubtless one and the same building. Additional buildings to the south making a change of number necesssary.

Imprints of 1796, 1797, and 1798 give Dickins' place of business as "No. 50 N. Second St." The Philadelphia Directory of 1797 lists Dickins as "stationer, No. 50 N. Second St."

On February 27, 1798, Dickins died of yellow fever and was buried at the southeast corner of St. George's. Elizabeth Yancy, whom he married in North Carolina, survived him.

On the death of Dickins, Ezekiel Cooper was appointed to fill his place. A brief sketch of Cooper, also, may be appropriate here.

Ezekiel Cooper, one of ten children of Richard and Ann Broadway Cooper, was born in Caroline County, Md., February 22, 1763, and converted under the preaching of Freeborn Garrettson. On the inside cover of his pocket Bible he wrote: "I began to preach and travel at the same time, November, 1784. My first sermon was in Johnstown, Del:. from I Pet. 4: 17. My first circuit was Caroline, extending from Choptank to Delaware Bay, Lewistown." In 1785 he was sent to Long

Island. From 1786 to 1793 he was Presiding Elder of the Boston District, which embraced a large part of New England.

We print the Agreement between Cooper and the Philadelphia Conference, whose duty it was at the time to appoint the Book Committee.

"Memorandum of an Agreement entered into this twelfth day of June, 1799, by and between the Ministers and Preachers composing the Methodist Conference held in Philadelphia, in the State of Pennsylvania, on the one part, and Ezekiel Cooper on the other part; witnesseth, that the said Ezekiel Cooper on his part doth agree as Agent and Agent only in the name and behalf of the Conference to take the station of the General Book Steward and therein to superintend the printing, enter into and make all contracts, answer orders, receive and pay away money, keep accurate and true account of all matters relating to the said business and generally to do all matters and things which his duty as Agent and Book Steward require, to the best of his knowledge and understanding, and further the said Ezekiel Cooper promises and agrees that he will not by himself or in connection with any other person follow any other mercantile or other temporal business except taking care of his own private concerns during the time he is employed and acts as Book Steward, and further that he will engage in all matters relating to the kind of books to be printed, follow the orders and directions of the Conference, and generally to conduct himself in the business according to the rules and customs heretofore established and pursued by the late Book Steward, and further when thereto required by the said Conference to lay before them the books of accounts for examination. And in consideration that the said E. Cooper does and shall well and faithfully perform the duties and comply with the stipulation herein before mentioned the said Ministers and Preachers, comprising the Philadelphia Conference, do engage and agree to allow and pay him as a compensation for his labour, trouble and attention to the said business the yearly salary of two hundred and fifty dollars clear of any deduction whatever and further to allow him all necessary expense of board, room rent and fuel and candle therefor, and the same to pay out of the moneys belonging to the Book Fund, and further the said Con-

ference do agree that they will not release and discharge any person or persons who now are or hereafter may become indebted to the Book Concern without the previous consent of the said agent. And it is further understood that the said E. Cooper is to stand in connection with and be subject to the control and direction of the said Conference in regard to his ministerial functions so far as the same shall not interfere with his duty as agent and Book Steward. In testimony whereof the said Philadelphia Conference by their President and Bishop F. Asbury on their part, and the said E. Cooper on his part have set their hands and seals on this day and year first above written."
Sealed in the presence of
    Thomas Haskins
    Jesse Lee
    Jno. ------?
    Lem'l Green

                      Francis Asbury (SEAL)
                      Ezek. Cooper (SEAL)

"N.B.—It is agreed by the parties to this instrument that in all cases where the Book Steward may judge proper he may consult and take the advice of the *Trustees of the Charter Fund* in relation to the pecuniary concerns and finances of the Book Business—and further the Conference direct that whenever the Book Steward may want advice and assistance on anything relative to the business of the books he may consult the *stationed preacher* and such of the local preachers as he may judge proper.

"N.B.—The Conference agree that the Agent may, provided he can get a suitable piece of ground build a small book room, and provided *he will loan the money* to defray the expense of building, the Conference agree to pay him the interest thereon out of the Book Fund till the principal is refunded."

According to Ezekiel Cooper's personal check book (in possession of St. George's) on the Bank of the United States, Cheque No. 1, dated November 1, 1880, he made "A Loan to Book Concern $800."

The General Conference of 1800 appointed Cooper Superintendent of the Book Business, with authority "to publish any books or tracts which at any time may be approved of or recommended by the majority of an Annual Conference, provided the same be approved of by the Book Committee which shall be appointed by the Philadelphia Conference."

At the General Conference of 1804 the Book Business was moved from Philadelphia to New York. Cooper was continued at its head with the title of General Book Steward. The duty of appointing the Book Committee was transferred to the New York Conference.

At the General Conference of 1808 Ezekiel Cooper presented his resignation as Editor and General Book Steward. The Conference requested Cooper to continue, and voted him "an extra compensation for his services the first five years" of $1,000. Cooper, however, insisted on retirement, and John Wilson, appointed assistant in 1804, was elected General Book Steward at $750 a year.

Sunday, June 6, 1813, Asbury writes in his Journal, "Knowing the uncertainty of the tenure of life, I have made my will, appointing Bishop McKendree, Daniel Hitt and Henry Boehm my executors. If I do not in the meantime spend it, I shall leave when I die an estate of two thousand dollars, I believe: I give it all to the Book Concern."

The first Sunday School publication (1823) was *The Youth Instructor and Guardian*, containing thirty-six pages and issued monthly. The first *Advocate* was issued September 9, 1826.

In 1824 Nathan Bangs became Book Agent. At that time the business was carried on at No. 14 Crosby Street, New York. In 1833 the Concern was moved to 200 Mulberry Street.

Cooper died February 21, 1847, and was buried just outside the door of Old St. George's, with which he had maintained close relations for many years and which he had severd as pastor.

In the course of time the two separated bodies, the Methodist Protestant Church and the Methodist Episcopal Church, South, both established their own concerns. Under the Plan of Unification the three concerns were merged in one great establishment, "The Methodist Publishing House."

When Ezekiel Cooper succeeded Dickins as General Book

Steward in 1799, the assets of the Concern were only $4,000. On retiring, Cooper reported that in 1804 the Capital was about $27,000, and in 1808, $45,000. Today the Methodist Publishing House enjoys the distinction of being the oldest publishing house in America and the largest religious publishing house in the world, with a total investment estimated at over one billion ($1,162,230,000) dollars.

The Chartered Fund

At the Christmas Conference in 1784 when the Methodist Episcopal Church was organized, a regular plan was adopted, as we have stated in a preceding chapter, for raising money to support or help "superannuated preachers, and the widows and orphans of preachers."

The fund was called the "Preachers' Fund." Every travelling preacher was to contribute two dollars yearly at the Conference. Everyone, when first admitted as a travelling preacher was to pay $2.67. Nothing, apparently, was to be asked or expected of the laymen. It was in every sense indeed a "Preachers' Fund." There were to be 'three treasurers, three clerks, each of whom shall keep a separate account; and three inspectors, who shall annually lay before the conference an exact state of the fund." The nine specified were to "form a committee for the management of the fund. Three of whom shall be competent to proceed on any business, provided one be a treasurer, another an inspector, and a third, a clerk."

Out of the Fund provision was first to be made for "the worn out preachers, then for the widows and children of those that are dead. Every worn out preacher shall receive, "if he wants it," $64 a year. Every widow of a preacher shall receive yearly, "if she wants it," $53 and 33 cts. Every child of a preacher shall receive once for all, "if he wants it," $53 and 33 cents. But none shall be entitled to anything from this fund till he has paid $6.67 cents. Nor any who neglects paying his subscription, for three years together, unless he be sent by the Conference out of these United States, etc."

While we are told that most of the preachers were subscribers to the Fund and that it afforded relief to many, it, nevertheless, was soon discovered that the plan was not comprehensive enough. Nothing was done, however, in the matter at the General Conference in 1792, and by 1796 the Church had lost 106 preachers.

It is evident that the matter was discussed by Asbury, the Officials of St. George's, and John Dickins, who at the time was Book Agent at Philadelphia, active in the Church and also a Trustee of St. George's.

On August 1, 1796, Asbury "drew the outlines of a subscription that (he hoped) might form a part of the constitution of general fund for the sole purpose of supporting travelling ministry." In a few days he submitted his suggestions to the officials of St. George's, going "from house to house" for the purpose.

In a short time Thomas Haskins, Treasurer of St. George's, drafted "THE ARTICLES OF ASSOCIATION of the TRUSTEES of the FUND for the RELIEF AND SUPPORT of the ITINERANT, SUPERANNUATED and WORN-OUT MINISTERS and PREACHERS of the METHODIST EPISCOPAL CHURCH in the UNITED STATES OF AMERICA, their Wives and Children, Widows and Orphans." The instrument was signed by Haskins, John Dickins, Jacob Baker, Henry Manly, Burton Wallace, Josiah Lusby, Hugh Smith, Caleb North, and Cornelius Comegys, all Trustees of St. George's, who probably collaborated with Haskins, and are all designated in Article I as "The Trustees of the Fund."

In October, 1796, "The Articles of Association, etc." as the Fund was at first called, "were submitted to the General Conference and received its unanimous approbation and sanction."

The instrument contained ten Articles. Article 1 gave the name, style, title of the corporation, and the names of the Trustees, who were the original framers and presenters. Article 8 provided: 1. No sum exceeding $64 was to be applied in any one year to an itinerant, superannuated or worn-out single preacher; 2. No sum exceeding $128 to a married one; 3. No sum exceeding $64 to a widow; and 4. No sum exceeding $16 was to be applied for the use of a child or orphan of an itinerant, superannuated or worn-out preacher.

Among the regulations adopted by the General Conference of 1796 to govern the Fund were the following: 5. Elders and those in charge of a circuit were to collect the money; 6. Money was to be sent by post to John Dickins, at Philadelphia, and he in turn was to pay it to the trustees; 7. No money was to be drawn until August 1, 1798; 8. Interest was to be divided into six parts, and each of the Yearly Conferences were authorized to draw that sixth part according to regulations prescribed; 9. Produce of sale of books after books' debts are paid and sufficient capital provided to carry on business is to be paid regularly into the Charter Fund.

On November 23, 1796, application was made to the Commonwealth of Pennsylvania for incorporation as follows:

"The undersigned members of the Methodist Episcopal Church in the city of Philadelphia (St. George's) having associated themselves for a charitable and religious purpose, and being desirous to acquire and enjoy the powers and immunities of a corporation or body politic in law, beg leave to exhibit to Jared Ingersol, Esq., Attorney-General of the Commonwealth of Pennsylvania, as also to the honorable judges of the Supreme Court of the Commonwealth, the following instrument of writing, wherein are specified the objects, conditions, and name for and under which they have associated in pursuance of a law of the Commonwealth, aforesaid, entitled, 'An Act to confer on certain Associations of the City of this Commonwealth the powers and immunities of Corporations or Bodies politic in Law.'"

John Dickins
Jacob Baker
Burton Wallace
Hugh Smith
Thomas Haskins
Henry Manly
Josiah Lusby
Caleb North
Cornelius Comegys

Philadelphia, November 23, 1796.

The charter was approved by Governor Mifflin, and the body incorporated and enrolled January 18, 1797.

According to Ezekiel Cooper's personal cheque book, Bank of Penna., he drew "Phila. Aug. 4, 1800 Cheque No. 8 to Col.

North, Treasurer of the Charter Fund for the M. E. Church $500."

In 1805 the Trustees memorialized "the Bishops and Preachers composing the several district Conferences of the Methodist Episcopal Church in the United States of America," as follows: "It is with extreme regret your memorialists have understood that attempts have recently been made to question the expediency and generate doubts as to the utility of continuing the operations of the Charter Fund on the ground of its being the cause of the deficiencies in the Quarterage of the preachers in some of the Circuits, etc."

On January 29, 1817, the Trustees, in a letter to "the Members and Friends of the M. E. Church in America," stated that "the capital of the Fund amounted to $20,712," "the profits for the years 1816 to 1817 amounted to $1,430, and was divided among eleven (11) Conferences and 700 preachers besides the widows and orphans of deceased preachers."

In 1832 the following resolution was presented by the Trustees and adopted by the General Conference:

"Whereas some difficulty has arisen to the trustees in the management of the fund under their charge, in consequence of two items in the present act of incorporation, to wit: 1, In its title, which is 'The Trustees of the Fund for the Relief, etc.,' the same being so long that cases occurred where legacies have been left misnaming the fund and that in consequence of which law suits have occurred. 2, The annual income being limited to 500 pounds in the original Act of Assembly, April 6, 1791, it has been argued before court that inasmuch as the income has exceeded the legal limit the charter is legally void."

Whereupon, Resolved, That application be made by the president and secretary to the General Conference that if the trustees shall deem it expedient to apply to the Legislature of Pennsylvania to remedy these cases, that they may be authorized so to do and to change the name of the Fund to "The Chartered Fund of the M. E. Church in the United States of America," and to enlarge the income as they may deem expedient.

The assets of the Fund at the present time amount to approximately $152,000. The distribution of this fund is simple. The total income for the year is divided by the number of Annual Conferences in the United States, and each Conference is entitled to one full share, regardless of the size or condition of the Conference.

Allotments to the various Conferences of the Methodist Episcopal Church up to 1939 were made at the rate of $60 to each Conference annually.

Up to 1932 the Fund was handled by Philadelphians. By action of the General Conference of that year, "the Chartered Fund" was placed in the hands of the Trustees of the Board of Pensions and Relief, "the principal of said Fund to be held intact and only the interest to be distributed."

In 1876 a resolution was presented to the General Conference of the Methodist Episcopal Church to establish a "connectional agency" to create and administer a fund for the relief of superannuates and ministers in distress. This fund later called the Permanent Fund was to be money raised "by collections, grants, wills, etc." In 1888 a "Board of Conference Claimants" was created. In addition to administering the Permanent Fund, this Board was given the authority to administer contributions from the Annual Conference and profits from the Book Concern. In 1892 the "Board of Conference Claimants" established in 1888 was abolished and a new Board, having the same name, was created. The new Board was authorized " 'to build up and administer a permanent Connectional Fund,' so that the Preachers and people of the stronger Annual Conferences may be united with those of the weaker Conferences in one Connectional plan." Profits from the Book Concern were eliminated from the administration of the new Board. These were disbursed directly by the Book Agents. In 1928 the name of the organization was changed to the Board of Pensions and Relief.

CHAPTER XIV

The Sunday School, Cokesbury College, First Missionaries

In 1737 John Wesley started a school on Sunday in Christ Church, Savannah, Georgia, and under his direction Mr. Delamotte included the children of the church.

Simpson says that in England, as early as 1769, Miss Hannah Ball gathered together a number of the children of the poor and neglected and taught them on Saturday and Sunday, and reported to Mr. Wesley the progress she made in her work. Other isolated instances of a "Sunday School" being held may be found, but nothing like a general system of teaching the young on Sunday, whether in secular or religious learning, was known prior to 1781.

The system that then arose was purely philanthropic in its design, and in its origin contemplated only local results. In the City of Gloucester, England, pin-making was an important industry. This industry employed a great many children, not only resident in Gloucester, but from the surrounding country.

"Vast numbers of these children, who," we are told, "were wholly uneducated and without parental restraint or moral supervision, fell into disorder and immorality, especially on Sunday, when unemployed."

The first person who undertook to remedy this condition was Robert Raikes, a printer, of Gloucester, and a member of the Church of England. He found persons who were used to instructing children in reading and engaged their services to receive and instruct such children as he should send to them every Sunday.

Several Sunday Schools were opened in Gloucester, each accommodating about thirty scholars. The results were amazing. "Even the parents of these pupils began to show reform when they realized what the Sunday School had done for their children. The development in the intelligence and morals of the children surpassed even the hopes of Robert Raikes. When visitors were taken into the school and shown the results—

clean, well-behaved children repeating Bible lessons, catechism, and singing hymns—they were astonished." William Fox, the philanthropist, Mr. Wilberforce and others visited the schools.

When once the idea of Sunday instruction for the ignorant children of Great Britain was fairly developed, it was seen not only to have great intrinsic merit, but to be perfectly adapted to other places.

In Wesley's Journal, July 18, 1784, he says he found Sunday Schools springing up wherever he went.

Very early the instruction of children claimed the attention of the American itinerants.

Minutes of 1779—"What shall be done with the children? Ans. Meet them once a fortnight and examine parents which regard to their conduct toward them."

At the organization of the Church in 1784—"Question 5. But what shall we do for the rising generation? Who will labour for them? Let him who is zealous for God and the souls of men begin now. 1. Where there are ten children whose parents are in society, meet them at least an hour every week. 2. Talk with them every time you see any at home. 3. Pray in earnest for them. 4. Diligently instruct and vehemently exhort all parents at their houses. 5. Preach expressly on education, etc."

In 1786 a Sunday School was held in Hanover County, Virginia, at the home of Thomas Cranshaw and under the direction of Asbury.

In 1789 a change was made in the requirements for the instruction of the children. They are now to be met an hour once a week; but where this is impracticable, once in two weeks. The itinerant was advised also to "Procure our 'Instructions' for them, and let all who can, read and commit to memory."

In 1790 the question of the poor arises. "What can be done" it is asked, "in order to instruct poor children, white and black, to read?" Ans. "Let us labor as the heart and soul of one man, to establish Sunday Schools in or near the place of public worship. Let persons be appointed by the bishops, elders, deacons or preachers to teach (gratis) all that will attend and that have the capacity to learn, from six in the morning till ten, and from two o'clock in the afternoon till six; when it does not interfere with public worship. The church shall compile a proper school book to teach them learning and piety."

After 1790 Sundays Schools were established in several places. In January, 1791, as we shall see, 3 schools for the poor were established in Philadelphia, one of them under the direct supervision of St. George's.

The teachers in the early Methodist Sunday Schools took nothing for their services. The greater part of the scholars were black children whose parents were backward about sending them. Few of them were regular in attendance and in a short time the teachers "were discouraged and having no pay and but little prospect of doing good soon gave up" and the matter of instruction of children was for some time neglected.

In 1796 the Bishops (Notes on the Discipline, by Coke and Asbury) called upon the preachers to meet the children weekly, visit with them and pray with them in their homes, giving notice beforehand of their intention. "Let us labor among the poor in this respect, as well as among the competent. O if our people in the cities, towns and villages were but sufficiently sensible of the magnitude of this duty and its acceptableness to God, if they would establish Sunday Schools wherever practicable for the benefit of the children of the poor, and sacrifice a few public ordinances every Lord's Day to this charitable and useful exercise, God would be to them instead of all the means they lost."

From the foregoing it is evident that the Sunday School was in the beginning generally established for "the poor and neglected." The Methodists in America at first provided for the instruction of the children of parents "who were in Society," but it was not specified that the instruction should be on Sunday. In time "children of the poor and neglected," regardless apparently of the relationship of the parents to the Church, were provided for, and the "Sabbath" was designated.

Whatever may have been the character of the instruction contemplated by Asbury and his co-workers, however, they may have begun or carried on their work among the children, the Sunday Schools in America soon attempted what Raikes attempted in England—to give the children of the poor not only a religious but a common school education.

In 1791 three "Sunday Schools were established" in Philadelphia with a combined enrollment of 900 scholars, under the auspices of "The First Day or Sunday School Society." This organization, as far as we have been able to discover, was the first interdenominational Sunday School Association in America, having been formed January 11, 1791, by representatives of the Churches in Philadelphia, including St. George's Methodist.

The character of the instruction given in the Sunday Schools in their formative period is indicated by the following extract from the "Rules of the First Day or Sunday School Society":

"It is a particular rule with the Society that the scholars come clean to the schools and attend the place of worship to which they respectively belong.

"By this benevolent institution the children of many of the poorer part of the community who would otherwise have been running through the streets, habituating themselves to mischief, are rescued from vice and inured to habits of virtue and religion, and it is with pleasure that the Board of Visitors have observed the improvement in reading and writing made by the children in the schools, answers their most sanguine expectations."

Old quill pen ink-wells, sand ink-blotters, slates, etc., of the early Sunday School period are still preserved by St. George's.

As the public school system came into existence and developed in America, the Sunday Schools confined themselves more and more, and eventually, exclusively to religious instruction. The School that with us was first for the "children of parents in Society," then for the "children of the poor and neglected" regardless of whose children they were, finally embraced both children and adults without distinction.

The first Sunday School Union of the Methodist Episcopal Church was organized in 1827, and reorganized and recognized by the General Conference of that church in 1840.

Cokesbury College

Shortly after the meeting of Dr. Coke and Francis Asbury in the latter part of 1784, they consulted as to the advisability of building a school or college. The matter was brought before the Christmas Conference in 1784, and it was agreed that the work should be undertaken. Later "A plan for erecting a college intended to advance religion in America, to be presented to the principal members and friends of the Methodist Episcopal Church," and signed by Coke and Asbury, was published.

The college was to be built at Abingdon, Maryland. It was "to receive for education and board the sons of the elders and preachers of the Methodist Church, poor orphans, and the sons of subscribers, and other friends. A moderate sum for tuition and board was to be paid by those who could afford it. Others were to be taught and boarded, and if finances allowed it, clothed gratis." The institution was to be for the benefit, also, of young men called to preach, and for the time being under the presidency of the Superintendents. Yearly collections and endowments were to support the institution.

When the plan was published January 3, 1785, the statement was made that subscriptions amounting to £1,057 17s had been received.

For the sum of £60 four acres of ground eighteen miles east of Baltimore, in Hartford Co., Maryland, were purchased from Mr. J. Dallam.

On June 5, 1785, the cornerstone of the building was laid by Asbury. "I rode," says he, "to Abingdon, to preach the foundation sermon of Cokesbury College; I stood on the ground where the building is to be erected, warm as it was, and spoke from Psalm LXXVIII-48." The building was built of brick, 108 feet long, 40 feet wide, three stories high, and stood in the center of a six-acre lot. The cost of the structure, the equipment, and the library was upward of £10,000.

The name given to the institution, Cokesbury, is a combination of Coke's and the latter part of Asbury's surnames.

On Wednesday, June 12, 1787, Asbury went to the College to fix the price of board and the time of opening. "Thursday, December 6," says he, "we opened our college and ad-

To preserve St. George's on its original site the plans for the Delaware River Bridge were changed, putting the roadbed 14 feet further south

mitted twenty-five students. .... On the Sabbath I spoke on, 'O man of God there is death in the pot.'"

In 1791 the College had an enrollment of seventy students with a faculty of five members. In 1794 it was incorporated, and its management transferred from the Conferences to the trustees named in the charter.

On December 7, 1795, fire, which some think was of incendiary origin, destroyed the entire building. No attempt was ever made to rebuild it. "January 5, 1796," Asbury writes in his Journal, "we have now a second and confirmed account that Cokesbury College is consumed to ashes, a sacrifice of $10,000 in about ten years. .... Its enemies may rejoice and its friends not mourn. Would any man give me $10,000 per year to do and suffer again what I have done for that house I would not do it. The Lord called not Whitefield nor the Methodists to build colleges. I wished only for schools; Dr. Coke wanted a college."

Writing to Thomas Haskins (in a letter in the possession of Old St. George's) under date, Charleston, January 11, 1796, Asbury says:

"Charleston, January 11, 1796.
"My own dear Son:

"As Cokebury .... attention will be turned toward the spiritual interests of our Society chiefly. This hath perhaps been one cause of its consumption. I wished and prayed if it was not for his glory it might be destroyed. It hath taken up my time, consumed my spirits and would eventually have rendered me useless if I had not given it up. As to the bill for the fund, it must be drawn according to the section in the form of discipline on the subject. 3,000 pounds will be sufficient. The subject of relief of the superannuated preachers and widows and orphans of preachers, as are this order in the minutes and recommended from year to year by the Bishop and Conference or President and Conference held in any part of the U. S. Oh, my dear Bro. how I pant for thy soul to be wholly alive to God and flowing with holy love. I hear of a stir of religion in York, and we have had the city in motion here. God is with and hath been through every Conference in the Union. The Virginia Conf. hath perfectly recovered its love, once distracted with Solomon wronghear. It is very low times here with the separate people. Our Society is greatly augmented with the return of old and increase of new members. Dr. Coke writes me he is now about to sail for Timboo in Africa with six companions. One of the kings hath invited him. I am in great hopes God will work upon our prosperous darker continent. I am solemnly happy in God, but I am pained to be cooped up here 2 months, but the winter campaigns are the cause of my pain. So I must submit. My love to .... Norths and Bakers and all that ask after me—thrice more than even,

F. Asbury.

The first Saturday in March I march for about 2,000 miles before you see me in Philadelphia."

In the opening part of his letter from Hanging Rock to Thomas Haskins, and from which we have quoted an extract (see Chapter XII), Asbury refers first to the affairs of John Dickins, then in no happy vein, to Cokesbury College.

"Hanging Rock, 20 miles Northwest of
Camden (N. C.), October 17, 1807.

"My dear Son:

"Grace and peace from him that was, and is, and is to come. Amen. John Dickins knew his real friends, both to his temporal and spiritual interests. He wisely made choice of you at his death as his friend and, a friend to the connection; you performed your trust. Happy it might have been had all things continued in your management to the end; but of that no more, it is done. The widow writes me her friend Amatt (Armatt?) is no more. May he rest in peace. I must request you if possible to take up the settlement of that broken Estate; if you do not, who will? I do not expect that the widow or her children will receive any more benefit; no, they must seek support from other sources as they have done for four years past. I wish only that the profits may go to the suffering creditors, only this I know that Mrs. Dickins will feel more at ease of mind when she knows where she stands, although she has little or no hope of receiving any relief from that quarter, except it is mental. I hope you can begin where Mr. Amatt left it, as he had progressed. For my part I have always been poor but now I am in debt. I gathered up the fragments of Williams Books and deposited the hundred pounds sterling, which is burnt up in Cokesbury and Mr. Rankin made me executor, without my will. I told what I had done. He now demands the money and I must pay my Brother Rankin or that part of my character will not come up to the other. I must pay 100 sterling out of my own pocket. You see now how you and I have gained by the College with my ten years of toil, and drudgery, and abuse, if any are made we may expect the college will come up. Our dearly beloved Coleman has published Jarratts Life in letters, with a kick at Cokesbury (Shoemakers and Tailors) to set up a college. I have this pleasure that we have the greatest possible harmony in the Conferences. All the Conferences are satisfied with your conduct, as trustees, your correctness and fidelity, and so they would were you to publish as your fund expense, a few hundred copies of the charter, with a fervent letters and you would have supplies from the living or the dead or both."

The college bell is now in possession of Goucher College, Baltimore. In the yard of the Abingdon Methodist Church four stones designate the corner locations of the building of what was once American Methodism's first college.

Methodism was not, however, to be deterred either by the financial difficulties that attended her first institution nor by the disaster that eventually overtook her. Cokesbury College was but the beginning. Today's Methodism boasts that Universities, Colleges, Seminaries, Training Schools, Professional Schools, etc., under her auspices are to be found throughout the land. Her oldest College is Dickinson, located at Carlisle, Pa.

First Missionaries

The first "Missionaries" were sent out by the Christmas Conference in 1784—Freeborn Garrettson and James O. Cromwell to Nova Scotia, and Jeremiah Lambert to Antigua. In 1812 the General Conference authorized the raising of money for missionary purposes. On April 5, 1819, "The Misisonary Society of the M. E. Church in America" was organized in New York, at the Bowery Church. In 1820 Rev. Ebenezer Brown, the first missionary of the Society, was sent to labor in Louisiana among the French. In 1828 "in America" was omitted from the title of the Society to permit work in foreign countries.

In 1833 Rev. Melville B. Cox, of Virginia, the first foreign missionary of the Methodist Episcopal Church, went to Liberia, Africa.

CHAPTER XV

The Colored People in Early American Methodism

The early Methodists labored zealously and impartially for the welfare of the colored people, both slave and free, in America. In consequence large numbers of them in Philadelphia, New York, and elsewhere became Methodists.

From the very beginning colored folks were numbered in the membership both of the New York and the Philadelphia Societies. At St. George's the colored membership kept fair pace with the white and at one time (1805) almost equaled it.

In his letter to Wesley from New York on November 4, 1769, Boardman said: "The number of blacks that attend the preaching affects me much. One of them came to tell me she could neither eat or sleep because her master would not suffer her to come to hear the word. She wept exceedingly, saying, 'I told my master I would do more work than I used to do if he would but let me come; nay I would do everything in my power to be a good servant.'"

Writing in his Journal, at the same city, Sunday, January 27, 1771, Pilmoor says, "After preaching I met with the Negroes apart and found many of them very happy. God has wrought a most glorious work in many of their souls, and made them witnesses that He is no respecter of persons." On his trip south from Philadelphia to Savannah, on frequent occasions he had colored folks in his congregations. On one occasion at Norfolk, Va., to assure the whites an opportunity to get into the house to hear Pilmoor, men "were appointed to stand at the doors to keep all the Negroes out till the white persons were got in." Eventually he had "a noble congregation of white and black." On another occasion "a vast multitude of colored people stood around the outside."

In the Minutes of 1787 the question was asked: "What directions shall we give for the spiritual welfare of the colored people?" The answer was, "We conjure all our members and preachers by the love of God, and the salvation of souls, and do require them by all the authority invested in us to leave nothing undone for the spiritual benefit and salvation of them, within their respective circuits and districts; and for this purpose to embrace every opportunity of inquiring into the state of their souls, and to unite in Society those who appear to have a real desire of fleeing the wrath to come; to meet such in class and to exercise the whole Methodist Discipline among them."

The first report in the Minutes, of the colored members, was in 1786. At that time there were 1,890. In 1792 there were 3,871 reported; in 1808, 30,308.

From the colored converts two outstanding colored Methodist preachers were raised up, namely; Richard Allen and Harry Hosier, better known as "Black Harry."

Richard Allen was born a slave of Benjamin Chew, in Philadelphia on February 14, 1760. He was sold to a Mr. Stokley of Delaware and converted near Dover. During the Revolution he drove an army wagon. After the war he joined St. George's and was licensed by that church in 1784.

Often from three to four times a day, beginning at five o'clock in the morning he exercised his gifts by preaching in Old St. George's. He labored among his own people in Delaware, Maryland and New Jersey also. In 1786 Allen purchased his freedom and, in the same year, organized, at Philadelphia, with forty-two members, the first class of colored Methodists in America—with himself as leader, teacher, and preacher.

In 1787 Allen made a second purchase, this time of an old blacksmith shop which he hauled to a lot previously acquired, at Sixth and Lombard Streets. Having transformed the shop into a "House of Worship," he preached within it to his own race. In 1794 a new place of worship was built, dedicated Sunday, June 29, 1794, by Bishop Asbury and christened "Bethel" at the suggestion of John Dickins.

In 1799 Allen was ordained by Asbury, thus gaining the added distinction of probably being the first colored man to be ordained in America.

The Bethel congregation remained under the supervision of St. George's until 1816.

Of the early life of "Black Harry" Hosier little seems to be known. He is said, however, to have been born at Fayetteville, North Carolina. The first mention we find of Harry is in Asbury's Journal. Writing at Todds, North Carolina, Thursday, June 29, 1780, he says, "Read several chapters in Isaiah. I have thought if I had two horses, and Harry (a coloured man) to go with, and drive one, and meet the black people, and to spend about six months in Virginia and the Carolinas, it would be attended with a blessing.

"Sunday, May 13, 1781, Preached at the chapel (at Mr. Adams near Baltimore) afterward Harry, a black man, spoke on the barren fig tree. This circumstance was new, and the white people looked on with attention.

"Tuesday, May 21," (Virginia) "I preached in the afternoon at P. H.'s, and had liberty in urging purity of heart. Harry spoke to the negroes, some of whom came a great distance to hear him; certain sectarians are greatly displeased with him because he tells them they may fall from grace, and that they must be holy."

Saturday, October 27, 1781, at Philadelphia, Asbury writes: "My soul is drawn out to God to know whether I ought to go to Virginia this winter, in order to prevent the fire of division. I do not look for impulses or revelations—the voice of my brethren and concurrent circumstances will determine me in this matter. Harry seems unwilling to go with me. I fear his speaking so much to white people in the city has been or will be injurious; he has been flattered and may be ruined." Asbury does not say whether or no Harry finally accompanied him although it seems he did.

At the close of the meeting at Barratt's Chapel in November, 1784, Asbury says: "I was very desirous the Doctor (Coke) should go upon the track I had just been over, which he accordingly did." Lednum says, "Asbury provided him with a carriage and horses and Harry to drive and pilot him round the Peninsula. By the time they reached John Purnell's, Worcester County, the doctor observed, 'I am pleased with Harry's preaching.'" Harry travelled with Garrettson and Whatcoat also.

After a temporary lapse Harry was reclaimed. He died in Philadelphia in 1810 and was buried, it is said, in the Palmer Burying Ground in Kensington.

Of the colored converts to Methodism many remained

within the parent fold and were organized into separate Societies and Conferences such as the Delaware and the Washington Conferences of what became the northern branch of the Methodist Episcopal Church. Eventually, and comparatively soon, two great colored denominations sprang from the labors and ingatherings of the early Methodist itinerants, namely, The African Methodist Episcopal Church and The African Methodist Episcopal Zion Church.

The African Methodist Episcopal Church, organized in 1816, in Philadelphia had as its nucleus Bethel Methodist Episcopal Church (1787), founded by Richard Allen, a member of St. George's, and supervised by that church until the new denomination was formed. On April 9, 1816, a committee of five colored delegates from Philadelphia, seven from Baltimore, three from Attleborough, one from Salem, N. J., and one from Wilmington, Delaware—seventeen in all—met and organized the African Methodist Episcopal Church. On April 10, Allen, who belonged to and who had been licensed by St. George's and ordained deacon by Bishop Asbury, was elected bishop. He was consecrated to that office the following day.

The African Methodist Episcopal Zion Church (1820) had as its nucleus Zion Methodist Episcopal Church organized in 1796 from John Street Church, New York. In 1820 the Zion congregation, led by James Varick, Abraham Thompson, and William Miller, seceded from the Methodist Episcopal Church, and with several other groups formed the new denomination, using the name of the principal seceding church to distinguish it from the African Methodist Church, organized in 1816. In 1821 the first Annual Conference, attended by 22 ministers and reporting 1,426 members, was held in New York.

Not wishing at first to be wholly independent of the Methodist Episcopal Church, "it was proposed," says Simpson, "that their association should be treated as a distinct and separate Annual Conference under the patronage and government of the Methodist Episcopal Church." Bishops of the Methodist Episcopal Church, believing they could not do so officially, declined the invitation to preside at the Conferences in 1821 and 1822. Bishops Roberts and George, however, urged delay of permanent organization until the next General Conference of the

IN ENGLAND AND IN AMERICA

Methodist Episcopal Church. The African Methodist Episcopal Church, through Bishop Allen, on the other hand, urged union with that body.

For seven years successively a Conference, each of which elected its own president, was held. In 1828 Rev. Christopher Rush was elected Superintendent for four years. James Varick was their first Bishop.

Chapter XVI

Some Early Methodist Customs

DRESS

In a sermon on I Peter 3: 3-4, John Wesley says, "I conjure you all who have any regard for me shew me before I go hence, that I have not laboured, even in this respect, in vain, for near half a century. Let me see before I die a Methodist congregation full as plain drest as a Quaker congregation. Only be more consistent with yourselves. Let your dress be cheap as well as plain. Otherwise you do but trifle with God and me and your own souls. I pray let there be no costly silks among you, how grave soever they may be. Let there be no Quaken-linen, proverbially so called for their exquisite fineness; no Brussels lace, no elephantine hats or bonnets, those scandals of female modesty. Be all of a piece drest from head to foot as persons professing godliness, professing to do everything small and great with the single view of pleasing God."

At the Wesleyan Conference in Leeds, England, August, 1766, in answer to the question, "Should we enforce the rules regulating to ruffles, laces, snuff and tobacco?" the answer was given, "Enforce them vigorously, though calmly. When any person is admitted into Society good breeding requires him to conform to the rules of that Society."

The early Methodists in America, especially at St. George's, however, evidently did "conform."

Speaking of the dress of the early Methodists, Watson's "Annals" say: "They aimed in general to dress like the Friend:, except that they intended not to be mistaken for them, and therefore they wore collars to their coats, and their clothes of various colors—avoiding only such as should be esteemed gray, and such as were drab, because that color was then a much more prevalent one among the Friends than now.

"The men all wore shad brested coats and low crowned hats, the women all wore plain black satin bonnets—straw bonnets were never seen among them. No white dresses, no jewelry, no rings.

"No male persons were to be seen with tied or queued hair, but lank, long locks straitly combed down in thick, natural profusion.

"The females wore no curls, no side locks, or lace or ornaments.

"Their ministers, as such, could be readily recognized when abroad in the streets. They never wore black, but what was called a 'parson's gray'—a gray in which a proportion of blue was given. Their coats were without lapels, and their hats were generally white and large brimmed. They wore small clothes and vests of cotton velvet of olive colour, and sometimes of black lastings, such as are now used in shoes. Their bishop, Asbury, wore an entire suit of blue-gray cloth, with a big white hat, and a fine, venerable-looking man he surely was. He had greatly the dignity and port of a ruler."

It is said that when George Cookman came from England he landed in Philadelphia. As he walked along the streets to find the Methodist Church, when nearing 4th and Arch Streets, he saw three women with plain bonnets and dresses walking up 4th Street. He concluded they were Methodists and followed them, which attracted their attention and naturally annoyed them that they should be followed by a stranger. However, Cookman was not mistaken, they were Methodists and they led him direct to St. George's.

Notwithstanding the injunction for plainness in dress and habit so persistently urged by Wesley, he nevertheless, as another points out sought to engraft upon the new denominations a Liturgy to be used in churches by ministers in black gowns, bands and cassocks. Wesley himself clung to the vestment of the established Church.

The Superintendents, Asbury included, and some of the Elders in America early introduced the custom of wearing gowns and bands, but it was opposed by many of the preachers as well as the members. They having taken a stand against it, after a few years it was given up.

It is said that Henry Willis started to wear a black gown at

St. George's in 1791, but it gave offense to many, and he finally discarded it.

SEATING

At the Wesleyan Conference in 1765 the question was asked, "Shall the men and women sit apart everywhere?" The answer was, "By all means. Every preacher look to this."

In 1766 an exception was made to the above as follows: "In those galleries where they have been accustomed to sit together, they may do so still. But let them sit everywhere apart below, and in all new erected galleries."

The 75th question discussed and answered at the Conference of 1784 in Baltimore was. "Is there any exception to the rule 'let the men and women sit apart'? Answer: There is no exception. Let them sit apart in all our chapels."

The Methodists at St. George's followed until a late date the Wesleyan custom.

The colored folk were also seated by themselves.

March 17, 1837. "The Committee appointed to draft Rules and Regulations reported the following: *Females* will occupy the south side and from end of the gallery except that part taken up by the singers in the choir; also to occupy the south side of the lower floor under the gallery and the north center block; *men* to occupy the north side under the gallery and the south center block; *Colored Persons* to occupy the seats in the gallery usually appropriated to them."

At the Wesleyan Conference in Manchester in 1765, backs to seats in Methodist Chapels were prohibited.

The question was asked, "Is anything further advisable with regard to these houses?" (Chapels.) Ans. "In all our future buildings:

1. Let all the windows be sashed, opening downwards.
2. Let there be no tub-pupits; and
3. No backs to the seats."

The first seats at John Street and St. George's were "slat-backed," i. e., they were made with a narrow strip of wood across the top. The present benches with backs were soon installed. In some instances, evidently, the wish of Wesley in regard to "tub-pulpits" was disregarded. The first permanent pulpit of Old St. George's was such a pulpit.

EVOLUTION OF THE COLLECTION PLATE

In the early days in some churches (St. George's) they did not "pass the plate." Membership dues were received in the Classes by Leaders. Loose collection at the services was received at first in "boxes." It is said that in the beginning the entire congregation, one after the other, much after the manner of our present day colored churches, walked up to the front and placed their gifts in a box. Reference to the "box" collection is made in the old Cash Book, April 14, 1794:

Received box collection Thursday night, 4.0½
do do Sunday, 27th, 1,17.5. Total, 2.1.5½

After 1811 we read no more of a "box" collection, but instead of a "bag" collection. The first reference to this we found dated June 5, 1812. One of these "bags" which is made of plush is fastened at the end of a pole, has been preserved.

In 1839 "baskets" supplant "bags" and we read of "basket collections." In time plates replaced baskets.

MEMBERSHIP TICKETS

The custom of issuing tickets to members of Society was begun, as we have seen, very early in England. After having personally seen and inquired into the spiritual condition of the members, those deserving were given a ticket by the assistant quarterly. Apparently no one would receive a ticket, nor would a ticket be renewed if a member were delinquent in dues. Tickets were not given unless the member was recommended by the Leader with whom they had been two months on trial.

"In Philadelphia there are 182 in Society to whom I have given tickets and they meet in class and attend all the Discipline of the Methodists as well as the people in London or Bristol. This is God's own work. He has wonderfully made bare His arm in the sight of the people, and His right hand has got Himself the victory." (Pilmoor, March 23, 1770.)

The oldest membership ticket, if it be such, extant, although mistakenly claimed to be a "love feast" ticket is one given October 1, 1769, by Robert Williams to Hannah Dean, a member of the John Street Society. By whose authority and under what circumstance Williams would issue any kind of a ticket we do not know. On October 1, 1769, he had been in the country a month, and as far as we know, only ten days in New York. Furthermore he had not come as an accredited representative of Wesley.

In America as in England only those with tickets were admitted to Love Feasts and Meetings of the Society. Unconverted persons were as a rule excluded. Asbury thought it wrong to admit to Love Feasts anybody but those holding membership tickets. "The idea," as another expressed it, "was that the people of God should be by themselves without anything to distract from the deep devotion and close personal examination condutced for the soul's welfare."

At the Christmas Conference in 1784 in answer to the question, "How shall we prevent improper persons from insinuating into the Society?" it was answered, "Give tickets to none till they are recommended by a Leader with whom they have met at least two months on trial."

Again, in 1784, the question was asked, "Should we insist on the rules concerning dress?" Answer, "By all means. This is no time to give any encouragement to superfluity in apparel. Therefore give no tickets to any, till they have left off superfluous ornaments. Allow no exempt case, not even of a married woman. Better one suffer than many. Give no tickets to any that wear high heads, enormous bonnets, ruffles or rings."

Concerning these tickets Asbury and Coke in their "Notes to the Discipline in 1796" say: "This is of no small moment for the preservation of unawakened persons to our Society meetings and love feasts, would be to throw a damp on those profitable assemblies, and cramp, if not entirely destroy that *liberty of speech*, which is always made a peculiar blessing to earnest believers and sincere seekers of salvation. Beside this regulation affords the preacher who holds the office now under consideration an opportunity of speaking closely to every person under his care on the state of their souls."

In 1820 the "Tickets" were made to cover admission to love

feasts, especially. After "tickets" was inserted "for the admission of members into love feast." The Membership Ticket thus became in a sense a Love Feast Ticket. In time "Strangers" were permitted to attend Love Feasts—"with the utmost caution; and the same person on no account above twice or thrice, unless he become a member."

PREACHERS' CARE, ACCOMMODATIONS AND PARSONAGE

In the beginning the preachers did not receive salaries for their services. The preacher's necessities were cared for by the church—travelling expenses, postage, clothing, washing, shaving, "shewing" (shoeing) of their horses, lodging, and in fact everything essential to their comfort and appearance was provided.

St. George's Old Cash Book records the following:
1769
Sept. 2, pd. Mr. Williams traveling expenses £1.2s 6d.
do for washing for Mr. Williams 5s 7½d.
do for Shrub for Mr. Williams in Boat 2s 2½d.
Nov. 6, To Mr. Williams traveling expenses £1.2s 6d.
pd. for Mr. Williams Horse 3s.
pd. for 1 gal. wine 7s 6d.
pd. for 2 quarts Shrub 3s 9d.
pd. for 7 Bottles for Mr. Williams 2s 8d.
Nov. 9, pd. 4½ days & washing for Mr. Williams 1.5s. 9d.
Provision was made for Williams at St. George's, periodically until 1771.
Dec. 2, pd for 10 yds plaid @ 3/6 d for Mr. Pilmoor's Nightgown £1.15."
"1770—Feb. 17 pd for Mr. Pilmoor for Lissy the maid—7s. 6p."
"Nov. 1 for shaving of Mr. Pilmoor etc as per Bill £1-6-6
"Feb. 24, 1770 paid Mr. Ohara for a wig and shaving for Mr. Pilmoor, 3-10."

"1770—May 4 pd Jos. Jenkins 2 weeks Lodging and Diet for Mr. Boardman, £1-10."
"June 18 pd for 1 pr of silk stockings for Mr. Boardman 13s."

It should be said to Mr. Boardman's credit that on July 16 he repaid the 13s.

"July 6, 1770 paid for Hinges etc to Mr. Boardman's Wigg Box—3s"

"June 2, 1771 pd for 4 months shaving and one bleeding for Mr. Pilmoor, £1 8s 8d

"Feb. 11, 1772 for making 4 shirts for Mr. Wright to Mrs. Thorn 16s."

Mrs. Thorne, probably a seamstress, is said to have been the first woman Class Leader. She was appointed by Pilmoor in 1769 and was the recipient of a number of letters from both Pilmoor and Boardman, who addressed her as "Dear Mollie." She dwelt at the home of John Dowers, trustee of St. George's.

"Jan. 6–1773 paid to George Kheemle for shaving preachers in full Jan. 1, 1773"

"June 23, 1773 to washing Messrs. Asbury's, Rankin's and Shadford's linens to Nancy Parks 7s. 3d."

"June 25, 1773 for Mr. King's Horse at Cooper's Ferry—3s. 2d."

Most of the expense incurred for Asbury was for postage, horse shoeing, quarterage, washing, shaving and an occasional gift such as a coat, hat, and spectacles, a pair of which is preserved at Old St. George's with those of Bishop McKendree. No lodging or board bill appears. He apparently was too much "on the go" to incur either.

John Street's Old Cash Book records the following:

Sept. 20th, 1769. To cash paid to Mr. Jarvis for a hat for Mr. Williams £2. 5s.

Sept. 22 to cash for book for Mr. Williams 9d.

Oct. 9 to cash paid Mr. Newton for three pair of stockings for Messrs. Williams and Embury 31s. 9d.

Oct. 9 To cash for trunk for Williams 12s. 6d.

Oct. 30 cash paid for cloak for Mr. Robt. Williams £3 6d.

April 10, 1770 To cash paid Mr. Boardman, to pay his expenses to Phila. £1. 4s. 0d.

May 16 1771 castor oil for Pilmoor 3s.

May 1771 Cash paid to bring Boardman from Phila. to New York 2 9s.

Aug. 1771 salary paid Pilmoor for one quarter 7. 8s.

Richard Boardman, as we have seen, on November 1, 1769,

entered into an agreement with the John Street Society, "That each preacher having labored 3 months in New York shall receive 3 guineas to provide himself with wearing apparel."

In time the itinerants received "quarterage" for their personal needs in addition to their board and traveling expenses. Quatrerage seems to have been at the rate of £6.18s or from $60 to $80 a year. Entries for 6.18s are recorded in St. George's Cash Book as paid to Pilmoor, Boardman, Asbury, Rankin, Shadford, and Wright.

September 7, 1772, is the following entry: To Mr. Boardman to be taken from Mr. Wright's Quarterage £1.14s.

At the Second Conference of American Methodism "Every preacher (was) to be allowed 6 pounds, Pennsylvania currency, per quarter and his traveling charges besides."

At the Third Conference it was decided that "the preacher's expense from the Conference to the Circuit be paid out of the yearly collection."

The Christmas Conference (1784) fixed the salary of Elders, Deacons and helpers at $64 annually "and no more." The same Conference fixed the allowance of the preacher's wife at the same figure and for "each child under six, $16 and "from six to eleven, $21.33."

Still later the value received in clothing etc. was appraised, counted with the money and any deficit was supplied by profits from books and Conference collections.

On April 27, 1815, according to the minutes of the Trustees of St. George's, Manning Force "demanded salary for his wife" but was refused on the ground that "he was a single man at the commencement of the year and appropriations had been made for him accordingly." It was resolved, at the time, "that if a preacher marry hereafter during the year it should remain with the trustees to determine whether he shall be paid any salary for his wife or not."

The first parsonage provided in America was that provided by the John Street Society adjoining Wesley Chapel, New York. Wakeley in "Lost Chapters" states, "It was a little old building that stood upon one of the lots the trustees purchased from Mr. Forbes. David Morris, who did much of the carpenter's work to the preaching-house, repaired this house. This record in the 'old book' is found on page eleven, 'April 28, 1770, To cash paid David Morris, on account of work done to the preaching-house and dwelling-house £25.'"

It would seem from the old records (1768-1796) of the Society that record the following purchases of the trustees, that the parsonage was not completely furnished until June, 1770.

June 12, 1770. To cash laid out by Mr. Newton and Mrs. Benninger for the preacher's housekeeping £5. 13. 0.

June 12. Feather bed, bolster and pillow weight 67 pounds at 2 s. 4d. £7. 16. 4. Small furniture £0. 15. 0. 11 yards sheeting for a pair of sheets £1. 6. 7.

July 15. Pair sheets bought by Mrs. White and Southwell, £1. 0. 0.

July 26. One bedstead and sofa, £2. 0. 0.

Sept. 20. To cash paid for preachers housekeeping, £3. 15. 1.

Nov. 22. Pair blankets, £1. 8. 0.

Nov. 22. To cash paid Mrs. Southwell for saucepan, £0. 7. 0.

Nov. 26. To cash for plates 7s. 6d.

Nap-cloth and tape 5s. 6d., £0. 13. 0.

NOTE—The above is taken from the old records, 1768-1796, found by Dr. Wakeley in 1856.

It is not definitely known who first occupied the John Street parsonage. Embury lived at No. 10 Augustus Street until until he left New York early in 1770. Boardman and other early itinerants lodged in New York at the home of Richard Sause, a trustee of John Street and one of those under suspicion of writing derogatory letters to Wesley about Pilmoor and Boardman. According to the "Old Book" Sause received in January, 1770, £12 "for boarding Mr. Boardman, one Quarter." John Dickins is said to have been the first married itinerant to occupy the John Street parsonage. Unfortunately the first parsonage like Wesley Chapel was not preserved.

In Philadelphia, as in New York, the itinerants at first lived in private homes. For a time Pilmoor roomed with a Thomas Wakefield, who evidently rented or permitted the Philadelphia Society to occupy another room in the same building, No. 8

Loxley Court. On November 2, 1769, St. George's paid Wakefield "£1.2s.6d for one week's board and washing" for Pilmoor. On November 6, 1769, while the meeting of the Society was in progress, Pilmoor, writing in his Journal, says, "As I sat in my room my mind was impressed with a strong desire to go down and join with them. I did so."

In 1770 or early in 1771 a house was secured and a housekeeper installed for the preacher in Philadelphia. A Mrs. Gardner seems to have been the housekeeper for both Pilmoor and Boardman. Asbury, also, was probably looked after for a time by Mrs. Gardner. This arrangement definitely ended in May, 1773, when the homes of the members were thrown open to the itinerants.

Asbury, for a time at least, stopped in Philadelphia at the Wilmers. May 14, 1772, he writes in his Journal, "Here (Phila.) I found a change. Brother Pilmoor was come and the house was given up which pleased me well, as it was a burden to the people. Bro. P—e went to Mr. W's and I went to Mr. W—rs.

"Friday night I was heavily afflicted and dear Sister Wilmer took great care of me."

The General Conference of 1800 recommended that the friends of the church purchase a lot of ground on each circuit, build a house and furnish it "at least with heavy furniture."

The first "parsonage" in Philadelphia, of which we can find any record was rented in 1805 for William Colbert.

BURIAL GROUNDS

It was the custom in the early days for churches to own "burial grounds" not only for the accommodation of the members but for the revenue derived from the sale of lots and for the opening of graves. These grounds were connected with or close by the church. Later vaults were built in churches to care for bodies when the weather was too inclement to inter them at once.

St. George's, Philadelphia, had several of these grounds, one of which was in use from 1795 to 1833. In 1847 it was definitely abandoned and of the 367 bodies removed 365 were reinterred in 14 wooden boxes beneath the lower vestibule of the church. Other bodies were buried either originally, among them Thomas Haskin's wife, or later in the rear of the church. John Dickins was buried at the southeast corner and Ezekiel Cooper just outside the front door.

BIBLIOGRAPHY

Where two or more references in a chapter are from the same source, the source is given but once.

Chapter I

John Wesley's "Character of a Methodist."
Wesley's Journal.
Tyerman's "Life of Wesley."
Charles Wesley's Journal.
Dr. Frederick Platt, Warden of "The New Room."
Whitefield's "Short Account of God's Dealing with the Rev. Mr. Geo. Whitefield, etc." (1739).
Wesley's Funeral Address on Whitefield.
Autobiography of Benjamin Franklin.
Letter of Franklin to Whitefield.
* Joseph Pilmoor's Journal.

Chapter II

Wesley's Journal.
"Minutes of the Methodist Conferences" (British, Vol. I, 1744-98).
Whitefield's Journal.
"Life of Whitefield," Belcher.
Letters of John Wesley.
"The Religious Revival in England," Wesley, 1744.
Lloyd's "Evening Post," 1769.
North Bristol "Review."

Chapter III

"Minutes of the Methodist Conferences" (British, Vol I).
Wesley's "Plain Account."
Dr. Frederick Platt.
Wesley's Journal.
Letter of Pliny, the younger, to Emperor Trajan (about 110).
Acts XXVII-35, I Cor. XI, 27, 28, 33, 34.
Tertulian (160).

Works of Wesley, Vol. VII.
Address: "Settlement of Preaching-houses." Dr. Thomas Coke.

Chapter IV

"Methodism, Old and New," Flanigen.
Whitefield's Journal, ("Short Account Ek").
Philadelphia Gazette, 1739.
Autobiography of Benjamin Franklin.
Watson's "Annals of Philadelphia and Pennsylvania."
"Life of Whitefield," Belcher.
Letter of Whitefield to Captain Joss, 1769.
Extract of Letter of Thomas Taylor to Wesley.
Pilmoor's Journal.
"History of the Methodists, etc.," Jesse Lee.
"History of American Christianity," Bacon.

Chapter V

"History of Old Philadelphia Churches."
Watson's "Annals."
Pilmoor's Journal.
"History of the Methodists, etc.," Lee.
"Rise of Methodism in America," Lednum.
Minutes of the American Conferences.
Asbury's Journal.
"Minutes of the British Conferences," Vol. I.
Wesley's Journal.
"Historical Statement," *Discipline*, 1790-91-92-96-1939.
"Maryland Methodism." Mrs. Arthur Bibbins.
"Lost Chapters." Wakeley.
"Story of Old John Street," Upham.
Archives of "John Street."
Archives of "Old St. George's."

Chapter VI

Extract of Letter of Thomas Taylor to Wesley.
Wesley's Journal.
"History of the Methodist Church," Bangs.
"Rise of Methodism," Lednum.
Minutes of the Methodist Conferences (British) Vol. I.

"Western Pioneers," Lockwood.
Archives of Old St. George's.
"History of the Methodists in America," Lee.
Pilmoor's Journal.
Leed's "Intelligencer," August 8, 1769.
Wesley's "Ecclestical History," Vol. IV, page 261.
Letter of Richard Boardman to Wesley, dated New York, November 4, 1769.
Letter of Pilmoor to Wesley, dated Philadelphia, October 31, 1769.

Chapter VII

Pilmoor's Journal.
Minutes of the American Conferences, 1791.
General Conference Journal, 1792. Lee. Neely.
Archives of Old St. George's.

Chapter VIII

Pilmoor's Journal.
Minutes of the American Conferences.
Letters of Wesley to John King.
Minutes of the Methodist Conferences (British). Vol. I.
Asbury's Journal.
Minutes of the American Conference (1779).
Archives of Old St. George's.

Chapter IX

Archives of Old St. George's.
Minutes of the Methodist Conferences (British). Vol. I.
Pilmoor's Journal.
Asbury's Journal.
Letter of Wesley to George Shadford.

Chapter X

Archives of Old St. George's.
Minutes of the American Conferences.
Pilmoor's Journal.
Asbury's Journal.
Autobiography of William Watters.

"A Prophet of the Long Road," Tipple.
"Address on the Death of Asbury," Ezekiel Cooper.
"History of the Methodists, etc.," Lee.

Chapter XI

Wesley's Journal.
Minutes of the American Conferences.
"Minutes of the Methodist Conferences" (British). Vol. I.
Dr. Frederick Platt.
Certificate of Ordination of Thomas Coke.
Asbury's Journal.
Letter of Wesley addressed to Coke, Asbury, etc.
Bangs "History of the Methodist Episcopal Church."
Lee's "History of the Methodists in America."
Journal of the General Conference of 1792. Lee-Neely.
Journal of the General Conferences of 1796-1824.

Chapter XII

Steven's "History of Methodism."
Cooper's "Funeral Address on Death of Asbury."
Asbury's Journal.
Letter of Asbury to Thomas Haskins (extract). Possession of C. F. Eggleston.
Letter of Asbury to the Society at Norfolk, Va. Archives of St. George's.
Discipline of 1787.
Letter of Wesley to Asbury, dated September 20, 1788.
Archives of Christ Episcopal Church, Philadelphia.
Letter of Wesley to Ezekiel Cooper.

Chapter XIII

Archives of St. George's.
Lee's "History of the Methodists, etc."
Asbury's Journal.
Bangs "History of the Methodist Episcopal Church."
Minutes of the Conferences.
General Conference Journals of 1792 to 1808.
Imprints of Publications by Dickins and Cooper.
Philadelphia City Directory, 1793, 1797.

Agreement between Philadelphia Conference and Ezekiel Cooper. Archives of St. George's.

Chapter XVI

Simpson's "Encyclopedia."
Wesley's Journal.
Minutes of the American Conferences.
Archives of St. George's.
Asbury's Journal.
Letter of Asbury to Thomas Haskins. Possession of C. F. Eggleston.
Letter of Asbury to Thomas Haskins. Archives of Old St. George's.

Chapter XV

Archives of St. George's.
Letter of Boardman to Wesley, dated New York, November 4, 1769.
American Conference Minutes.
Pilmoor's Journal.
Asbury's Journal.

Chapter XVI

Sermon on "Dress," John Wesley.
Annals of Philadelphia, Watson.
Minutes of the Methodist Conferences (British). Vol. I.
Archives of Old St. George's.
Archives of Old John Street.
Pilmoor's Journal.
Asbury's Journal.

* This name, though variously spelled, is generally spelled "Pilmoor." The bearer of the name spells it Pillmore, Pilmore, and Pilmoor. Boardman spelt it "Pilmoor." On the Deed of Old St. George's it appears both as "Pilmoor" and Pilmoore," "Pilmore" is carved on the tomb beneath the chancel of St. Paul's Episcopal Church, Phila.

We have used the general spelling except when quoting.

www.ingramcontent.com/pod-product-compliance
Lightning Source LLC
Chambersburg PA
CBHW070247230426
43664CB00014B/2436